White Privilege

THE PERSISTENCE OF RACIAL HIERARCHY
IN A CULTURE OF DENIAL

White Privilege

THE PERSISTENCE OF RACIAL HIERARCHY
IN A CULTURE OF DENIAL

Ninochka McTaggart and Eileen O'Brien

University of California—Riverside • Saint Leo University

David Brunsma, Advisory Editor

SAN DIEGO

Bassim Hamadeh, CEO and Publisher
Seidy Cruz, Specialist Acquisitions Editor
Gem Rabanera, Project Editor
Christian Berk, Production Editor
Emely Villavicencio, Senior Graphic Designer
Trey Soto, Licensing Coordinator
Natalie Piccotti, Director of Marketing
Kassie Graves, Vice President of Editorial
Jamie Giganti, Director of Academic Publishing

Printed in the United States of America.

3970 Sorrento Valley Blvd., Ste. 500, San Diego, CA 92121

Brief Contents

Detailed Contents

Acknowledgments

Joint Acknowledgments

We are especially grateful to Dr. David Brunsma for coming up with the idea of a text on white privilege and for thinking of us to write it. We also are appreciative of everyone at Cognella, past and present, who supported us in the long journey of seeing the text from an idea, to a prospectus, to a final product—every step of the way, from collecting peer reviews to formatting. This includes Gem Rabanera, Seidy Cruz, and Jim Brace-Thompson. We also are grateful to a number of anonymous peer reviewers who offered feedback at both the prospectus and chapter draft stages. Additionally, our colleague Ted Thornhill, who teaches a nationally renowned course on white racism, offered very detailed feedback, corrections, additional references, and many other enhancements for which we are deeply grateful. The time they took greatly enhanced the project, while any remaining deficiencies are most certainly our own.

Eileen's Acknowledgments

Writing about white privilege is not nearly as intellectual of a challenge (all the evidence is there!) as it is a deeply emotional one. Researching and writing for a decade now with my colleague and dear friend Nosh began with our study of Asian American participation in hip hop music and culture. That was a "fun" topic, but it was also a topic which heavily rests on choice. Those who birthed hip hop chose to conceive it under the direst of circumstances in the poverty of the South Bronx, but it was a choice nonetheless—a creative choice, at that. There is joy in creative power, and agency. Likewise, it is agency and choice that draw Asian Americans and Pacific Islanders to contribute to hip hop and to form a multiracial community. Our research on this topic was an intellectual choice and an emotional one, but the emotion was often joy and delight. We had such fun working together!

When we switched to writing together about this much-needed topic of addressing white privilege, it was an abrupt shift, and a difficult one. As two scholars of race and two deep thinkers (dare we say over-thinkers) leading multiracial personal lives, white privilege was hardly new or unexamined territory for us. After all, my dissertation was on white antiracist activists challenging white privilege, and I lead community workshops on white privilege, teach about it, write about it, and all that. Yet this deep dive into white privilege we undertook together to complete this project was like nothing either of us had done before. Even we were not fully prepared for the heavy weight of it all. It is something none of us chose, yet we must live it out every day. If it were not for the tremendously exceptional human being that my coauthor is and the beautiful friendship we have built as a result, I do not know how we would have ever finished this project.

I have worked with many coauthors over my career, but none have evolved into this type of friendship, which is truly a testament to the special person Nosh is. During the particular years we birthed this book, each of us celebrated tremendous professional achievements—between us earning a PhD, tenure, and promotion, and co-curating a museum exhibit, among others. At the same time, we each experienced tremendous grief and loss too personal to recount here. As two people who care deeply for humans of different racial and ethnic backgrounds, all too often we witnessed firsthand the very topics we were writing about and how they impacted our personal relationships. And then we had to come back and keep writing about it all, as if we were not also a part of it somehow. It seemed that nearly every day, one of us was messaging the other about yet another incident in the news, or another study that again and again touched on the deadly and near-deadly (and sometimes just plain stupid) consequences of white privilege. The gift of being able to write this book with Nosh is that a most wonderful, supportive friendship evolved between us by this shared work together. By friendship, I mean not just cheering each other on and encouraging each other, but also sharing tremendous anger and sadness with each other, and finding support—that is, not the kind of person who wants to smooth over and gloss over your anger and sadness, tie it up in a bow and send you on your way, but real sitting with another's emotion and just letting it be what it is. When you are studying white privilege and also living with its consequences, day in and day out, there is no escaping that kind of outrage and despair. And really, this is a metaphor for life in general, in all its messy realities. As a result of the unique combination of the type of work we were doing and the type of people we are, we formed the type of bond that I honestly do not share with any other sociologist over a twenty-year career. Words cannot begin to express my gratitude to Nosh for just being who she is, both intellectually and personally. It has been truly an honor and a gift.

Besides my coauthor, there are many others who have also supported me during this project in various ways. The deep dives that several of my friends and colleagues have taken with me on race-related conversations have enriched my thinking on this project in ways they probably did not even realize. Maybe some of them did not even know I was writing this book at the time. But I consider them to be resources that I have drawn upon to do better thinking on white privilege as a result of their insights. Discussing racism and white privilege with a white woman requires making oneself vulnerable to someone who, based on history, with good reason should not always be trusted. Discussing everything from my state's governor wearing black-face, to school mistreatment of my biracial children, to me walking up to a black man at a conference and calling him by the wrong name, I counted on my friends to be real with me and tell me what they really thought, even if they disagreed with me. And they did not let me down. And for that, I am truly grateful. Likewise, some trusted me to tell them when white privilege and racism reared its ugly head in their lives and careers, and it is through their sharing that I always learned something new about every sneaky which way racism works. I am likely forgetting someone, but for starters, in alphabetical order by last name: Eduardo Bonilla-Silva, Joe Feagin, TJ Ghose, Travis Harris, Joe Healey, Jimmie Johnson, Xavier Joyner, Ainsley Lambert-Swain, Jessica O'Brien, Iyabo Osiapem, Ebony Perez, Carletta Perry, Janis Prince, Bedelia Richards, Deidre Royster, Andrea Simpson, Yvette Smith, Duane Stephens, Ramona Taylor, Megan Underhill, Robert Vinson, John Whitley, Lekesha Williams, Tammy Wilson, and D'Shawn Wright. Whether you are white or black or somewhere in between, I respect your deep thinking and critical reflection about race and about humans. It takes a fellow student of humans to know one, and not everyone "goes there," so I appreciate you going there with me. This work is no doubt better, but I am most certainly a better person, because of you.

This book is written for students, some of whom are likely to be coming into contact with some of these concepts for the first time. We could not have been writing in a voice that spoke to students without listening carefully to our students over the years. I am especially grateful to those special students—the ones who speak out in class, the ones who are angry, and the ones whose lives are forever changed, the ones who contact me even many years later—to tell me the impact my class had on their thinking about race, and on their ability to exchange in productive dialogue with others about race and white privilege. This book is written with you in mind, and with the hope that there will be many others after you to follow.

Finally, and most importantly, in order to write about white privilege and its heavy toll, it is hard to go on and persevere without also being fortified by joy! My beautiful children, Kaya and Kaden, are my number one source of joy in this world, so I am eternally grateful for every minute with those blessings! I am also grateful to their father and stepmother (Kendall and Vicky James) who are able to care for them when I can't. For the smiles and laughter they brought me while I was working on this book, I also thank the following friends and family (again in alphabetical order): Anne Batten, my BBD the Movement family (especially D'Shawn and

Trey), Sarah Bunn, Sydney Covey, Amy DeLorenzo, Justin Dovi, Amy Etheridge, Judy Fuss, Doug Godfrey, Milton and Lois Green, Alex James, Lori Janke, Karen Johnson, Xavier Joyner, Jean Kelly, Mo Mathews, Shari O'Brien, Anna and Kent Potter, Traci Powers, the Roache family (especially Kathy), Kerry O'Brien Smith, Leigh Starr, and Michelle Taliaferro. And since I've worked at quite a few universities that were low-joy situations, I am especially grateful to the joy I get from my Saint Leo colleagues and community and especially the support of my chair, Janis Prince, and dean, Heather Parker. The fact there is still so much joy despite all that's wrong in this world gives us a reason to go on; thank you! May we redouble our efforts to see to it that this joy one day triumphs over injustice.

Ninochka's Acknowledgments

I would first like to express my immense appreciation to my coauthor and dear friend, Dr. Eileen O'Brien. Your intelligence, creativity, and guidance have made a huge difference over the past decade. I am proud to call you my friend and colleague. Your kind heart, laid-back nature, and wonderful sense of humor have made this process so much fun. I've enjoyed our adventures together all across the country and am excited we were able to make this collaboration happen. You are such a shining light in this world, and I am grateful for that every day.

I would like to express my sincere thanks to my mentors. Dr. Karen Pyke, your guidance, motivation, and patience have been invaluable. I admire your excellence in teaching and upholding a high ethical standard in all that you do. I am extremely grateful for your support during this entire process. Dr. Scott Brooks, thank you for your wisdom, acceptance, guidance, and your strong commitment to your students. I thank Dr. Julie Albright for opening up my sociological imagination during my undergrad years. Your immense knowledge, kindness, and warmth are unmatched. Thank you for believing in me and being an example of a stellar scholar, professor, and mentor.

My friends have played a huge role in providing much-needed support during the writing of this book. To my dearest friends, Sharon Dahan, Carie Martin LAc, Tania Verafield, Nicole Weiss-Calamar, Jessica Felman, Ani Galyan, Sarah Cespedes, Jenna Heffernan, Dr. Whitney Mannies, and Dr. Elizabeth Hughes, thank you for providing me with lots of laughs, adventures, great memories, and most importantly emotional support and guidance during this process. I thank Dr. Caroline Heldman, Dr. Ian Breckinridge-Jackson, Isabelle Shuman, LAc, Sara Choi, and Rocky Davis for always providing me with kindness and with a sense of community and comfort.

Finally, I would like to thank my family for being a wonderful source of love and support. To my parents, Ricardo and Claudette, you have always supported me in all my endeavors wholeheartedly and without hesitation. You have taught me how to be hard-working, empathetic, and dedicated. I know that it took much courage to leave Jamaica for an unknown future in America, but your sacrifices have made this incredible process all possible. I love you both immensely. To my grandfather, Irving Meyer, I am forever grateful for your unwavering support. You have always taught me the importance of education and hard work and always pushed me to achieve greatness, even when I thought I was not capable. I love you so much and you have made such a great impact in my life. I would also like to thank my brother, Michael McTaggart, for being an irreplaceable source of support, my number one concert companion and twin in spirit. Love you, bahd. To Mum and Grandma, thank you for always showering me with your warmth and love. To my sisters, Althea and Claudia, you are amazing women and are wonderful examples of loving and caring mothers, who also excel in their careers. Kimani, Taryn, Kino, and Chai, I love you dearly and I'm so thankful to be your Auntie Nosh. To Kathie and Sam, I love you both and wish you only the best in your grad school journeys. To Murray and Laurel, thank you for always showing me lots of love and support for all of these years. You are both wonderful, kind people whom I love. To Uncle Johnny, thank you for being a source of levity, humor and kindness in my life.

Preface

SOME UNIVERSITIES ARE still naming their race and diversity courses with titles like "Minorities in Society," and many textbooks that focus on race and ethnicity still have Tables of Contents with a chapter for virtually every group *except* whites. W.E.B. Du Bois long ago drew critical attention to the question often posed to him: "How does it feel to be a problem?" In doing so, he was challenging the notion that racial inequality exists because there is something wrong with African Americans or other people of color. He was also contesting the assumption that a "race problem" is a "person-of-color problem." We wrote those books for all those who want to study racial inequality from the vantage point of the unfair advantages conferred upon the dominant group, whites. Scholars of color, often from the margins of the academy and/or outside the academy, were the first ones to investigate from this angle, and others eventually followed, but there is still a long way to go; thus, we hope our book continues to grow the teaching of racial inequalities in this direction.

We are only all too aware that the very concept of white privilege is fraught with contention and even anger and indignation. During the years we were working on this text, if it ever came up in casual conversation that we were writing a book and people asked what it was about, at times we would be met with resistance—the kind of resistance one does not always anticipate when trying to make light, chatty dialogue! To merely invoke the term *white privilege* is apparently a battle cry for some—and most often, such people identify as white. Such conversations can tend to take the shape of a clash of two totally different worldviews, not a mere difference of opinion. Despite the fact that this is an evidence-based text, the teaching of the topic of race is often an emotionally laden topic. Individuals can frequently string one or two personal experiences together, and in their minds it supersedes much more systematic patterned evidence, so it can be difficult to advance such conversations forward in a productive manner. We explicitly designed every aspect of this text with all this in mind.

It is our hope that the multiple "real-life examples" we have inserted into each chapter, only after presenting the preponderance of evidence, serve the purpose of meeting students where they are. In this way, they might ideally be able to apply the concepts and patterns presented here to their everyday lives and the lives of others around them. Another factor that may make the facts of white privilege difficult for some people to digest is we are so much more than just a "race"—we all also occupy many other statuses, including, but certainly not limited to, social class, gender, sexual orientation, religion, age. So to the extent to which these and other experiences may hold people back, they may not really be feeling the idea of being privileged due to race. Thus, we have also inserted "intersectionality" boxes into each chapter to help students see how the material we present on white privilege is compatible and relative to many other social statuses and experiences. Finally, we fully acknowledge that most of the world is not made up of social scientists and gets most of their information these days from pop culture and media while believing that these sources of information make them mini-experts in any given topic. Thus, unlike many race textbooks, we have a full chapter devoted solely to media and pop culture, so we can address some of these issues head-on; again, hopefully meeting students right where they are. Of course, these enhancements alone cannot altogether make white privilege completely digestible or palatable to all. But it is our hope that we have written an accessible text despite the challenging nature of the material herein.

One of us saw a close friend eventually lose a dating partner when the topic of white privilege was broached, and the other of us saw her daughter get accused of being a racist herself by two family members—when she merely pointed out a disciplinary case at school where white privilege was most certainly at work. These events both happened during the short space of writing this text, but much longer we have both sat through many classroom situations witnessing white privilege being a difficult and contentious concept for folks to grasp. We undertook this task knowing full well it would not be an easy one. However, our aspiration is that our work here has made such a path even a tiny bit easier for others, and that ultimately the evidence and the analytical tools we provide here can be useful as our readers go out into the world and face these difficult conversations and occurrences. Ideally, we look hopefully forward to the day when there is no white privilege left to discuss. But in the meantime, our goal is that we have better equipped our readers with the means to expose and resist it, and in so doing, build a fairer, more just, and more equitable world we can all share.

CHAPTER 1

Race

What Is It? Who Decides?

Y OU ARE READING this book in order to study race. You are probably assuming you are going to study people you know of as white, black/African American, Latino/Hispanic, Asian American, Native American, and so on. You may even think of them as white, black, and brown people, even though they do not actually match those colors in the crayon box. At some level, you may already know that these race categories—which we tend to treat as reality in everyday life—can get a bit slippery. You may want to insist we are really all just one race—the human race. And technically, biologically, this is true. But yet there is this thing called white privilege—in fact, it's even in the title of this book. You may know that all 45 US presidents but one have been *white* men, and concerns about *white* supremacist terrorist violence are in the news (Buncombe 2017). You may know that February is *Black* History Month in the United States, and people are marching in the streets for *Black* Lives Matter—not only in the United States, but in Canada, England, France, Senegal, South Africa, Ireland, and Germany (Fadal 2016). These and many other social facts we observe each day indicate to us that there is something called race, with which many people strongly identify, and by which society is organized and interpreted. But it did not always exist. How did it get there? Understanding how "race" got here (in this chapter) is the key to understanding what white privilege is (in all subsequent chapters.)

Before Race

Human beings have been walking the earth way longer than race has existed. Socially, humans organized themselves in various ways, whether it was as clans rivaling for resources or property, royalty attempting to subjugate the masses, or religions clashing for control of a nation/region. Feudal and caste systems do predate the concept of race. Prior to dividing power and resources along racial lines, class/property and religion were two major criteria of human hierarchies. In fact, slavery predated our conceptions of "race." But in the case of a religious monopoly

1

of a region, rulers often would conditionally allow those they subjugated to convert over to the dominant religion. Or in the case of slavery, this often involved an indentured servitude that individuals could work off after a number of years. In other words, this idea of a "race" as an unchanging birth-to-death essential condition did not yet exist (Allen 1994; Roediger 1991).

It was not until the advent of colonialism—and with it, the perceived need to establish ideological (and material) dominance over an entire people—that race was created, precisely to justify one group's control of another (Desmond and Emirbayer 2010). And that controlling group, with its European aristocratic origins, would come to be known as white. But it is important and even crucial to emphasize that this was not always the case. There is no white privilege without whiteness, and there was no whiteness until relatively recently in human history.

It has been supported by both genetic and fossil evidence in the scientific community that the *Homo sapiens* species originated in Ethiopia (in Africa), so we all trace back to a common ancestor there (Stringer 2003). But cross-continental migration further away from the equator allowed for surface-level genetic variations to emerge in our species, creating some skin color differences that we notice today. At the same time, our society has trained us to even notice such human differences in a way that we now assign meaning to them. Yet much more genetic variation exists within animal species such as fruit flies, deer, gray wolves, and even our closest relatives—the chimpanzees—than does among human beings. As evolutionary biologists observe: "Genetic substructure does exist in humans, but there are no natural divisions in our species equivalent to biological races" (Graves and Rose 2006). We humans are much more alike as a species than we are different. Even the "genetic tests" being marketed to consumers today to find out "where they come from" (such as ancestry.com) are based on highly suspect science and tend to reveal that anyone—whether categorized as "black," "white," or something else in today's US society—has some mix of European, African, and Native American ancestry, usually incorporating that common original African ancestor and indicating *continent* of origin rather than "race" (Graves 2015; Herbes-Sommers 2003). Thus, before the invention of race as we know it—and also after—according to biological science, there has always simply been one race: the human race.

So when we speak of **race** today in the social sciences and in society at large, we are speaking of what is now understood as a *pseudoscientific category*. That is to say, early understandings of science were used (as religion was also used) by those in power to make it appear as if race were an unarguable, scientifically supported category system of human beings. *The surface-level genetic variations of skin color, eye shape, and hair texture among people that the human eye is now trained (by many societies) to see and assign meaning to* is now the pseudoscientific category known as **race**. This makes **race** real as a *social construct*, much more than a scientific classification of humans. *Legal and political restrictions that shape life chances* have been now attached to race for centuries, and these dividing lines were only erected in order to preserve material and social advantages (now known as white privileges) for the elite European male landowners of the imperialist, colonialist, and aristocratic class (Feagin and Ducey 2017). As we shall see, who was and is to be included in the "white" racial category (and thus who was to enjoy such legal and political advantages) is the key organizing principle motivating the various shifting definitions of race that have occurred across time and place.

Creating Race: Whiteness as a Racial Bribe

The invention of the concept of different races of human beings was a gradual process that cannot be pinned down to a single date, since as a social construct it had to take hold among a critical mass of those in power. Generally, the 1700s are marked as the point of solidification of race as a fundamental organizing, rank-ordering principle of legal and social consequence, although certainly the groundwork was being laid well before then—since the various Spanish, French, and British exploration voyages to other continents beyond their own, especially Christopher Columbus's 1492 arrival upon the Americas. These centuries of humans from different lands coexisting on one soil were fraught with conflict and attempts to dominate and conquer. More specifically, native, indigenous peoples had to fight off takeovers of their land by Europeans who would eventually come to be referred to as white in subsequent generations. Creating an ideology that fused religious thought with new scientific ways of understanding the world was central to European colonialist justification of their violent takeovers of foreign lands (Culotta 2012; Feagin and Ducey 2017).

In the American context, historians often cite an event now known as Bacon's Rebellion, which took place in the British colony of Virginia in 1676, as a turning point for British landowners' trajectory toward solidifying whiteness—and thereby race—as a social and legal distinction of humans (Alexander 2010; Allen 1994). During this armed conflict aimed at Native Americans, a British man named Nathaniel Bacon was able to organize working-class peasants and slaves with various continents and countries of origin, fighting together as one united and powerful front (Allen 1994). European elites viewed the success of this working people's alliance as a threat to their continued chances of maintaining a subjugated, cheap labor force, and thus began attaching social and legal advantages to those deemed "white"—advantages that would not cost elites any extra in terms of pay, but were aimed at fracturing continued labor alliances. It was, in effect, a "racial bribe" (Alexander 2010), or what W.E.B. Du Bois termed the "psychological wage," that was offered to the lighter-skinned Europeans who had previously worked and socialized with their fellow African-origin indentured servants (Roediger 1991). As laws and social codes gave "whites" greater freedom of movement, the ability to live and shop where they chose, and eventually condemned Africans to lifelong/birth-assigned chattel slavery, the notion of different races of humankind took root just as a nation called the United States of America was about to be born. White privilege, born through this creation of race, thus became foundational to the budding nation.

Yet all over the world—whether it was the British in North America, the Spanish in Latin America, or the French in Africa—it was European Christianity's hierarchical ideas about divine rights to land, combined with new ideas of scientific classification, that imperialist colonialists fused together in order to justify what they deemed their God-given conquest of others' land, livelihood, and even personhood. Franz Fanon ([1952]1967), among others, has analyzed how the guilt of the colonizers needed to be projected off onto an "other"—indeed, all the capacity for violence Europeans had come face to face with in themselves, they began attributing to blackness and all others deemed not white. Thus, it is important to emphasize that race is a *relational* category. In other words, there would be no need for human "races" without the need to erect boundaries between this privileged category called "white" and something else. As Ta-Nehisi Coates has written:

> But race is the child of racism, not the father. And the process of naming "the people" has never been a matter of genealogy and physiognomy so much as one of hierarchy. Difference in hue and hair is old. But the belief in the preeminence of hue and hair, the notion that these factors can correctly organize a society and that they signify deeper attributes which are indelible—this is the new idea at the heart of these new people who have been brought up hopelessly, tragically, deceitfully, to believe that they are white. (Coates 2015:8)

In saying that race is a "child," Coates further illustrates that, once the need for creating a hierarchy of humans for imperialist domination was established, elite Europeans got to work creating the reality of race, in order to fence off a privileged status of whiteness from the rest. Thus, it is not the case that racial differences always existed among humans, but then some "bad apple" had to go and attach biased assumptions to one group over another. Rather, the very act of setting out to distinguish human races had at its core the intent to justify unequal relations between the elite European (males) and the rest.

As natural science began to develop classifications of various other animal and plant species, European scientists became accomplices in creating the pseudoscientific basis of race. Johann Blumenbach, a professor in Germany who was a student of Carl Linnaeus, was the first to combine intelligence testing and physical appearance observations to propose five categories of humans—Ethiopian (African); American (Native); Malayan ("brown"); Mongolian ("yellow"); and Caucasian (European/"white") (Desmond and Emirbayer 2010). You may sometimes hear some people prefer the term "Caucasian" over "white" when they are trying to sound more neutral, scientific, or proper, but the selection of this term itself is at best arbitrary and ironic. Blumenbach thought the people of the Caucasus Mountains in Russia were the most beautiful light-skinned people he had ever seen, so he decided to name his "white" category after them (Witzig 1996). The irony is that with migration changes, this region of Russia later became inhabited with slightly darker-skinned peoples, so Caucasian is in effect a meaningless label within an already scientifically meaningless classification system. Yet, it is a term that continues to be used by many with little understanding of its origins.

Blumenbach was hardly alone in the European academic community in his zeal to categorize humans in rank-ordered categories—rank-ordered categories that always placed whiteness at the top. The late 1700s was a period in which a multiplicity of scholars solidified this way of thinking. For example, German philosopher Immanuel Kant in 1790 used his own observations on the human diversity of temperament and reasoning ability to create a four-category system, solidifying the idea of whiteness as a privileged status (Larrimore 2008). Later, these practices would come to be known as scientific racism, but a plethora of scholars since the late eighteenth century have continued to use some combination of skull size measurements, intelligence testing, and other methods in attempts to lend this kind of pseudoscientific backing to a classification system which is largely legal, social, and environmental—with little to no true biological basis. Such attempts to use the language of science while practicing questionable methods are characteristic of the larger pattern of making whiteness and race appear neutral and normal.

Races as Pan-ethnic Categories Aimed at Preserving White Advantage

In understanding race as a social construct created to preserve white economic, legal, and political advantage, it is also important to acknowledge that races are pan-ethnic social groups. That is, they often combine various ethnic backgrounds and cultural practices under one umbrella for the purposes of classification and treatment under the law. These groupings may or may not be meaningful designations for the practitioners of such ethnicities, especially at first. An **ethnicity**, or **ethnic group**, is a *group that shares a common ancestry and/or cultural practices and heritage*. For example, many diverse Native nations who considered themselves rivals, spoke different languages, and had differing cultural practices came to be treated as one racial group (American Indian/Native American) for policy purposes by federal US agencies like the Bureau of Indian Affairs and Bureau of the Census. Likewise, the many tribes from the continent of Africa, such as Yoruba, Wolof, and Mande, who survived the Middle Passage on slave ships—speaking different languages and practicing different religions—eventually developed a newly created African American culture because of their subjugated treatment in the US context as one "black" race. Thus, when we study white privilege, it is instructive to take note of how diverse ethnicities combine within the racial category of white. Sometimes, people may refer to whites as European Americans, but in fact, an examination of the US Census and other legal decisions in the country over time reveals that it was not just European Americans alone to garner the white distinction. And conversely, not all European Americans were always considered white. The invention of race was to preserve hierarchy and advantage for certain elites over others.

Ethnic groups such as the Irish and Russian Jews were not readily welcomed into the socioeconomic advantages of whiteness in their early immigration history to the United States, but eventually became white (Brodkin 1998; Ignatiev 1995). Many other ethnic groups, however, were never permitted to be included in the legal status of whiteness, though many would try. One important component of race being a social construct is that the way it is defined varies across time, place, and society. Hence, the various ethnic groups who have been considered white over time and place have rarely been consistent. During apartheid in South Africa, two ethnic groups that are today considered part of the same race (Asian American) in the United States—Chinese and Japanese—were treated distinctively, with the Japanese enjoying the racial freedom of movement afforded to whites, while the Chinese were relegated to the more provisionally situated "colored" racial designation. Various "racial middle" ethnic groups have shifted from being considered white to not white throughout US history (O'Brien 2008; Rodriguez 2000; Tuan 1999).

Particularly in the lengthy period between 1790 and the mid-twentieth century, one could not become a US citizen at all unless categorized as white (Desmond and Emirbayer 2010; Taparata 2016). Due to this legal roadblock, members of various ethnic groups over time attempted to petition the courts to get themselves reclassified as white so that they could enjoy basic citizenship under the law. For example, in 1922, in the case of *Ozawa v. United States*, the US Supreme Court told a Japanese American man he could not be white (and thus never become citizen), and then in 1923, in the case of *United States v. Bhagat Singh Thind*, the same fate befell Mr. Thind, who was of Indian descent (O'Brien 2008; Smith 2003). Both cases decided the fate of thousands of hardworking families who had known nothing but the United States since they could remember—some who had even previously been considered citizens had their citizenship revoked as a result of this ruling (Taparata 2016). In the words of legal scholar John Powell, there are many things that are "slick about whiteness" (Smith 2003), and one is that whiteness becomes whatever those in power say it is. As Michael Eric Dyson writes: "Whiteness only has two modes: it either converts or destroys" (Dyson 2017:49). In the history of deciding which ethnic groups would become white and not, we can see that race has never been merely a scientific classification for categorization purposes alone. Whiteness is a category that reserves full citizenship for a select group and is subject to change as social and political boundaries shift.

When these socially constructed pan-ethnic racial groups are created, something called **racial formation** occurs (Omi and Winant 1994). Sociopolitical interests shape and reshape what constitutes a race. The boundaries of whiteness have thus both expanded and contracted over time, depending on the socioeconomic, political, and legal conditions of any given society. Certain ethnic groups, such as the Irish and the Russian Jews, were seen as inferior and racially different from whites in earlier periods, but by distancing themselves from blacks and becoming more accepted into economic and political spheres of influence, they came to be known as white (Warren and Twine 1997). For the Irish Americans, it was a tough choice—Irish Catholics in particular had just come from their homelands where they were persecuted for religious differences, and many felt a kindred cause with African Americans, who were subjugated in the labor market, housing, and other areas of social life, even in the North. While some, like Father Daniel O'Connell, remained a staunch abolitionist leader, others took that racial bargain, leading the way for Irish Americans to eventually become part of the political machine by distancing themselves from African Americans (Ignatiev 1995). Likewise, Jewish Americans—although seen as inferior throughout the early half of the twentieth century and excluded from universities and various forms of work—were able to benefit from the GI Bill's housing benefits at the conclusion of World War II in a way that fellow African American veterans could not (Brodkin 1998). Not that GI Bill housing benefits were not afforded African Americans, but the US Federal Housing Authority still approved of racial discrimination in home buying, mortgage lending, and insurance practices, so African Americans were excluded from purchasing in the newly created suburban neighborhoods that became wealth generating for Jewish Americans and all others considered white. Some have referred to this period in US history as "affirmative action for whites" (Desmond and Emirbayer 2010) because it gave all those who were considered white by that time an economic boost, simply due to racial group membership.

Likewise, racial formation—creating a race by combining different ethnic groups for sociopolitical purposes—can also occur "from below." That is, rather than the government using its power to define who is and is not part of a racial group "from above," occasionally social movement efforts can effectively petition the government to become reclassified. Such efforts are typically more successful when the reclassification being requested does not involve becoming "white." Thus, while Ozawa and Thind were both unsuccessful in petitioning the US Supreme Court for "white" classification in the 1920s, by the latter part of the twentieth century, things had changed significantly—not only for Japanese and Indian Americans, but for many other ethnic groups with ancestral ties to Asia, such as Chinese, Korean, Filipino/a, Vietnamese, and other such Americans. Some of these Asian American ethnic groups had been in the United States for just as long, if not longer, than groups like the aforementioned Irish and Russian Jews. Significantly, the 1965 Immigration and Nationality Act finally lifted racially biased national-origin quotas that had severely restricted migrants from Africa, Asia, and Latin America prior to that time, which brought greater immigration from these areas. Around this same time, the African American–led civil rights movement inspired other groups, like Native Americans, Mexican, and other Latino Americans, to challenge their lack of representation (socioeconomic, cultural, political) and equal treatment under the law. This and other factors inspired a collection of diverse ethnic groups—with ancestral ties to many different Asian and Pacific Island nations—to unite and successfully get the US Census to add an "Asian Pacific Islander" racial category in 1990 (Espiritu 1993; O'Brien 2008).

Although this racial category was added due to successful coalition building among these Asian Pacific Islander groups, it is important to also underscore how white perceptions (or more accurately, *mis*perceptions) factored into this pan-ethnic racial formation. Incidents like the hate-crime killing of Vincent Chin, a Chinese American man, on the eve of his wedding night (in 1982) demonstrate how white scapegoating of the other bears little resemblance to how members of ethnic groups actually view themselves. The white men (Ronald Ebens and Michael Nitz) who killed Chin mistook him for Japanese and mentioned being angry for having been laid off from auto-industry jobs, which they blamed on the Japanese (who would technically be in Japan, and not Americans) (Hwang 2000). What Asian activists and organizers of various ethnicities began to realize is that white perceptions of them lumped them together, which bound them in some kind of common fate, regardless of the lack of connection they felt to each other on the basis of ethnicity. They shared an increasingly similar racialized experience in the United States (O'Brien 2008). Having their "American-ness" questioned was not new in the 1980s. After all, the Chinese Exclusion Act of 1882 and the Japanese internment camps during World War II, are both part of a US history that alternately targeted these two ethnicities, albeit at different times, making it tempting to dissociate from one another for safety's sake. Yet as W.E.B. Du Bois outlined with his concept of **double consciousness**, people of color must be keenly aware at all times for their very survival, of both how they see themselves, and how whites view them. The Vincent Chin case was one of countless examples of white perceptions of foreign-ness attached to various Asian American peoples, regardless of ethnicity (Takaki 2000; Tuan 1999). Consequently, although the pan-ethnic Asian American Pacific Islander racial group may have been constructed "from below," it was nevertheless shaped by white power to mischaracterize, and even terrorize, groups based on notions of inferior race.

The Ethnicity Tradeoff for Whiteness

Because of the privileged legal, political, social, and economic status of white-ness, members of various ethnic groups have attempted to become accepted into whiteness over time, with varying degrees of success. As we have seen, one's access to jobs, citizenship, property, voting rights—and one's ability to avoid being a target for racist violence and oppression—has hinged upon the degree to which one can be racially categorized as white. Note that the white race is a construct with legal, political, and socioeconomic ramifications, but appears to be devoid of the distinct cultural heritage and practices typically associated with an ethnic group. This is because from its inception, whiteness was an invention that fused together different groups so it had enough of a critical mass to maintain its power. Whiteness has "ever-expanding boundaries" (Warren and Twine 1997:200), but its acceptance is conditional and subject to change (Bonilla-Silva 2017). Two of the most consistent conditions of being accepted into whiteness have been (a) distancing oneself from blacks; and (b) de-emphasizing ethnic markers. For example, many Russian Jews and other southern and eastern European families shortened or changed their surnames as part of the process toward being able to access the benefits of whiteness in the United States (Brodkin 1998; Takaki 2008). In his "Sermon to White America," Dyson aptly describes this historical process when he says:

> When your ancestors got to America, they endured a pro-
> found makeover ... All of your polkas, or pubs or pizzas, and
> more, got tossed into a crucible of race where European eth-
> nicities got pulverized into whiteness. (Dyson 2017:45)

Dyson's reference to polkas, pubs, and pizzas is a shorthand description of the process of cultural assimilation that many groups attempt in pursuit of structural assimilation—but even with all these efforts, only certain groups/persons were able to claim the white designation. As the organization People's Institute for Survival and Beyond explains, in this process of becoming white, ethnic groups have "traded culture for power" (O'Brien 2001:117). That is, they become less connected to the cultural practices that were once more salient for members of their ethnic groups. And in exchange, they may be able to access the benefits of whiteness in return. (Others can only get so far as "honorary whiteness," at best—which we discuss further in a subsequent section.)

Assimilation is a term that dominated the social science of race and ethnicity for quite some time. It is a concept that describes the process by which a minority group becomes absorbed into the dominant culture and eventually virtually indistinguishable—melting into the metaphorical melting pot. Milton Gordon

(1964) identifies six different types of assimilation—cultural, structural, civic, attitude-receptional, behavioral-receptional, and ultimately, marital. But his model is structured around earlier immigrant groups to the United States who arrived mainly from Europe and eventually became white (Feagin and Feagin 2010). While conforming to dominant cultural norms and patterns of behavior worked out fairly well for European ethnics seeking to become assimilated in the United States, other groups who played by the same rules were not as favored. But for those Italian, Irish, Polish, and others who did come to be regarded as white, over time their ethnic cultural connections became less salient in their everyday lives. Herbert Gans (1979) refers to this as **symbolic ethnicity**. Ethnicity encompasses cultural practices, and sociologists typically define culture as a way of life, so when someone's ethnicity is largely symbolic, it is no longer part of his or her everyday life practices. If someone only thinks about being Irish in occasional conversations about their last name or on special occasions such as St. Patrick's Day, we can say their ethnicity is mainly only symbolic. Whereas for folks whose ethnicity is practiced on a daily basis through the language(s) they speak, the food(s) they eat, the way they dress, it is no longer merely symbolic for them. Another useful way of thinking about this varying level of connection to one's ethnicity is **thick versus thin ethnicity**. This newer concept posits ethnicity on a continuum or sliding scale, to reflect varying levels of engagement. Older models proposed that ethnicity followed a fairly linear trajectory of gradually thinning with time and with generations. However, some research finds later generations may have a revived interest in reconnecting with ethnic traditions after the prior generation has attempted to distance themselves from them (Vasquez 2011).

One advantage of being white is the "option" to connect with one's ethnicity or not. If someone is racially marked as not-white, whether or not they feel much connection personally to their ethnicity, they are often perceived through the lens of that racial group and the ethnicity that is presumed to go with it. For example, someone who is Latino or Asian American may be complimented on their English skills, despite having lived for generations in the United States and knowing nothing but English. A similar instance is being constantly asked "Where are you from?"—also called the "ethnic game"—even when answering the question with a US town or state name, and the questioner does not accept that answer, instead continuing to ask, "No, where are you from, before that, before that?" (O'Brien 2008; Tuan 1999). Whites do not have to deal as much with this constant questioning of their own narratives of ethnic identity. Many white Americans are no longer even sure what ethnicities are part of their family tree (Waters 1990). They no longer live a reality where they are regularly called to account for it. (We present ample evidence of this in the coming chapters.)

Defining White Privilege

Throughout this brief introduction to defining race and ethnicity, we have already highlighted the various ways in which whiteness has been situated above other statuses, and by definition is a hierarchical concept. It should by now be evident how being white was invented as a locus of power and advantage, separating those deemed white from others with fewer resources and rights. But before we go any further, because it is the basis of this book, we want to make sure we lay out a clear, precise definition of white privilege. It is perhaps as important to grasp what white privilege is as it is to understand what it is not.

W.E.B. Du Bois was one of the earliest writers to describe in detail what would later be termed white privilege. We introduced his concept of double consciousness above, but in his own words, in his famed book *The Souls of Black Folk*, Du Bois wrote:

> It is a peculiar sensation, this double-consciousness, this sense of always looking at one's self through the eyes of others, of measuring one's soul by the tape of a world that looks on in amused contempt and pity. One ever feels his two-ness,—an American, a Negro; two souls, two thoughts, two unreconciled strivings; two warring ideals in one dark body, whose dogged strength alone keeps it from being torn asunder. (Du Bois 1996[1903]:5)

About a decade later, Du Bois wrote an essay entitled "The Souls of White Folk" in his book *Darkwater* (1920), in which he poses a stark contrast between this constant state of dual awareness blacks have in a racially stratified society and the *obliviousness* that whites have to this reality. Although not using the term white privilege, Du Bois marvels at how it is possible that whites can prevail over so much torture, lynching, destruction, and death, seemingly without even batting an eye. Whites only inhabit a world that seems fair and humane, without appearing to be morally disturbed by its injustice. Even writing this critique of whites' character—at a time where if a black man so much as met a white man's eyes he could be lynched with no hope of justice—was brave indeed.

By the 1960s (several decades later), Kwame Ture (then Stokely Carmichael) and Charles Hamilton wrote *Black Power* [1967] (1992), a critique of white racism—which they termed institutional racism—still a relatively rare implication of whites' role in prevailing over racial inequality. During the US civil rights movement, very often the frame of advocacy for full human rights for African Americans was one in which blacks asked for a fair seat at the table in an otherwise just system. Overt critique of whites and a white-designed system (publicly) was relatively rare. Du Bois echoed this undue focus on African Americans in the race discussion when he problematized the oft-asked question: "How does it feel to be a problem?" Du

Bois implored whites to look at their own role in the problem of racial inequality instead of merely seeing racial inequality as a black problem. Du Bois, and dozens of other African American thinkers throughout the twentieth century, proposed this kind of turning the tables (onto whiteness) for analyzing racism (Roediger 1999).

However, it was not until a white woman named Peggy McIntosh (1989) presented a paper at conferences (1986–1988) where she brainstormed a list of 46 white privileges she experienced as a white woman, in comparison to her African American colleagues, that the term **white privilege** itself gained momentum. A key component of McIntosh's essay is her focus on the obliviousness or invisibility of white privilege, and as a woman, she compares this component of white privilege to the obliviousness that she has encountered when talking to men about their own gender-based advantages. McIntosh writes:

> As a white person, I realized I had been taught about racism as something which puts others at a disadvantage, but had been taught not to see one of its corollary aspects, white privilege, which puts me at an advantage. ... I have come to see white privilege as an invisible package of unearned assets which I can count on cashing in each day, but about which I was "meant" to remain oblivious. White privilege is like an invisible weightless knapsack of special provisions, maps, passports, codebooks, visas, clothes, tools and blank checks. ... The pressure to avoid it is great, for in facing it I must give up the myth of meritocracy. If these things are true, this is not such a free country; one's life is not what one makes it; many doors open for certain people through no virtues of their own. (McIntosh 1989:10–11)

McIntosh also points out that in everyday language, the term *privilege* is used for something people earn—such as the privilege of a driver's license, which can be revoked when rules are not followed—and in that sense, is understood as something that is fair. So, when referring to white privilege, we must pay close attention to the fact that the word privilege is not used here in the traditional linguistic sense. Because whiteness is marked as neutral, normal, and the default, there is much that those humans assumed to be white can count on as they move through their daily lives. For example, a few privileges from McIntosh's list of 46 include: "Whether I use checks, credit cards, or cash, I can count on my skin color not to work against the appearance of financial reliability"; "I can do well in a challenging situation without being called a credit to my race"; and "I can take a job with an affirmative action employer without having coworkers on the job suspect that I got it because of race" (McIntosh 1989:11). **White privilege** is thus defined as unearned advantages that whites experience in a racially stratified society that often go unnoticed or taken for granted by them. White privilege can sometimes be blatant—as when a person of color gets a security screening while the white person with them does not—but more often it is unremarkable experiences, such as people being friendly and pleasant to you, or not asking you for identification when you write a check, or telling you that a home is available to buy/rent, or that an employer is currently accepting applications. As Michael Eric Dyson writes: "A great deal of white advantage has nothing to do with how you actively resist black success ... It's what you do for each other, how you take each other into account" (Dyson 2017:79) Thus, white privilege happens in both racially mixed and in all-white spaces. Yes, race is relevant even when people of color are not there.

Another oft-misunderstood point about white privilege: White privilege is not to be confused with living in the lap of luxury. White students of very humble backgrounds who are struggling financially often balk at the notion of white privilege. They do not feel very privileged living on some of the lowest rungs of the socioeconomic ladder and hanging on by a thread. Indeed, the wealth gap between the richest and poorest families in the United States has been growing and by 2017 was at the highest levels ever recorded (Kochhar and Cilluffo 2017). There are way more whites struggling than there are whites doing well. White privilege does not mean if you are white you will be rich and have no problems. Just as race itself is a relational concept, so, too, is the concept of white privilege. That is, white privilege highlights the unearned advantages that whites, even at the same income level as their not-white counterparts, can expect to experience based on race. Throughout this book, we will provide data and examples of how that happens. Certainly there are ample examples of financial white privilege (e.g., income, wealth) that we review in Chapter 3, but it is important to remember, as one writer puts it: "There are a lot of privileges that white folk get that don't depend on cash. The greatest one might be getting stopped by a cop and living to talk about it" (Dyson 2017:66). What sociologists refer to as life chances, or what the US Constitution refers to as "life, liberty and the pursuit of happiness," can be captured in many different measures, and we present those throughout this text.

White privilege also operates at both micro and macro levels. As we discuss more in Chapter 2, individual biases and prejudices occur among all racial groups and can be aimed at whites sometimes. As noted above, there is a great deal of denial and obliviousness about white privilege, and one way that denial can manifest itself is when whites point out a time or two when they have felt in the minority or mistreated because they were white. To say there is white privilege is not to say that white people never have negative experiences of mistreatment that might feel tied to their race. A white person might read McIntosh's #4 on her list of white privileges ("I can go shopping alone most of the time, pretty well assured that I will not be followed or harassed") and respond, "Well, I got followed in the store once, too." Individual experiences that run counter to the pattern does not mean that the overall larger pattern does not exist. In this text, we will encourage you to be skilled practitioners of reviewing data and evidence from large-scale studies and reliable sources. These skills will hopefully help you to discern between an "out-lier" (an atypical instance that is counter to the overall pattern) and an "illustrative example" (a case that typifies anecdotally a larger pattern). Both certainly exist, but we must place each in its proper context.

Finally, and most importantly, other systems of privilege and inequality exist besides just race. Such systems include, but are not limited to, gender, class, sexual orientation, age, and ability. How white privilege looks for an upper-class white straight male is going to be very different from how it looks for a white disabled lesbian female. But that does not mean they do not both experience white privilege. They do. As we have emphasized, white privilege is hardly an experience of riding off into the sunset with no problems or issues. Many whites face inequalities of other kinds, which may make white privilege even harder to see than it already is. But as Peggy McIntosh reminds us, privilege can often be more visible to those who don't have it than those who do. McIntosh maintains that indeed one is "care-fully taught" not to see privilege. The goal of this textbook is to make the invisible more visible.

White Privilege for Whites ... or for Non-blacks?

We have reviewed how race was defined and created to separate whiteness (a privileged status) out from the rest. We have also considered some historical examples of the various ethnic groups who were and were not permitted to be included in the category "white" over time. These examples illustrate how members of some ethnic groups who count on white privilege now could not always count on it in other times. Because race is a social construct, its boundaries have always shifted since its inception, and will undoubtedly continue to do so. One of the most vivid examples of the dynamic shape of race can be found in the US Census. An analysis of the racial categories of the US Census over time strongly emphasizes the pseudoscience of race. Race is *not skin color, but rather a sociopolitical and legal designation*—it is the law that changes it, not biology or science.

In Table 1.1, some interesting races—"Mulatto," "Quadroon," and "Octo-roon"—are listed in 1890. Note that they disappear after that year, but "Mulatto" makes a brief reappearance in 1910 and 1920. All these racial categories were placed on people whose skin color and features would likely be assumed to be white by today's US standards, but during this legal segregation period of history, would have actually been considered black. Here is where the pseudoscience of race becomes painfully evident. Legal proceedings used the notion of "one drop" of "black blood" in order to decide whether an individual was considered black or white. Blood is of course never actually drawn to make these determinations because blood types in biological sciences (e.g., A, AB, O) do not correspond to the socially constructed categories of race. Courts simply used the racial classification

Table 1.1 Racial Classifications in the US Census 1890–2010

1890	1900	1910	1920	1930	1940	1950
White	White	White	White	White	White	White
Black	Black	Black	Black	Negro	Negro	Negro
Mulatto	Chinese	Mulatto	Mulatto	Mexican	Indian	American Indian
Quadroon	Japanese	Chinese	Chinese	Indian	Chinese	Japanese
Octoroon	Indian	Japanese	Japanese	Chinese	Japanese	Chinese
Chinese		Indian	Indian	Japanese	Filipino	Filipino
Japanese		Other	Other	Filipino	Hindu	Other
Indian				Hindu	Korean	
				Korean	Other	
				Other		

1960	1970	1980	1990	2000*	2010*
White	White	White	White	White	White
Negro	Negro or Black	Black or Negro	Black or Negro	Black, African American, or Negro	Black, African American, or Negro
American Indian	Indian (American)	Japanese	Indian (American)	American Indian or Alaska Native	American Indian or Alaska Native
Japanese	Japanese	Chinese	Eskimo	Asian Indian	Asian Indian
Chinese	Chinese	Filipino	Aleut	Chinese	Chinese
Filipino	Filipino	Korean	Asian or Pacific Islander	Filipino	Filipino
Hawaiian	Hawaiian	Vietnamese	Chinese	Japanese	Other Asian
Part Hawaiian	Korean	Indian (American)	Filipino	Korean	Japanese
Aleut	Other	Asian Indian	Hawaiian	Vietnamese	Korean
Eskimo		Hawaiian	Korean	Other Asian	Vietnamese
Other, etc.		Guamanian	Vietnamese	Native Hawaiian	Native Hawaiian
		Samoan	Japanese	Guamanian or	Guamanian or
		Eskimo	Asian Indian		
		Aleut	Samoan		
		Other			

(Continued)

Table 1.1 Racial Classifications in the US Census 1890–2010 (*Continued*)

1960	1970	1980	1990	2000*	2010*
		Not Spanish/Hispanic	Guamanian	Chamorro	Chamorro
		Mexican, Mexican American, Chicano	Other	Samoan	Samoan
		Puerto Rican	Not Spanish/Hispanic	Other Pacific Islander	Other Pacific Islander
		Cuban	Mexican, Mexican American, Chicano	Some other race	Some other race
		Other Spanish/Hispanic	Puerto Rican	Not Spanish/Hispanic/Latino	Not of Hispanic, Latino, or Spanish Origin
			Cuban	Mexican, Mexican American, Chicano	Mexican, Mexican American, Chicano
			Other Spanish/Hispanic	Puerto Rican	Puerto Rican
				Cuban	Cuban
				Other Spanish/ Hispanic/ Latino	Another Hispanic, Latino, or Spanish Origin

*Beginning in 2000, individuals were presented with the option to self-identify with more than one race and this continued with the 2010 census. Beginning in 2000, the placement of the Hispanic origin question directly preceded the question on race.

*(Based on Lee, 1993; Snipp, 2003; Cohn, 2010; U.S. Census Bureau, 2001; U.S. Census Bureau, 2011)

on an individual's birth certificate (and also the racial classification of one's parents and grandparents) to determine how much "black blood" they had. The term *octoroon* was used to refer to someone who was one-eighth black; *quadroon* was for someone who was one-fourth black; and *mulatto* for one-half black.

Even though in 1890 chattel slavery was legally over, the legal segregation of Jim Crow continued to operate through these same racial categories (which we discuss more in Chapter 3). And during slavery, there came a point at which in the United States it was no longer legal for humans to be imported from other countries, with an act of Congress that took effect in 1808. So slave masters routinely raped enslaved Africans, and the offspring from these unions were still categorized as black and condemned to lifelong slavery, thereby increasing the number of slaves they owned (Brunsma and Rockquemore 2002). It was advantageous, then, for elite white landowners to follow this **one-drop rule** for determining who was African American—since anyone so categorized was legally permitted to be owned and subjugated as their property. The one-drop rule dictated that even the slightest bit of African American ancestry meant you were classified as black. And although the US Census only shows a "one-eighth" example (with "octoroon"), there were US states such as Louisiana where as little as one-32nd of so-called "black blood" was enough to make you black (Desmond and Emirbayer 2010). Laws like this demonstrate how the boundaries of whiteness and white privilege were tightly controlled.

Another interesting racial category on the US Census, appearing in 1930 and 1940, is Hindu. Although we have been mainly emphasizing how societies have combined different ethnicities/national origins to create race, it is important to note that neither skin color nor ethnicity alone can adequately describe what is race. During this period of global history leading up to World War II, the eugenics movement garnered worldwide attention, especially among elite white males continuing to seek justification for oppression and persecution. During the 1930s and 1940s, many large US corporations actually had financial ties to Nazi Germany with its racist ideas, including the idea that members of the Jewish religion were actually a racial group distinct from elite whiteness (Feagin and Ducey 2017). The inclusion of the Hindu religion as a racial category reflects eugenics ideology of the time period and demonstrates both how religions can be considered races and how strict boundaries continued to be drawn between people like Ozawa and Thind (plaintiffs in the 1920s US Supreme Court cases noted above) and whiteness. Religions becoming racialized continues into the twenty-first century with the experience of Muslim Americans as well (Selod 2018).

Although they may not have been officially categorized as white, in places where dividing lines between black and white were clearly drawn, sometimes racial middle groups like Latinos and Asian Americans basically were forced to pick a side. Chinese sharecroppers living in the Mississippi Delta during the Reconstruction period were able to change their names and distance themselves from blacks to the point where they moved from being excluded to being included in the highly segregated US South—into white-only schools and other avenues of social life (Loewen 1988; Warren and Twine 1997). As we have seen in the cases of Irish and Jewish Americans, distancing oneself from blackness has been one successful way to cash in on white privilege—or what some have termed light-skinned privilege (Hunter 2011).

Many lighter-skinned African Americans (especially those who might have been classified as mulatto, quadroon, or octoroon by the US Census) practiced what is known as **passing** in order to gain access to jobs and other resources, especially during the period of legal segregation (1865–1965) in the United States. Individuals like Plessy from the noted *Plessy v. Ferguson* US Supreme Court case (1896) (where "separate but equal" was upheld as legal) often attempted to access white-only accommodations like train cars and schools by performing whiteness (Desmond and Emirbayer 2010). Both the necessity of distancing oneself from blackness to gain legal and economic opportunities, as well as the cultural valuation of whiteness over blackness globally, have created a situation where there exists light-skin privilege, even among nonwhites. Among Latinos, for example, housing segregation is greater for darker-skinned than lighter-skinned Latinos, and standards of beauty favor the lighter skin and features over the darker (O'Brien 2008). This is not merely a personal preference, but a cultural ideal conditioned by a society that favors and privileges whiteness. Darker-skinned African Americans have lower self-esteem on average than lighter-skinned African Americans, and they are also discriminated against more in the job market and other areas of life (Thompson and Keith 2001; Hunter 2007). This lighter-is-better ideology exists across the globe, especially where colonialism's influence has been most pervasive—North America, South America, and Africa. At its most extreme, the marketing of skin-bleaching creams (despite health risks) and cosmetic surgery, especially for women, to approximate white features, demonstrates the far-reaching consequences of distancing oneself from blackness in order to get closer to white privilege (Hunter 2011). This practice of **colorism**, or *the favoring of lighter skin tone over darker skin tone among communities of color*, cannot be understood without taking into account the ubiquitous influence of the European colonialist elevation of whiteness and lightness as the preferred and most-prized standard.

Honorary Whites—White Privilege and Light-Skinned Privilege

Whiteness was invented, and we have seen how the creation of whiteness has been a dynamic and ever-changing process. Although since its inception whiteness has been the most privileged racial status, some have questioned what might happen to the privileged status of whiteness if and when people of color come to outnumber whites. Some are optimistic that white privilege might go away altogether if society becomes increasingly multiracial, assuming power might then be shared more equally, while others think whiteness will just keep including more "honorary whites" so that whiteness retains dominance and power (Bonilla-Silva 2017; O'Brien 2008; Warren and Twine 1997; Yancey 2003). Latinos and Asian Americans are the two fastest growing racial groups in the United States, and many are already identifying as white by various measures: on the US Census, for example, millions of Hispanics switched from choosing "some other race" to choosing "white" between 2000 and 2010 (Cohn 2014). Children of interracial marriages (with one white parent) are much more likely to consider themselves "white" if their other parent is Latino or Asian American than they are if their other parent is black (O'Brien 2008). It is evidence like this that leads many leading scholars in this area to predict that even as societies become more multiracial, white privilege is not going to end (Bonilla-Silva 2017; Warren and Twine 1997).

In particular, a more likely scenario is that the racial stratification system would become less dichotomous (white over black) and more multifaceted, but with whites still on top. With a history of less rigid miscegenation laws than the United States, Latin America has a more sizable racially mixed (*mestizaje*) population and has been characterized by more of a three-layer stratification system—with its mixed population in the middle, enjoying greater levels of prestige and opportunity than darker-skinned people, but still not as much as those deemed white (Bonilla-Silva 2017). Also, there are more flexible boundaries between white and nonwhite in many Latin American societies than in the United States, but still very much tied to power and prestige. For instance, in Brazil there is a saying "money whitens," and indeed the data bear this out—that even with darker skin, parents who are more educated are more likely to classify their children as "white" than those who are less educated (Schwartzman 2007). This example further underscores the point that it is very inaccurate to define race as "skin color." Race is a social construct that combines a variety of sociopolitical factors, and thus race changes as societies change.

Taking a look at the various ethnicities most populating the United States in the early twenty-first century, Eduardo Bonilla-Silva (2017) predicts that groups like Japanese, Korean, Chinese, Indian, and Filipino Americans, along with Middle Easterners, light-skinned Latinos, and most people who are multiracial, will eventually become part of a middle "honorary white" status between white and black. Alternatively, he predicts Vietnamese, Laotian, and Hmong Americans, as well as darker-skinned Latinos and West Indian and African immigrant blacks, will fall into a "collective black" category, in terms of the pattern of socioeconomic conditions and treatment they can expect to experience. He makes these predictions based on a variety of income, housing, and intermarriage data. "Honorary white" status—like that which the early Mississippi Chinese sharecroppers experienced—is tentative. Bonilla-Silva compares it to the "coloureds" in South Africa during apartheid. They enjoy more freedom of movement and basic human rights than blacks, but they are never actually seen as fully white. Moreover, in times of economic uncertainty, their status can be revoked and they can become vilified as scapegoats for others' economic woes, as in the case of Vincent Chin described above. Thus, there is white privilege, and there is also light-skinned privilege, but it is never quite the same as white privilege.

A Multiracial Future?

Fifty years after the historic 1967 *Loving v. Virginia* US Supreme Court ruling where laws against racial intermarriage were deemed illegal, it was reported that interracial marriage rates were higher than ever before. Specifically, only 3 percent of all marriages were interracial in 1967, but by 2015, it was 17 percent of all marriages (Livingston and Brown 2017). Under Milton Gordon's (1964) old assimilation theory, marital assimilation is the ultimate step in blending into the proverbial melting point—at that point, we expect a formerly distinct minority group to be indistinguishable from the majority group, or so the theory predicts. But we now know that a key missing caveat to that prediction is that it assumes that the offspring of those marriages would be categorized as "white." Perhaps the more important question is not who is marrying whom, but how are the subsequent generations from those unions being perceived racially? Of all the racial groups, whites were the least likely to racially intermarry (Livingston and Brown 2017), so they are preserving their white advantage into the subsequent generations. And almost half (47 percent) of all the intermarriages reported were between a white person and a Hispanic person, further illustrating the black/nonblack divide with lighter-skinned Hispanics becoming "honorary whites" (Bonilla-Silva 2017; Yancey 2003). When intermarriage is between a black and a white American, their children are considerably less likely to be considered white (Bonilla-Silva 2017; O'Brien 2008). The one-drop rule, although invented for white slave-owner purposes, has a striking persistence into the present day—Barack Obama is just as much white as he is black, yet is considered the first black US president; Tiger Woods is considered a black golfer, when blackness makes up a small part of his Native American, Asian, and European ancestry. Even with more racial mixing than ever, old habits die hard, with divides between who is black and who is white being still closely guarded and socially controlled. The "last taboo"—intermarriage between black and white—is still the least likely to occur (Qian 2005).

White privilege is still preserved by a group's distancing itself from black-ness. As we shall see in the evidence presented in the subsequent chapters, there

still remains a striking divide between white advantage and th[e]
faced by people of color. With every piece of data presented [c]
ties faced by African Americans, Latino Americans, Asian A[n]
Americans, and other nonwhites, therein lies a white privile[g]
as society becomes more and more multiracial these inequal[ities]
points <u>not</u> to inadequacies of people of color, but rather to t[..] ...,
racialized system that was built from its inception to unfairly advantage whites.
But just as a system is built by humans, it can also be dismantled by humans.
To the extent to which only disadvantage is being addressed, there is little hope
of that system being disrupted. But as the focus points more and more toward
making invisible privileges visible, there is greater possibility of more fully
understanding the <u>totality</u> of the racially stratified system and thus greater possibility of change. We invite you to that journey of greater understanding in the
subsequent pages.

Real-Life Example

"What Are You?"

Who is asked "What are you?" and what does that tell us about the role of white
privilege in defining and constructing race? (three examples: A, B, C)

(A) "Debbie" is a light-skinned biracial American who was adopted by an African
American family in the 1960s—note white privilege in adoption process—
who can "pass" phenotypically but has an African American family/cultural
frame of reference; she was "outed" to her classmates when her mom brought
in cupcakes for her birthday, and they assumed she was white until they saw
her mom.

(B) One coauthor is white, sometimes assumed not to be the parent of her own
biological children due to phenotype differences with them; she was not asked
about sickle cell running in her family while pregnant (attending appointments
alone) because medical checklists says only ask this question if African American. White privilege, assumed to be healthy/without health risks.

(C) "David," like many other respondents in *The Racial Middle* (O'Brien 2008) is
asked, "What are you?"—white privilege is most whites are not asked this question—and has traveled extensively internationally, so has been assumed Italian/
Sicilian when in Italy; Mediterranean when in Spain; Middle Eastern/Muslim
when being profiled by TSA at airports, but he is the son of Indian (dad) and
Russian Jewish (mom) parents, had a Bar Mitzvah, etc.

Student Question: Discuss your own real-life example, from yourself or someone
else you know, and analyze how white privilege shapes how we define race.

Gender and Biracial Identification

As the United States becomes an increasingly multiracial nation, interracial relationships and marriage are more commonplace than in past years. Biracial individuals have been a part of the American race relations for centuries; however, biracialism is now a more salient issue than ever. Although black/white biracial people may be labeled as black by the broader society, they may categorize themselves as mixed race or biracial. Due to the changing nature of the American racial hierarchy, rigidity between racial categories have eroded somewhat and changed the nature of racial identification. Some biracial individuals choose an identity that blends both of their racial backgrounds; others choose the racial identity of one parent; and some shift back and forth from black to white, depending on context. Still others choose to avoid racial classification altogether.

Gender also plays an integral part in identification for biracial individuals, as skin color stratification has become a gendered phenomenon for women. For instance, lighter-skinned black women have more social desirability in the arena of the marriage market (due to their proximity to European beauty standards), earn higher incomes, attain higher education levels, and are assessed as more attractive than dark-skinned women. Light-skinned women, cognizant of these privileges, could encounter resentment or repudiation from other blacks and may even feel a lack of belonging to the black racial group. For mixed-race women, their gendered identity presents a unique location where they experience racialization (Rockquemore 2002).

Things to Consider: How will current racial categories change in order to account for biracial and multiracial individuals? How do biracial individuals who are not black/white experience the racial hierarchy differently? In what ways are appearance and identity magnified for biracial women?

Credits

Tbl. 1.1: Source: http://futuresinitiative.org/wp-content/uploads/2016/02/diversity-research-table-1.png?x91120.

CHAPTER 2

Prejudice, Discrimination, and Racism

"THAT'S RACIST!" IN this early part of the twenty-first century, in many postindustrial democracies, particularly in Europe and the Americas, being "racist" has become a dominant cultural insult or accusation that many attempt to deny. This "r-word" seems to be a label that many whites would like to avoid at all costs, at least publicly. Even news journalists seem to bend over backward to avoid using the word "racism," tiptoeing around with euphemisms like "racially charged," "racially tinged," or "racial undercurrent" rather than overtly identifying something as racist (Glickman 2018). Yet those social scientists who study racism would likely use the term racism to describe many aspects of everyday life—such as media/advertising, government, schools, health care—and even to describe everyday language, such as terms like "blackmail" and "black market." Indeed, as we have already established, we currently live in a nation and global society that rests on white privilege as its foundation. But as long as experts are using the word "racism" one way and everyday citizens are understanding it differently (as a "bad guy" insult reserved for only the most egregious things), we are likely to be "talking past" each other (Blauner 1994).

In everyday language about race, we often hear the terms *prejudice, discrimination*, and *racism* used interchangeably, but to social scientists, each has a precise meaning. In this chapter, we will focus on distinguishing racism from prejudice and discrimination, while also demonstrating how they are interrelated and how they were created by white privilege. While not even among social scientists is there complete and total agreement on how to define these terms, it is our aim to synthesize some of the key literature in the field to arrive at some definitions that frontline white privilege. Indeed, because some of these terms have existed for over a half century, invented during times when scholars of color and women were not even permitted in universities, it is necessary to unpack some of the older (or less insightful) definitions of these terms to make more visible prior blind spots and/or current misapplications. As we shall see, one of the key issues in some prior and even current models of prejudice, discrimination, and racism is conflating *intent* with effect or outcome.

To the extent that some definitions seek to frontline the intent (i.e., "well-meaning") of individual actors, white privilege is preserved. In this textbook, then, we seek to correct for such blind spots as we arrive at our definitions. It is our goal that these definitions will become useful analytical tools for the institutional arrangements analyzed in the remainder of the text as well as in your own social environments.

Prejudice

One of the earliest concepts to be defined in social science literature about racism and white privilege was prejudice. The goal of much sociology around the mid-twentieth century was to develop grand schemas that could be applied to a variety of intergroup contact situations—whether it be black-white contact in the United States, relations between the Polish and the Irish as immigrants to the United States, or relations between the Jewish and the Nazis in Germany. Gordon Allport, known for his book *The Nature of Prejudice* (1954), defines prejudice as "an avertive or hostile attitude toward a person who belongs to a group, simply because he belongs to that group, and is therefore presumed to have objectionable qualities ascribed to the group" (Allport 1979 [1954]:14–15). Allport's approach is cognitive and individualistic—that is, even though these "objectionable qualities" are learned and taught by society, they are believed by an individual, who can also be taught to unlearn them if s/he chooses. Allport is attributed as one of the earliest theorists of the **contact hypothesis**, which proposes that *individuals' prejudices about a group can decrease with actual contact with members of the group about whom they hold prejudices*. In other words, if I believe Asians are quiet and passive, for example, the more contact I have with various Asians, the less likely I would be to continue to hold this prejudice against them. This is because I would realize there is much more variety within the group than the stereotypical notion of them suggests.

However, there are several issues with the applicability of this definition of prejudice. It is overly focused on negative beliefs ("avertive," "hostile," "objectionable") and it also does not adequately treat the larger societal context of these beliefs. Writing just a few years after Allport, Herbert Blumer (1958) made something of a critique of this idea of prejudice as a "set of feelings" that is "lodged within individuals," emphasizing that race prejudice is most fundamentally a "sense of group position" and is thus better understood as a "collective process" rather than a set of "individual dispositions" (Blumer 1958:3). What is important about this definition of prejudice is it problematizes and centralizes the persons holding a sense of superiority over another group, whether or not those feelings involve overtly negative associations like "antipathy, hostility, [or] hatred" (Blumer 1958:3). Blumer's concept of prejudice thus goes beyond just the negative and also moves the discussion of prejudice away from being an individual-level personality trait, by investigating how society defines who belongs in a racial group and communicates that in-group/out-group status to its members.

Yet it must be emphasized that well before these 1950s definitions of "prejudice" by white male sociologists, scholars of color were publishing these same ideas about racial group position being taught by society. Although perhaps not using the concept of "prejudice," African American sociologist W.E.B. Du Bois published his essay "The Souls of White Folk" in *Darkwater* as early as 1920 and analyzed how white workers accepted a "psychological wage" to feel superior to blacks, even though both groups earned a paltry working-class wage as compared to the ruling (white) class. Likewise, Oliver Cromwell Cox published his book *Caste, Class, and Race* in 1948, arguing that the ruling class uses race as a concept to keep the human race divided and oblivious to our shared international connections and global heritage. Both Du Bois and Cox wrote well before Allport and Blumer to voice the concern that humanity was being corrupted by this fiction of "race"—first and foremost on a societal level. So to the extent to which individuals internalized beliefs of superiority/inferiority about each other, in the form of "prejudice," this was not at all natural or automatic. Individuals become conditioned to think of themselves as racialized beings and are not born that way. So in other words, the societal arrangements come before the individual behavior. Thus, we can understand individual prejudices as a byproduct of a racist system, not the cause of it.

This is not to say that humans do not fall prey to categorical thinking and overgeneralization that does not serve them well, regardless if the topic is race or some other social category. Psychologists like Gilbert and Malone (1995) found that fundamental attribution error (or correspondence bias) can cause people to attribute enduring characteristics to others when they are simply a result of a situational circumstance. Likewise, social psychologist Claude Steele coined the term **stereotype threat** based on his studies where subjects were told that members of their particular group tend to perform better (or worse) on this test, and then indeed their *performance on the test conformed up (or down) to those expectations.* While race was one of the stereotypes used in these studies, gender was also effective (Spencer, Steele, and Quinn 1999; Steele and Aronson 1995). Categorical thinking is clearly not limited to race. Yet is it simply the case, as some students assert, that if humans did not have "race," they would just find some other status to develop some kind of pecking order among themselves? The Museum of Tolerance in Los Angeles, California, gives guests a choice of two doors to enter through—one for the prejudiced people, and one for the unprejudiced people. As it turns out, those who choose "unprejudiced" will find they cannot enter at all—the museum's way of emphasizing that prejudice is inevitable and no one is above it.

During the 2016 US presidential debates, candidate and former secretary of state (and senator) Hillary Clinton used the term "implicit bias" to also assert that everyone has prejudices, as the candidate outlined her thoughts on mandatory bias training for police officers as a solution for racial profiling. Clinton's use of this term "implicit bias" relies on social psychological research from Harvard (Greenwald, McGhee, and Schwartz 1998) that has popularized a diagnostic test anyone can now take online at implicit.harvard.edu (Implicit Association Test 2011). Test takers have to respond very quickly to pictures of people and word associations with positive and negative adjectives and personality traits. The popular interpretation of this test is that it somehow proves that racial prejudice is impossible to cognitively avoid. Yet even the website itself reports that nearly all test takers, regardless of reported racial identity, show a preference for European Americans over African Americans. This finding, and many others like it, suggest that the commonly held conventional wisdom that all humans automatically have an in-group favorable preference and an out-group negative bias is actually inaccurate. That is, racial prejudice cannot simply be reduced to some kind of a "fear of difference" or "fear of the unknown." If people, regardless of race, are evaluating *whites* more favorably on an implicit association test, then something else is going on besides just in-group preference.

For the purposes of this textbook, we shall define racial **prejudice** as an *assumption (or presumption) made about an individual (whether deemed "positive" or "negative") based on his or her perceived racial group membership.* We shall also add the caveat that *prejudice is socially embedded, so that the dominant/advantaged group in society is the group that people are least likely to hold prejudices about, regardless of their own group identity/membership.* (The fact that there even exists a dominant racial group in society is the product of racism, which we define in a later section.) This tendency of relatively few prejudices about the dominant group (whites) in society is yet another example of white privilege.

It is striking to examine the research on antiblack prejudices by race. Who is most likely to hold antiblack prejudices? Asian Americans are even more likely to hold antiblack prejudices than whites are, and African Americans are much more likely to hold antiblack prejudices than they are to feel prejudiced against or distant from whites (Bonilla-Silva 2017). These prejudices are often deeply embedded because the training starts early: researchers have found striking differences between black and white children as young as age seven, with white children having a much stronger in-group bias than black children (Newheiser and Olson 2012). These study results taken collectively tell us that it is *not* the case that all people regardless of race similarly hold prejudices against unfamiliar/outsider groups. Prejudices that individuals hold are thus not primarily individual products. Rather, they are reflections of white racial privilege on a societal level. <u>One privilege of whiteness, then, is to rarely experience being the target of racial prejudice, as compared with any other racial group</u>.

Moreover, the tendency of many social science textbooks to continue to define prejudice as an unfavorable or negative attitude also privileges whiteness and white intent. Because white interests in racialized societies create the road map through which individuals map out their prejudice and it is no longer popular or favorable to be accused of being "racist," white interests have recently begun to frame many racial biases as so-called well-intentioned "positive prejudices"—like "blacks are great dancers and athletes" and "Asians are smart and good at math." The speaker of such stereotypes is often characterized as someone with good intentions, who is paying the target a compliment, even. Yet this dynamic reveals a privileging of white so-called-good intentions, and a silencing of the feelings and experiences of people of color. Indeed, research reveals that such so-called "compliments" are nevertheless perceived negatively by those targeted by them (Czopp 2008). The stereotype that blacks are great with their bodies (dancers, athletes) is steeped in a mind/body dichotomy that negates the intellectual abilities of African Americans and also makes invisible and uncomfortable those blacks who aren't interested (or as skilled) in such physical activities. The recent cultural phenomenon of the label "BLERD" (for black nerds) is a reclaiming effort to make visible the African Americans these stereotypes and prejudices render silent. Conversely, the stereotype of the "book-smart" Asian renders invisible the other assertive, social, gregarious qualities of Asian Americans (that exist just as much in them as in other members of the human species). Research on the "bamboo ceiling" reveals there are serious consequences of this stereotype that Asians are bookish nerds—it leads to assumptions about weak social and managerial skills that undergird wage and promotion penalties experienced by those with even higher levels of education than their counterparts (McTaggart and O'Brien 2014). So even when prejudices are disguised as "positive" and "paying someone a compliment," upon closer examination, the privileging of white "good intent" in these so-called positive framings obscures the negative unintended consequences such assumptions can create for the targeted individuals.

Another concept worth noting is **interethnic prejudice**. Recall in the previous chapter we distinguished between race and ethnicity. Heretofore we have raised examples of prejudices between races. However, within races, interethnic prejudice also exists. Interethnic prejudice refers to *members of a same "race" making assumptions about an individual of a different ethnicity based on his/her ethnic group membership*. For example, Cuban Americans and Puerto Rican Americans may see themselves as superior to, or hold prejudices about, Mexican Americans. Japanese Americans and Chinese Americans may make generalizations about each other, even while distancing themselves from Vietnamese Americans and/or Filipino Americans. Italian Americans may tell derogatory jokes or use slurs about Irish or Polish Americans. This may lead an untrained observer to conclude that prejudice is just everywhere, it is an equal-opportunity offender, and there is no white privilege to be seen here. However, upon closer inspection, the light-skin privilege and colorism we covered in the previous chapter clearly informs much of the interethnic prejudice that occurs. For instance, some Latino parents discourage their children from marrying a member of another Latino ethnicity but encourage and support marrying a non-Hispanic white person; or some may hold stereotypes about darker-skinned Dominican and Mexican Americans' neighborhoods as crime ridden or unsafe (Bonilla-Silva 2017; O'Brien 2008). Such instances of interethnic prejudice clearly reflect white privilege by elevating lighter-skinned members of "nonwhite" races over others and associating them with more positive characteristics, while assuming darker-skinned members of these groups hold less desirable traits.

The data show us that, indeed, prejudice is not an equal-opportunity offender. Not only is prejudice more likely to be directed at groups perceived as not conforming to the socially constructed category of whiteness, but when you are a member of a nonwhite group in society, it is actually more common for you to hold prejudices about your own group or other nonwhite groups than it is for you to have prejudices against whites. In fact, antiwhite prejudices are the least commonly reported prejudices of all, for everyone, regardless of race (Bonilla-Silva 2004). So it is not the case that prejudice is a naturally human preference for one's own group over others. Not only does society teach you what group you are in, but it also teaches you what the preferred or more valued group is in society, and your own self-evaluation becomes affected, for better or for worse, by these prejudices. This pattern points to another white privilege: low likelihood of ever experiencing what is known as **internalized racism**—internalizing wider society's ideology that whiteness is the preferred norm, the standard of beauty, and negatively evaluating oneself and one's own group against that standard. Internalized racism has been studied since the 1950s when Kenneth and Mamie Clark used black and white dolls in experiments with young children to see which dolls they would prefer, and this research has been replicated in modern times with similarly racialized results (Kohli 2014; Pyke 2010). Both whites and African Americans (and other Americans of color) tend to attribute the white dolls as the more beautiful, virtuous, and so on. So the concept of internalized racism and the research exploring it serve to further highlight that prejudice is not just equal opportunity across the racial landscape, but rather is socially patterned.

And more to the point, it is a white privilege to *not* experience internalized racism, to inhabit the world with relatively greater confidence that prejudice is less likely to be directed against you because of your race. That is not to say that all whites experience unfettered self-confidence, as there are a host of other factors influencing people's confidence, that we know from the research on intersectionality—societal messages about gender, social class, sexual orientation, age, physical appearance, and various other environmental influences also play a role in how we see ourselves (McMullin and Cairney 2004; Steele 1997). Yet as we shall see in the subsequent sections on discrimination and racism, when society is already erecting barriers from without, to also be battling these inner beliefs about one's own self-worth and the societal devaluation of one's own racial group membership (e.g., the negative prejudices, the so-called positive prejudices) simultaneously is exhausting, and has negative physical and mental health consequences (Van Ryn and Fu 2003; Williams and Williams-Morris 2000). In sum, racial prejudice exists, and members of every racial group can hold prejudices about any and every racial group; however, the preponderance of evidence makes it plain that prejudices are not simply personal/individual level beliefs, because if it were a matter of simple in-group preference and out-group bias, then there would be much more antiwhite prejudice than currently exists. On levels of prejudice typically measured and reported about their racial group, whites clearly get a "pass." This is not to say whites never are targets of race-related prejudice—far from it. But it tends to exist in small pockets and does not have the societal consequences in terms of discrimination and racism that we turn to in the next sections.

Discrimination

It is common for race and ethnicity textbooks to distinguish between prejudice and discrimination by identifying prejudice as attitudinal, cognitive, and emotive, while contrasting with discrimination as behavioral and active. One of the biggest misconceptions emanating from this approach is the assumption that discrimination is the case of individuals "acting out their prejudices." As early as the late 1940s, sociologist Robert Merton challenged this notion by developing a four-category framework within which to understand the interplay between prejudice and discrimination (Merton 1949). The most instructive takeaway point of Merton's contribution is this: one does not have to be prejudiced to discriminate, and one does not have to discriminate to be prejudiced. While Merton identifies instances of prejudiced discriminators ("all-weather bigots") and unprejudiced non-discriminators ("all-weather liberals"), perhaps the more interesting categories were the other two: the "fair-weather liberals," or unprejudiced discriminators, and the "timid bigots," or prejudiced non-discriminators. These latter two types underscore the social context of discrimination. Many people discriminate due to social pressure. For example, they laugh along with or even tell racist jokes in order to fit in with a group. They may or may not personally believe prejudices about the group against which they discriminate. Conversely, some people may not reveal their prejudices through discriminatory actions, especially not consistently. Merton's classification system, though old, can be useful if not conceptualized as any certain personality types or fixed labels for individuals, but rather as a device for understanding that prejudice and discrimination have a complicated relationship to each other and can easily fluctuate as context shifts.

To define racial **discrimination**, we specify here that it is an *action that excludes individuals based on perceived racial group membership*. For example, a teacher may not offer the opportunity for after-school math help to an Asian American student if she perceives this person as a "model minority" who does not need such assistance. A realtor may not show a home that is for sale in a predominantly white neighborhood to an African American family—this action is taken because the realtor perceives the family as belonging to a group who would not want to live there. Note that whether the realtor loves black people and has black friends matters little here. The action of exclusion is based on perceived racial group membership. It *does not have to be based on animus or ill will* to constitute discrimination. But certainly discrimination can exist along with assigning notions of inferiority and/or outsider status to the perceived racial group. For instance, a group of white teenagers may not think to ask their Mexican American classmate for help with an assignment because they do not think s/he speaks English well, even though they have never conversed with the classmate enough to know for sure. Exclusion can also consist of being singled out for stigmatized treatment; it is not merely avoidance. Take, for example, the case of an airplane passenger with a Muslim name and brown-skinned appearance who is selected for special screening based on these two characteristics alone. His ethnic identity has in effect become racialized, and this is where the word "perceived" in the definitions of prejudice and discrimination is important. This person may not even be a practicing Muslim, this person may have dyed their hair darker or spent some time tanning on vacation to temporarily achieve this skin tone. But the discriminator reacts to social cues and symbolic meanings associated with "race" at this time and place, and the exclusion act is, in effect, excluding the passenger from the expedited and unencumbered passage through security that members of the dominant group (whites) expect, and get.

A somewhat useful distinction is made in many race textbooks between individual and institutional discrimination. These constructs are helpful in that they emphasize both micro- and macro-sociological levels of discrimination. Keep in mind that both individual and institutional discrimination are not mutually exclusive because institutions are comprised of individuals. Both could be happening simultaneously. Generally speaking, though, we can define **individual discrimination** as *acts of discrimination carried out against others as part of individual choices and actions*, while **institutional discrimination** is *discrimination carried out by agents of institutions and/or as implemented by policies that have discriminatory effects*. The student, realtor, and airport security examples discussed above could all be individual discrimination; however, when a realtor collaborates with a lending agency that routinely assesses "higher risk" to homes in predominantly nonwhite neighborhoods, that realtor could also be part of institutional discrimination. Likewise, when an airport security agent uses racial profiling techniques that are a matter of policy for the organization, the agent is also exemplifying institutional discrimination. Making this distinction between the individual and the institutional discrimination allows us to further accentuate how irrelevant blatant prejudice can be when assessing the impact of discrimination on targets. Very often with institutional discrimination, it is not as simple as a single "bad guy" or "bad apple" on which to assign blame.

While there was a time in the late 1960s and early 1970s when the US Supreme Court applied a more effect-based (less intent-based) model of evaluating whether something was discriminatory, by the late 1970s and on through the twenty-first century, discrimination lawsuits often place the burden on the plaintiff to prove discriminatory intent. For example, in 1996, Texaco had to pay a $176 million lawsuit after a US district court determined that African American employees were being discriminated against there, but only after a recording of a top executive using the n-word and referring to "black jellybeans" was used to prove discriminatory intent (Mulligan and Kraul 1996). Institutional decision-making processes both in and outside the courtroom rely heavily on equating discriminatory intent with past use of racial slurs. One of the many cases in point is former Los Angeles Clippers owner (and real estate mogul) Donald Sterling, who paid multiple settlements to tenants alleging racial discrimination over the years, but it was not until a recording was exposed (by his girlfriend) of him using racial slurs and racially charged language that the NBA dismissed him (Goyette 2014). Incorrect understandings like these that equate discrimination only with prejudicial intent, and only with individuals, demonstrate white privilege by negating the discriminatory impact felt by the targets. Efforts to pinpoint a confirmed white "bad apple" before an action is categorized as discrimination thus exemplify white privilege. To minimize white privilege in the study of race, then, we must define discrimination as any act which excludes a person based on racial group membership, <u>whether or not it occurs at the hands of a confirmed biased/prejudiced individual</u>.

Such a definition also allows ample room for institutional discrimination, since rarely can cases of institutional discrimination be distilled down to one person. Other noted examples of institutional discrimination include the 100-to-1 disparity in sentencing for crack versus powder cocaine, which disproportionately targets racial minorities and the poor, even though the two types of the drug have similar effects on the body. The Anti-Drug Abuse Act of 1986 made this law in the United States, which was only changed to an 18-to-1 disparity in 2010 with the Fair Sentencing Act—reducing substantially but not eliminating the discriminatory impact of the original law (Zimmerman 2014). This law literally targets a type of drug, not a type of person, but in its implementation, the discriminatory impact is clear. It privileges elite whites who can afford to buy cocaine in its powder form. The separate-but-equal education systems that were made legal by the 1896 *Plessy v. Ferguson* US Supreme Court case were exemplary of institutional discrimination, but so is the current process of funding schools with local personal property taxes, since the quality of schools is notably higher in richer, whiter neighborhoods (Walters 2001), and white flight to charter schools and private schools as a way to circumvent legal desegregation also contributes to the discriminatory results (Saporito and

Sohoni 2006). Thus, it is highly erroneous to reduce racial discrimination to merely individual "bias" and "hate," since discriminatory policies as a whole have a far wider-reaching impact. Rigorous social science does better to take into account impact over intent, since establishing intent is highly subjective at best.

A final example of white privilege (and white misinformation) to cover in this section is the term "reverse discrimination," which is actually a popular phrase, not a concept existing in social science or law. However, it is pervasive enough to warrant some brief attention here, as it can sometimes come up with students. As noted above, we have defined discrimination as an act of exclusion based on perceived group membership. Thus, to truly "reverse" this process, one would need to see acts of inclusion without regard for group membership, or what is scientifically and legally known as nondiscrimination. Indeed, the same discrimination law applies in a court of law whether it is a white person or not who files the lawsuit. So, yes, when it happens to whites, it is still simply identified as racial discrimination. We can identify "reverse discrimination" as a popular social construction, which is ultimately meant to be pejorative, and perhaps better understood as a perceived "reduced opportunity" (Pincus 2002). And it is more of an aggrieved perception than an actual confirmed pattern of behavior. As we shall see later in the chapter when we discuss color-blind racism, storylines that get repeatedly told begin to get believed, regardless of their veracity or basis in evidence.

The concept of reverse discrimination came to be used to challenge affirmative action policies by characterizing them as unfair to whites. This fiction relies on a framing of jobs (or other opportunities) as somehow inherently belonging to whites, thus "unfairly" taken away when equal opportunity measures attempt to provide equally qualified candidates from historically underrepresented groups (e.g., women, people of color, veterans) with consideration for such slots. Although this may be a semi-popular perception, the irony is that evidence shows that the umbrella of legal guidelines known as "affirmative action" have actually benefited white men (and white women). Not only have white women benefited as an underrepresented group, but white men actually benefited by the practice of affirmative action. This is because affirmative action policies have encouraged businesses to stop relying solely on word-of-mouth insider networks to fill open positions, as they often did previously (and still do). Even when businesses may have an internal candidate in mind for filling a position, affirmative action policies have made it more compulsory to actually publicly post jobs, which makes everyone more aware of potential openings, including white men (Desmond and Emirbayer 2009; Thompson and Armato 2012). Yet again the privileging of perceived white racial interests over the democratic ideals of equal access for all created the climate, which allowed a misunderstanding like "reverse discrimination" to flourish. The fact that actual cases of whites being targets of discrimination due to their race are relatively rare, isolated, and not institutionalized, yet there nevertheless exists a popular concept attempting to render special focus on it, over and above the inclusive term *discrimination*, further exemplifies white privilege.

Racism

We have already established in the previous chapter that, if it were not for the invention of "race" as a hierarchical stratification system privileging whiteness, racial prejudice and discrimination would not exist. To understand racism, then, we must first be grounded in an understanding of race as a pseudoscientific category and a social construct aimed at dividing and unequally distributing societal resources. We must also understand that supporting the creation of the idea of race, then, was an ideology. **Ideology** is *a belief system aimed at rationalizing and justifying existing social arrangements*. All, regardless of their position in the social structure (whether dominant or subordinated), tend to at some level buy into this ideology in order for it to stay in place. Because theoretically, if enough people resisted the ideology, the existing social arrangements might perhaps be transformed. Racial ideologies get encoded into various socialization agents and social structures—they are how many of us explain away why so many black and brown people live in inner cities in impoverished conditions or why they are disproportionately in prison, but also why so many white men are in power. Many come to believe they have worked harder, are more intelligent or somehow more deserving of being there. These ideologies are not always as evident as strong pronouncements of innate superiority and inferiority. They can be couched in well-meaning advice, such as the white person who advises the black or brown person to tone down their language, change their hairstyle or style of dress, or way of talking, in order to secure a desired resource like a job, house, or political position. It can be disguised in comments that have nothing to do with anti-blackness, such as calling someone "white trash"—this conveys the message of deviance from a hegemonic whiteness that is elevated as pristine, virtuous, and the ultimate in so-called civilized behavior. So the extent to which someone whose phenotype might be categorized as white deviates from this ideal, he or she is rejected as "trash." It all relates back to the ideology justifying a racially stratified society where those deemed "white" are somehow more deserving of being on top of the hierarchy. If we can grasp what an ideology is and how it can be held on to by people on all rungs of the social ladder (no matter how high or low), then we can better understand what racism is.

Racism is more of a broadly encompassing concept than either prejudice or discrimination. In order to define racism precisely and effectively, it is also necessary to define the concepts of dominant and subordinated groups in society. Sometimes the terms *majority* and *minority* may be used, but these terms can be quite misleading. Majority and minorities, numerically speaking, connote population proportion differences—that is, we might expect a "majority group" to at least hold a 51 percent (or more) share of the population and minority group members to be much fewer in number. Yet even when whites were a numerical minority in apartheid South Africa, they still were the dominant group in power, controlling the vast majority of resources (Seidman 1999). Likewise, women are a global majority numerically (as are people of color) but are a subordinated group worldwide because of their disproportionately smaller share of political power, wealth, income, and physical safety (Charles 2011; Watts and Zimmerman 2002). So terms like majority and minority that suggest one group is larger and the other smaller in size cannot adequately describe the societal relationship between the group that is in power and the group that is not. This is how terms like *dominant* and *subordinated group* contribute to a more accurate assessment. The **dominant group** *is the group that controls a disproportionately larger share of power and resources and greater life chances*, while the **subordinated group**[1] *controls a disproportionately smaller share of power and resources and lesser life chances in society*. For these definitions, the size of the group matters little compared to the degree of political and economic power they hold in the society.

As we have already seen, but will continue to review evidence of throughout this text, whites are the racial group considered the dominant group in many, if not all, societies that were formerly colonized by Europeans—Europe, North America, South America, Australia, and even in parts of Africa and Asia where numbers might be small. There still exists an ideology that elevates whiteness as a desired and privileged status, even where few whites are physically present in those societies. Western media images and past colonial control have far-reaching consequences. The prevalent sale of skin-bleaching products in places like Jamaica, Nigeria, South Africa, and India, and even cosmetic surgery to approximate certain Eurocentric features like nose shape and eye shape, demonstrate the power of colonial ideology of white supremacy (Hunter 2011). Long after the ownership of the political structure and the land is officially terminated, the ideology remains in how individuals see themselves and each other and in how society is structured to differentially reward those who most resemble the white supremacist ideal. As also discussed in the previous chapter, the persons considered to be in the dominant group of "white" is socially constructed so it can sometimes shift with changes in a society, because whiteness is not based in genetics or natural science, but in the reigning laws and practices of a society. So when we identify whites as the dominant group, we are speaking of this sociopolitical category.

Likewise, because we have already established race as a relational category, then, subordinated groups become any group that is not deemed white. When we

---

1   Here we have selected the term *subordinated* rather than subordinate in order to emphasize that individuals designated in this category are not doing it to themselves; it requires a dominant group to do the subordinating. We are grateful to Dr. Ted Thornhill for this valuable insight.

refer to **people of color**[2] in this text, we are referring to *subordinated racial groups*, although we know individuals can be subordinated to varying degrees. These are groups that have been oppressed, controlled, manipulated, and marginalized by the dominant group's structures, customs, and practices due to their perceived "race." But as we have reviewed in the previous chapter, they are actually hardly different genetically and biologically—the ways they are different culturally, if at all, are largely due to the historical external environmental influences of the structure of race and racism. As we shall see in more detail as we continue through this text, it is indeed a white privilege for one's culture to be considered as the norm, the standard, and in some ways unmarked or unremarkable, because indeed every social group has a culture and cultural practices. But we are carefully taught to mark some cultures in different ways according to "race."

Grounded in the knowledge of what racially dominant and subordinate groups are, we can establish a clearer definition of racism. Following the work of Beverly Daniel Tatum (2017), we define **racism** as *a system of advantage for the dominant group (whites) in society*. A crucial component of this definition is that it is not merely the sum of prejudice and discrimination; indeed, racism can occur even without prejudice or discrimination being identified. Tatum uses the analogy of a moving walkway (like the people-movers at airports) to enable us to characterize several levels at which racism operates. We can think of the movement, like the current, steadily advancing the system in favor of whites (or those perceived as white). For those who are *prejudiced and/or discriminate in a way that favors whites* (which evidence above demonstrates is much more common than the reverse), we can compare these actions to those who get on the walkway and walk along with its current, further accelerating the movement toward white advantage than if they were just standing still. These are the actions that most firmly keep the system of white advantage in place, and what Tatum refers to as **active racism**. Then, there are also individuals who stand still on the walkway but nevertheless still move forward with white advantage. Tatum would describe such examples as passively racist. Incidents of **passive racism** occur *when a person witnesses an actively racist action*, such as a racist joke or discriminatory exclusion, *and does nothing to challenge it*.

Although Tatum refers to this as passive racism, it is clear that an individual makes a conscious choice to stay silent and not confront racism in such cases. In

---

2   Please note this term is quite different from the term *colored people*, which is considered pejorative. *Colored people* has been used historically and legally to exclude African Americans and other groups from basic freedoms. Note how "colored" is used as an adjective before the word "people." The preferred term (of the two—some do not prefer either, actually) begins with the word "people," shifting the humanity back into the term. However, one should be aware this is a catch-all term that glosses over many important differences. It should not be overused when a more specific term could do; but it can be used to connote solidarity across varied groups that have been excluded from whiteness to varying degrees.

many cases, passive racism may be motivated by fear of losing a tangible benefit such as one's job, housing, or even one's life/physical safety may be at risk. In other cases, the impetus behind passive racism may seem less compelling—not wanting to make waves, not wanting to be ostracized or seen negatively by one's peers, or simply not caring enough about racism to intervene or voice one's disapproval. As we shall discuss more in the next chapter on institutional racism in education, there are many times when whites are not conscious of any particular antiblack antipathy but nevertheless practice what might be categorized as passive racism when they hoard public resources for their own white children and families. They are choosing not to speak up against the unequal access to resources for black and Latino children because their primary focus is protection of their own, thus preserving white privilege. (This is also called opportunity hoarding, covered more in the next chapter.) Some analysts might argue that some of these behaviors are not quite as "passive" (in terms of impact) as they might appear to the uncritical eye. Tatum's primary emphasis, though, is on effect, or impact. Even as certain behaviors may be more or less passive, the flow of the moving walkway still maintains white advantage.

One other concept that Tatum incorporates into her moving walkway analogy that is also relevant for us here, especially in Chapter 5 of this text when we analyze it in much greater detail, is **anti-racism**. An **anti-racist** action would be one that *deliberately challenges and works against white advantage*. Tatum compares anti-racism to walking the opposite direction on a moving walkway or escalator— it is not easy to do! Anti-racism interrupts the normative flow of resources and advantages in the society, culturally and materially. Refusing to consume media or patronize businesses with known records of racist policies and practices is one way to be anti-racist. Exposing and confronting those who practice racism is another. The key distinction about anti-racism is it is active. It should not be confused with **non-racism**. A person who professes to be non-racist (although they are not likely to use this term for it) states that they are "not racist," or they might use the ever-popular "I don't have a racist bone in my body." As writer Joseph Barndt has famously penned: "Non-racists deny the prison exists. Anti-racists work for the prison's eventual destruction" (Barndt 1991). To be non-racist is to *seek to distance oneself from the label "racist" while remaining uncritical about the ways racism still exists in everyday life, and not taking any particular action to try to stop white advantage*. This is often coupled with color-blind racism as discussed in the next section. The moving walkway analogy is particularly effective for conceptualizing anti-racism because it emphasize the level of commitment and going-against-the-grain necessary to challenge and chip away at white societal advantage.

Many students struggle at first to understand why race-based actions that may individually exclude or demean whites do not fit into this definition of racism. Certainly, there are individuals who occasionally are biased against whites and even act to exclude them from certain circles. In other words, yes, prejudice and discrimination against whites does happen. But the vast majority of reliable social science evidence we have does not identify any systematic patterns of this happening on a large scale, and even if it hypothetically did, it does not fit the definition of furthering white advantage. So the terms prejudice and/or discrimination would better apply to such actions, not racism. Some instances that might appear to some to be exclusions of whites can be better seen as *reactions to racism*. They may even be part of a counterstrategy to resist racism. For example, some teenagers may create a clique that excludes whites because they are trying to create a safe space in a majority-white school where they feel outnumbered, or they want to discuss issues that are unique to them. Or another example of white exclusion as a response to societal racism is when the civil rights organization Student Nonviolent Coordinating Committee (SNCC) wrote a position paper in the 1960s that asserted the need for their organization to be black led (Farmer 2017). Interestingly, in most such cases where it might appear on its face that an official position is white exclusion, often certain whites are still conditionally admitted because they have demonstrated their anti-racism by agreeing to take a backseat and support black leadership for the purposes of creating a more equal society. For example, a white anti-racist activist interviewed for O'Brien's (2001) research recalls how she was still able to continue to be part of SNCC "when the whites were kicked out." This was because she had previously demonstrated anti-racist behavior consistent with the mission of the group and was not trying to co-opt or hijack the black-led agenda for liberation. And of course, on college campuses everywhere, there are student clubs intended to support subordinated groups on predominantly white campuses, such as the Black Student Union or the Korean Student Association, who routinely and gladly welcome whites into their events. Sometimes students may misunderstand spaces like these where whites seem not to be present as exclusionary and erroneously equate them with racism. But this is clearly a misapplication of this definition upon greater inspection and analysis.

A common way of misapplying the term racism is to confuse it with something that appears to be "race based." Just because a person discusses race or brings up race does not automatically make something "racist"—if anything, it could be anti-racist, for example, to stand up and point out in a group that is all white and not bringing up race at all that they are being racist by furthering white advantage. Let us be clear: to discuss race, or to bring up what we know to be the social construction of race, is not racism. One must name and discuss race in order to undo it. A key component of our definition of racism is a clear understanding of the difference between the relative levels of power and privilege between the dominant and subordinate groups in society. So, even when an action appears to be race-based exclusion (prejudice or discrimination), if it does not further white advantage/white privilege, it would not be racist by our definition. Similarly, even when only one "race" occupies a setting, it could still be racism if the actions are furthering white advantage. For example, some who misunderstand racism may react to an instance of police brutality against an African American as "not racism" when they find out the police officer who assaulted him was also African American. But this action is indeed racism because it furthers white advantage. The criminal justice institution (and other institutions such as family, education, and media) has socialized its members to react in antiblack ways that advance that moving walkway of dominant group privileges—regardless of what actual race they might embody themselves. While the officer is targeting this person, whether or not a crime has been committed, the officer is missing actual crimes (and likely worse) happening in gated, predominantly white communities. Understanding white privilege is thus key to grasping this racism definition.

Also, a focus on the group membership (dominant or subordinated) of the *victim/target* is another key to applying this racism definition. There are indeed some analysts of racism who may state unequivocally "people of color can't be racist" (and thus "only whites can be racist") because generally people of color do not have as much power or privilege in society as whites do to encode their biases into law, but there are a number of problems with this sweeping generalization (Eichstedt 2001; Omi 2001). We know from evidence we have already reviewed above that various people of color can exhibit antiblack beliefs and practices that privilege whiteness. Furthermore, knowing race is a social construct, there are a number of multiracial people (and indeed, at some level, everyone is multiracial) who are treated as "white" in certain situations but as nonwhite in others. To make categorical assertions about who can and cannot be racist neglects the reality that bodies do not have a "race" in and of themselves; rather, race (including whiteness) is constructed by society's cultural and legal normative practices. So regardless of who is doing the given action (and in the cases of many institutional-level practices, there may not be a single raced actor to distinguish as the culprit anyway), if the action targets and impacts people of color in a way that advantages whites and whiteness, further subordinating the subordinated group, then we would categorize it as racism by this definition.

We have developed this concentric circle diagram (Figure 2.1) in order to illustrate the relationship between the concepts of prejudice, discrimination, and racism. The biggest takeaway from this diagram is that a majority of what can be regarded as racism is not necessarily even always overtly prejudiced or discriminatory, but it is white privilege.

Notice how racism is the biggest circle here, and the circles for prejudice and discrimination are mostly inside the racism circle. This placement corresponds to the evidence reviewed above, demonstrating that most of the prejudices and discriminatory actions in society work toward the advantage of the dominant group, whites. However, there are some much less frequent instances where prejudice and discrimination are directed at whites, and those are depicted in

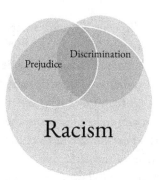

Figure 2.1 Prejudice Discrimination and Racism

---

the small part of the prejudice and discrimination circles that hang outside the racism circle at the top of the diagram. The overtly prejudiced and discriminatory acts that are explicitly aimed at advancing white supremacy would be placed in the center of the circle where it is darkest, as they fit the definition of all three concepts and form its core. Yet it is all that occurs outside the core that works to anchor it and keep it in place. As Robert K. Merton reminds us, there is prejudice that occurs without discrimination and discrimination that occurs without prejudice, signified in the above illustration by the parts of the prejudice and discrimination circles that are not overlapping with each other. But there again, these non-overlapping parts are still mostly inside the larger circle of racism—white privilege.

The most instructive part of this diagram is the bottom part, which is deliberately drawn as over half the total. It is indeed the visual equivalent of Tatum's notion of the moving walkway, flowing to white advantage even when whites are standing still on it. The "active racist" actions are in the smaller circles somewhere, but even those who are not being actively prejudiced or discriminatory are still taking advantage of white privilege, often without even intending to do so, by virtue of their *perceived* membership in the dominant group. (Some may not even personally identify as white but still get white privilege in some or many situations.) To use a sporting analogy, the active players (active racists) in the smaller circles are on the playing field, but even those sitting on the bench (in the bigger bottom part of the "racism" circle) are going to get a championship ring when the team wins. Those who are perceived as white are getting the racial advantages even when "sitting on the bench"—that is, not being actively racist themselves. The white family that gets the house or apartment after a Latino family is discriminated against, or the white employee who gets the job after the equally qualified Asian American candidate is rejected: these are examples of whites benefiting from racism, often without even being aware of it. They are part of the "winning team" (the dominant group), so they still get the "championship ring" (the advantages of white privilege) even when not actively choosing to do so.

This diagram makes plain how much racism occurs beyond the proverbial "bad apple" scenarios and allows us to better grasp why racism continues to thrive and remains so difficult to combat. Until more white people opt for the anti-racist path, by refusing to be the only ones who collect resources, there is this sizeable relatively unaddressed portion of racism that continues to occur. In subsequent chapters, we will address specific examples of the various forms such anti-racist actions can take. Inclusion riders happening in Hollywood and white parents who speak out against opportunity hoarding in school districts are just two examples which will be analyzed more specifically in later pages. We want to be clear that it is not inevitable that the bottom half of the circle in this diagram (racism) continues to exist just because people don't know it is happening. There are many forms of anti-racism that address the smaller/top circles (prejudice and discrimination) as well as the bigger bottom part of the circle (passive racism/white privilege). Historically, the burden of fighting racism has been shouldered disproportionately by people of color in society. Actions that work to change the dominant pattern are needed in order to change the dominant pattern. But why is there so much racism about which whites continue to be unaware? We tackle this a bit in our next section on color-blind and aversive racism.

Color-blind and Aversive Racism

The average person who has not studied racism extensively may be likely to only categorize as "racist" the types of actions that happen in the smaller two circles in our diagram—actively visible, overt acts of prejudice and discrimination. Yet much more of what fits our definition of racism here occurs outside of those simple boundaries, and often at the hands of people who see themselves as "not racist" (or non-racist). The very fact that many social scientists of race in recent years have coined all kinds of terms to refer to this kind of racism—modern racism, unaware racism, unintentional racism, symbolic racism—is truly reflective of white privilege at work in academia and in society. In effect, what the development of these concepts is doing is privileging intent (primarily white intent) over impact/effect. That is, the impact of racism on members of racially subordinated groups in society remains regardless of whether or not dominant group members *intend* to be racist. But since they tend to say they are not racist or do not believe they are racist, a number of social scientists have gotten to work to assemble the evidence and analysis to demonstrate that it is indeed possible for people to say "I am not racist" and yet racism still occurs. By far the most prominent work in this area has been Eduardo Bonilla-Silva's work on color-blind racism, and his aptly chosen book title *Racism without Racists* succinctly summarizes this very conundrum. The "racism without racists" are all the people and actions in the bottom half of the circle in our diagram. We may not be able to pin down an avowed "racist" individual to the particular action, policy, or practice, but it nevertheless still fits the definition of racism as the system of white advantage.

We cannot underscore enough that the very need for scholarly work demonstrating that racism still hurts even when whites "don't mean to" is in itself illustrative of white privilege. This academic work caters to whites' understandings of themselves as "good people," yet unconvinced that well-intentioned behavior still can have a deleterious impact on its targets. And we must still emphasize that race is a relational concept and a social construct, so rest assured it is not only whites who are raised on the dominant ideology of privileging white interpretations of race-related behavior and actions. As we review the concepts of color-blind and aversive racism here, we mean to emphasize how these interpretations of racial matters privilege whiteness, but it is not only whites who were studied in this research. They do, however, tend to be the group that exhibits these forms of racism the most. And even when people of color practice color-blind racism, it only further privileges whiteness, not themselves.

After conducting both interviews and surveys with many Americans across age, gender, race, class, and educational backgrounds, Eduardo Bonilla-Silva identified four frames of color-blind racism. He defines **color-blind racism** as an ideology that "explains contemporary racial inequality as the outcome of nonracial dynamics" and thus reproduces inequality by way of "practices that are subtle, institutional, and apparently nonracial" (Bonilla-Silva 2017:2–3). As he incisively points out, "the beauty of this new ideology is that it aids in the maintenance of white privilege without fanfare, without naming those who it subjects and those who it rewards" (Bonilla-Silva 2017:3–4). For example, one of the four frames of color-blind racism—cultural racism—does this by characterizing blacks and other minorities as lazy and not working hard enough. But this is often done through code words such as "ghetto," "low-income," and "at-risk" neighborhood without naming race directly. Another frame of color-blind racism—naturalization—asserts it's "just the way it is," that like gravitates toward like in residential neighborhoods and schools, as opposed to acknowledging any kind of race-based discrimination or unfair allocation of resources across districts. In other words, it reduces things like racial segregation to a seemingly benign personal preference/choice to be with those "like us," instead of race-based exclusion. A third frame of color-blind racism is minimization—which insists that complaints of racism are overblown, and in effect blames people of color for overreacting or "playing the race card," supposedly inserting a racial outlook into nonracial situations. The "they are the racist ones" projection rhetorical strategy is often part of this frame. This has also more recently been termed as "whitesplaining" (Greear 2017; Johnson 2016), as it elevates white privilege by advancing a race-neutral, well-intentioned explanation for a racist occurrence, minimizing and marginalizing the experience of the victim/target, who likely understands it better than an outsider.

Color-blind racism has a final frame called "abstract liberalism," which is yet another way of getting around addressing racial inequality with nonracial terms. Abstract liberalism takes collectively held values like fairness and equality and in effect, uses them as shields from critically thinking about how race has shaped people's chances. For example, people may oppose cultural competence training on the job because they profess to "treat everyone the same," framing such focus on diversity and difference as a diversion from the noble virtue of a liberal republic. Another way abstract liberalism is used is when people object to racial equality measures by stating that they interfere with individual choice or are "forced" on people. For example, if a certain percentage of bids must be considered by minority-owned contractors, people may use abstract liberalism to state they don't want to be "forced" to review these applicants. We know that blacks were excluded from union membership, from mortgages, from many other resources that would allow them access to capital accumulation on a *categorical/group* basis—they were not permitted to even be considered on their individual merit, they were forced out on the basis of their group membership. So to insist that individual merit is the only factor that should be considered elevates abstract ideals like "merit" and "fairness" to the point of ignoring the evidence that created the inequalities in the first place. Abstract liberalism thus elevates alleged race-neutral "intent" (as an ideal) far above the reality of racially unequal effects.

As Bonilla-Silva and many other analysts of color-blind racism have noted, these four frames are usually not utilized in isolation, and most often multiple frames are used in conjunction with each other. For example, in a study of letters to the editor in a Florida newspaper after the Trayvon Martin verdict (exonerating George Zimmerman for shooting the unarmed, walking boy), letter writers used the cultural racism frame to blame Martin's parents for "not educating a teenager to be more respectful of the neighborhood and the families that live there," as well as the minimization frame in chastising black community leaders for making it a racial issue: "The unfortunate death of the black teenager in Sanford has riled the black community, but there is no justification not to investigate the facts before arresting or not arresting the shooter. Would they want us to make a snap judgment had it been a black person shooting a white person?" (O'Brien and Prince 2015). Popular interpretations of this killing in the public eye combined the cultural racism frame and the minimization frame by implying that African American families are disrespectful and uneducated without explicitly mentioning race, and then criticizing those who actually did mention race as the ones causing the problem. Color-blind racism can thus be arguably more pernicious and difficult to combat than more overt, explicit racism because of the way it (1) uses seemingly nonracial language to transmit racist ideology; and (2) demonizes those who bring up race at all as the main problem.

Color-blind racism also exemplifies white privilege by presuming that majority-white-led power structures are inherently equal and fair minded in intent and practice. Its minimization of the racism frame, as well as its abstract liberalism frame, are consistent with the myth of "a few bad apples" about racism—there may be a few bad apples (active racists), but the majority would say they are not racist so it is (erroneously) assumed that for the most part, racism is a thing of the past. This ideological standpoint privileges the experiences of whites who say they are not racist over the experiences of those who experience racism. And it is worth repeating that many studies, including Bonilla-Silva's, demonstrate that it is not just whites who make use of color-blind racism frames. For example, some African Americans and other people of color may use the cultural racism frame to interpret why some blacks are not doing as well as others. Engaging in what some call "respectability politics," for example, some may buy into color-blind racism's notion that if black and brown folks would just dress and act in a more "respectable" manner, they would not become targets for police misconduct. When someone with a public platform makes such a statement, it tends to attract a lot of media attention, such as Bill Cosby's infamous 2004 "pound cake speech" at the NAACP Awards (Dyson 2005), or more recently, Pastor Jasper Williams at Aretha Franklin's funeral (Harriot 2018). As Bonilla-Silva's work brilliantly shows, color-blind racism is an ideology woven of stories people continually tell each other without the backing of evidence, but they tend to feel true to many because they have been told so much they start to sound familiar—such as "I did not get that job because of a black man" (Bonilla-Silva 2017). Just as the evidence does not exist to support the notion that affirmative action takes jobs from qualified whites and gives them to unqualified blacks, nor is there evidence to support the myth that blacks who act "respectfully" do not get targeted for police harassment—indeed, they do, and this evidence will be reviewed extensively in our next chapter. But these storylines told within the framework of color-blind racism uphold this notion of the "good intent" and inherent fairness of social institutions by blaming people of color and the occasional isolated "bad apple" when racial injustice occurs.

Likewise, the concept of **aversive racism** is another framework meant to shine a spotlight on how racism occurs even when people say they are "not racist." Developed through experimental psychology laboratory research, primarily by Samuel Gaertner and John Dovidio (1986; 2005), aversive racism can be defined simply as *racism without awareness* (Gaertner et al. 2005). More specifically, it is characterized by a cognitive state in which (typically white) individuals *state that they are not racially prejudiced but then exhibit racially biased nonverbal and implicit biases in interracial interactions*. The psychologists who invented the concept emphasize that the avoidance connoted by the word "aversive" is twofold: those who exhibit aversive racism both seek to avoid interracial *interactions* and seek to avoid the discomfort of the *contradictory self-awareness* they might experience by having to reevaluate their own biased behavior in light of their self-professed liberal-minded attitudes.

While concepts like symbolic racism and modern racism might also tap into this type of white contradiction, these types of racism are more characteristic of political conservatives, while Gaertner and his colleagues argue that aversive racism is more typical of liberals (Gaertner et al. 2005). According to the research on aversive racism, many self-proclaimed liberals will try to do the right thing (and not discriminate) when it comes to overt situations where the potential contradiction between their professed values and their behaviors would be too obvious to ignore. For example, when they have been a bystander to a black victim being harmed and 911 needs to be called, whites will overwhelmingly help if they know they are the only ones around to make the call. But if they know there are other people around, whites are far less likely to continue to be willing to help the victim (while blacks will continue to be willing to help in greater numbers, regardless of who else is around) (Gaertner and Dovidio 2005). In a wide variety of situations, the aversive racism hypothesis has been put to the test—from political, to employment, to medical, to educational—and the evidence consistently shows that whites' own evaluations of themselves and their racial beliefs tend to be more optimistic than their behavior suggests (Gaertner et al. 2005).

The aversive racism research is instructive because it also includes African American perspectives of the same interracial interactions. The social science research on racial prejudices over the past several decades has spent much more focus on white attitudes, with far fewer studies on the perspectives of African Americans and other people of color in terms of their racial views and attitudes (Nunnally 2009; Schuman et al. 1997). When our analyses of racial dynamics tend to privilege white "good intentions" interpretations, focusing more on white views, we pay less attention to how people of color might have been impacted by those supposedly well-meaning scenarios. Scholars studying aversive racism have effectively incorporated interracial subject pools in their experiments and measure not only professed attitudes, but also exhibited behavior, both from the perspectives of actors and targets. So, for instance, whites whom the researchers classified as aversive racists (they expressed egalitarian beliefs but were uncomfortable around blacks) evaluated themselves as friendly and pleasant in their interactions with blacks, while on the other hand the African Americans with whom they interacted did *not* feel those whites were friendly toward them. Indeed, of three groups of whites that African American subjects evaluated— those who would fit the "active racist" definition from earlier in this chapter; those who were "aversive racist"; and those whose egalitarian beliefs actually did match their actions—African Americans were most uncomfortable and distrustful about the aversive racists (Dovidio, Kawakami, and Gaertner 2002; Gaertner and Dovidio 2005).

This finding underscores a similar point made by the researchers on color-blind racism—that the increasingly common modern racism "without racists" is in many ways more harmful than more overt racism. It is harmful not only because its perpetrators are in denial and thus more difficult to identify, but because it induces a greater degree of mental harm and anguish on its victims by constantly keeping them ill at ease. Someone targeted by aversive racism ends up having to second-guess themselves and their own better judgment as they struggle to make sense of the disjuncture between the perpetrators' professed intentions and their treatment of them. As we shall see in the next chapter, this type of psychological distress has both mental and physical consequences, making what may seem like minor or "micro" incidents of racism not so minor after all. It has been the onus of racism researchers to assemble the evidence that racism nevertheless continues to exist despite white folks saying they are "not racist" or "did not mean" to harm anyone. The very scholarly work that continues to have to be directed at simply unmasking these "well-intended" proclamations in order to document what lies underneath is evidence in itself of white privilege. In effect, white professed intentions become privileged or elevated over the harm that is caused by racism on those whom it marginalizes and burdens. The bottom line is this: social science evidence is pretty clear at this point that whenever a statement is made about good intentions and not meaning harm, or that a person of color is overreacting or that something is being made a racial issue when it is not, we must look very carefully at these scenarios— perhaps even more carefully than those which overtly state racial intent.

Privileging Whiteness While Studying Race

In this chapter we have aimed to review common terminology used in the scientific study of race—prejudice, discrimination, racism—while emphasizing how white privilege has influenced both popular and scholarly misunderstandings of these terms. We have seen how prejudice has been misunderstood as only negative and as an equal-opportunity-offender, while the evidence shows prejudice can also be disguised as "positive" and tends to be directed at the subordinated groups in society much more so than the dominant group (whites). We have also seen how discrimination gets misunderstood as only "acting out prejudice," but it also occurs when individuals are not consciously prejudiced, and it occurs not even in individual actors necessarily but also in policies which sometimes do not even directly mention race at all (institutional discrimination). Further, we have analyzed how much of what fits our definition of racism does not even have to include explicit prejudice or discrimination, and occasionally is not even perpetrated at the hands of whites but nevertheless still advances white privilege.

As we have closed this section with more recently developed concepts like color-blind racism and aversive racism, it is worth noting that early scholars of color doing this work—such as W.E.B. Du Bois and Oliver Cromwell Cox—were not only few and far between (due to being excluded from universities), but are only now beginning to get the credit and recognition they deserve for their contributions to the development of the field. The more that the current generation of social scientists whose work illuminates white privilege continues to be incorporated more extensively into the academic textbooks and public discourse about race, the more likely we are to see more expansive definitions of these terms. We can no longer use limited notions of prejudice, discrimination, and racism and expect to dismantle white privilege. Our definitions can no longer tiptoe around concepts like prejudice and discrimination in race-neutral ways and limit what is categorized as racism to intentional/overt acts if white privilege is to be undone. As we move to studying evidence of racism and white privilege in several key social institutions in the following chapter, we seek to build on such expansive analysis. It is only by understanding something fully that we can attempt to address it.

Real-Life Example

"I'm Not a Racist"

Racism has become a loaded word in our culture, and few want to be associated with it. Racism is often associated with the actions of individuals, but it is essential to highlight how these intersect with racist practices at the institutional level. But does the way it is used in everyday life match its social science definition as outlined in this chapter? These three examples may help us to see how societal confusion about what racism is and is not makes productive dialogue challenging, to say the least. How might more societal consensus on what racism is (and is not) shed light on the following real-life scenarios?

(A) President Y: He is an Asian American university president. His goal is to raise the overall ranking of the school, and one way he can do this is by raising the SAT scores required of applicants. The school is the only public four-year institution in the metropolitan area, mostly first-generation college students who cannot afford the pricier local options. Many are transfers from the local community college. As a result, the school was quite racially diverse, but once the admission score standard is raised, the entering classes become less and less diverse and more and more white. The Black Student Organization stages a protest, accusing President Y of being racist. He cannot understand the accuracy of this charge, since he is a person of color also. How might the university president address the concerns of the Black Student Organization?

(B) Officer Smith: He is an African American police officer. A shooting of an unarmed young black boy by Officer Smith has the community in an uproar and protesting. He thought the child's toy gun was real and felt threatened.

Defenders of Smith say that policing is a tough job and he erred on the side of caution to save his life and potentially the lives of others around him. They say this has nothing to do with race, since both the officer and the victim were African American, so bias could have nothing to do with it. Protesters, on the other hand, claim this is racism—just another young, black male perceived as a threat. In what ways do institutional racism and the racial background of the shooting victim and police officer affect this scenario? What are some strategies/training that could be employed to combat racial profiling/implicit bias in police departments?

(C) Professor A: She is a white female who studies/researches race and gender. She identifies as non-racist, perhaps even anti-racist. One day while walking across campus, her purse kept falling down, and she kept having to pull the strap up every few steps. During one of those moves, she happened to pass by an African American male student on campus, who remarked to her, "Don't worry, lady, I'm not trying to steal your purse." Asking colleagues what she could have done differently, they reminded her it is a white privilege to not have to take the precautionary steps that people of color must take in public spaces in an attempt to minimize potential profiling (which can still occur even after trying to be overly cautious). Whites are often judged as individuals as opposed to a collective. However, people of color must regularly anticipate how their collective might be viewed, for the sake of survival. Wait until he passes, and then pull up your purse, they told her. How might the terms *anti-racist*, *non-racist*, and *passive racist* aid in understanding this discussion?

Student Question: Think of a time when you or someone you know felt unfairly accused of racism, seeing themselves as a "person without racial bias" to whom these terms did not apply. How might concepts in this chapter have aided that situation?

Intersectionality

Privilege and Oppression

In Patricia Hill Collins's *Black Feminist Thought: Knowledge, Consciousness, and the Politics of Empowerment*, she proposes a concept called the matrix of domination, which invites us to explore the idea that people can be both privileged and oppressed simultaneously, due to the different statuses they occupy in society.

Class can affect how people react to the concepts of racism and white privilege—for example, lower-class whites may not believe they have white privilege; and on the flip side, some people of color have privilege on the basis of class and educational attainment (their family may have generations of college education and wealth that is atypical of most), yet still are vulnerable to racism in areas such as public spaces and the criminal justice system. "Racism without prejudice" can happen in intersectional spaces (e.g., black trans concerns about violence getting raised within the Black Lives Matter movement or NFL kneeling protests first started by Colin Kaepernick).

Gender is also an important component in how white privilege operates. In a series of recent incidents, white women calling the police on people of color for seemingly frivolous reasons have gone viral for exhibiting racial prejudice. Through incidents like #permitPatty (a white woman who called the police about an eight-year-old black girl in San Francisco who was selling water without a permit) and #BBQBecky (a white woman who called the police on black men using a charcoal grill in a park in Oakland), we see the relationship of white women to racial privilege.

Things to Consider: How can social media and news outlets be used to expose instances of racial privilege? How does celebrity status affect the dynamics of oppression and privilege? In what ways can intersectional movements promote inclusivity in their base? What are other axes of identity that may privilege or oppress besides race, gender, and sexual orientation?

CHAPTER 3

The Microaggression to Institutional Racism Pipeline

Evidence of White Privilege Across Several Key Social Institutions

I T IS IMPOSSIBLE to analyze racism and white privilege without the appropriate
terms to discuss it, and racism and white privilege cannot be eliminated without
first understanding the extent of how it all operates. So far in this book we have
attempted to define some key terms so we can work from common vocabulary as
we evaluate the evidence of how white privilege works. In this chapter now, we turn
more directly to that evidence by focusing on three example social institutions: the
economy, the criminal justice system, and education. White privilege exists in many
other institutions, and we encourage you to seek out evidence in other institutions
using the conceptual tools we provide here as a foundation. In particular, we maintain that most dichotomous distinctions commonly used for the analysis of racism
(individual versus institutional; micro versus macro; covert versus overt; aware/
blatant versus unaware/unintentional) continue to privilege whiteness and white
so-called "good intentions," instead of focusing on the ultimate impact on those
excluded from white privilege. As a practical application of this approach, we will
begin with the concept of a "microaggression"—held conceptually by some as perhaps "not as" impactful as institutional racism, but our evidence will demonstrate
how "microaggressions" are the exact foundation that white privilege rests on,
enabling more systematic institutionalized racism and white privilege to flourish.
Indeed, it is the existence of white privilege in the academy and in the formalization
of knowledge that keeps the "micro" and the institutional in separate categories,
because both create great harm regardless of "intent"—as the evidence presented
in this chapter will make plain.

Our approach in this chapter will not be to bombard you with the preponderance of evidence of racism in these three areas because many longer race/ethnicity
textbooks in the field already do this well, and the evidence is there to be found once
you understand some basic patterns that you can research further on your own.
Our goal here is to conceptually link this evidence of the institutional racism—
traditionally taught as the disadvantages of people of color—to white privilege, in
ways that connect back to one's everyday experiences in human interaction. For

49

every transaction a white person makes during the course of their day is impacted by these patterns of racial inequality. By emphasizing what these large-scale patterns feel like in everyday interactions, we aim to translate large-scale numerical data tables that are already out there to be found back into lived experience. In effect, we peel back the curtain of the statistics about institutional racial advantage to examine how whites cash in every day, often without realizing it. Through this approach, we hope to empower you to see the ways you can impact these patterns in your everyday life. Institutions may feel large, but they are ultimately comprised of individual actors, each of us playing a role within them. As we shall see, despite the laws that have been passed in attempts to alter these institutions, there is still much work to be done to eliminate the white privilege they perpetuate.

Microaggressions

By the late 1980s/early 1990s, the first generation of African Americans who benefited from the 1960s public school desegregation began to study and write about racism, just as a recession hit the United States and there began a backlash against civil rights measures like affirmative action and busing. Titles like *Faces at the Bottom of the* Well by Derrick Bell (1993) and *The Rage of the Privileged Class* by Ellis Cose (1994) brought attention to the fact that despite institutional measures aimed at racism—such as desegregated schooling and public accommodations—there remained an enduring legacy of racism which was arguably even more painful than the form racism had taken previously. This was because certain African Americans and some other people of color were "let in" to institutions close enough to be able to feel that they deserved it, yet still were made to feel like outsiders within their own earned positions. It is akin to the difference between looking into a store window from the outside (not even allowed in) versus being inside the store with money, yet nevertheless thwarted from being able to make a purchase. Using interview data from black women in both the United States and the Netherlands, Philomena Essed (1991) coined the term "everyday racism" to refer to what Feagin and Sikes (1994) have also written about—the "daily murders" of racism particularly felt by the black middle class. Actions like being followed around in a store, being questioned as to whether you belong on campus, or a store clerk placing your money onto the counter rather than making skin-to-skin contact to place your change in your hand are all examples of what Essed's (1991) and Feagin and Sikes's (1994) interview research grouped into the category of everyday racism. An assumption that those who do not appear white "do not belong" guides much of these hurtful actions.

These sociological and critical race studies mirrored a term that was coined decades prior by Harvard psychiatrist Chester Pierce (1970)—*microaggressions*. However, it was not until a psychologist named Derald Wing Sue and colleagues revisited this concept in the early twenty-first century, applying it well beyond African Americans to Asian Americans and other people of color, as well as gender and sexual orientation, that it began getting widespread attention (e.g., Constantine and Sue 2007; Ong et al. 2013; Sue 2010; Sue et al. 2007a; Sue et al. 2008). These scholars define **microaggressions** as *"brief and commonplace daily verbal, behavioral, and environmental indignities, whether intentional or unintentional, that communicate hostile, derogatory, or negative racial slights and insults to the target person or group"* (Sue et al. 2007a:273). Microaggressions can be either verbal or nonverbal, are often described as "subtle," and notice the word "daily" in the definition is not unlike the aforementioned "everyday racism" concept. Researchers studying microaggressions maintain that nearly <u>every</u> interracial encounter includes some kind of "slight" such as this (Sue et al. 2008). Sociologist Joe Feagin (2000) has referred to this recurring barrage of commonplace racism as "woodwork" racism to emphasize the fact that some become so habituated to it that they may feel it is not worth noting. People of color may begin second-guessing themselves and/or decide not to confront it in order to preserve their mental health, and then whites are so infrequently challenged on it that they maintain it is "no big deal" or "no harm intended." Yet note that the definition of microaggression does not distinguish between whether it is intentional or not, which is a rare decentering of white intent in the scholarly study of racism, instead emphasizing the impact on the target. Microaggression studies maintain that even when **intended** impact is small or minimal, **actual** impact is devastating, cumulative, off-putting, and ongoing.

The prefix "micro" implies something small, but a growing body of research in the early twenty-first century links microaggressions to all kinds of negative mental and physical health outcomes for African Americans (Smith, Hung, and Franklin 2011), Latino Americans (Torres and Taknint 2015), Asian Americans (Ong et al. 2013), American Indians (Evans-Campbell 2008), and sexual minorities (Balsam et al. 2011; Frost, Lehavot, and Meyer 2013). It is because these frequent "slights" occur with such regularity that they can result in being more impactful on one's health than a single, blatant incident, which tends to be more visibly and readily validated. A major component of living a life of white privilege is that one's daily existence is not constantly assaulted with race-related microaggressions. Indeed, to quantify it a bit, being white adds about four years to your healthy life expectancy (Chang et al. 2013), because you are likely not dealing with these so-called "low-level" daily microaggressions. This life expectancy gap is also likely a conservative estimate—in more segregated cities in the United States, the gap can be as large as twenty years (Khazan 2018). Social epidemiological patterns such as the higher rate of hypertension among African Americans and some other nonwhite groups (Brondolo et al. 2011) provide further evidence of the white privilege of fewer microaggression-induced stressors.

Dividing these impactful stress-inducing behaviors into three subtypes—micro-assault, micro-insult, and micro-invalidation—can assist us in more precisely analyzing the forms they take in everyday life. We want to primarily focus on the latter two since they can tend to be less visible and thus more in need of greater study. While micro-assaults involve clear intent, such as the use of racial epithets and other racially explicit language, micro-insults and micro-invalidations often rely on some of the frames and styles of color-blindness we identify in the previous chapter. A **micro-insult** is defined by Sue et al. (2007b:73) as *"a behavioral action or verbal remark that conveys rudeness, insensitivity, or demeans a person's racial identity or heritage."* Many of the examples of micro-insults provided by Sue and colleagues bear a striking resemblance to the cultural racism frame of color-blind racism. For example, a white person tells their black friend they are "not like the others," relying on assumptions of criminality and amoral behavior on the part of the majority of African Americans. Notice that while this may appear to be a quite obvious instance of racial prejudice and bias, white speakers are often taken aback because they intend their comment to be a "compliment" to the person they have decided is the "exception." The rudeness or insensitivity is located in the fact that the speaker is more concerned with framing themselves as well intentioned rather than the target's feelings and mental health/well-being. The speaker does not stop to consider that they have actually insulted the very group with which the person identifies and from which they draw their identity, support, family heritage, etc.

Likewise, a micro-invalidation can also be misinterpreted by a white/dominant-group member as positive, when the vantage point of a person of color/subordinate-group member is not taken into account. Sue and colleagues define a **micro-invalidation** as *"actions that exclude, negate or nullify the psychological thoughts, feelings or experiential reality of a person of color"* (Sue et al. 2007b:73). One of many white privileges in a racist society is to not have to be educated about people of color's history, contributions, culture, and lived experiences. Because such education is not widespread, it follows that it would be virtually inescapable for whites to participate often, perhaps even daily, in micro-invalidations without realizing it. As Eduardo Bonilla-Silva (2017) notes, whites exist within a "white habitus" that inevitably shapes their point of view, and the way they see the world and their place in it. Teachers who assign students a "cultural heritage" project, depending on the parameters of the assignment, could very well participate in micro-invalidations by expecting African Americans to be able to point to a specific country or nation from where their ancestors came. This project assumes a white ethnic immigrant model that does not account for forced migration, annihilation, or exploitation. Another example of a micro-invalidation occurs when Latinos or Asian Americans are complimented on speaking good English. Again, this line of thinking emanates from an assumption of a very narrow and specific migration story that negates the reality of many fourth- and fifth-generation Mexican and/or

Chinese American families in the United States, for instance. It also makes a false equation of whiteness with citizenship and of non-whiteness with "foreign-ness," which is often not the case. Micro-invalidations marginalize people and make them feel invisible and/or as an outsider standing out from the group because of an artificial/assumed implied difference.

The white privilege here is twofold—immediate and cumulative. In the immediate sense, whites are exempted from these daily questionings of their character that are race or ethnicity based. As one of Feagin and Sikes's (1994) black middle-class interview respondents eloquently put it:

> [I]f you can think of the mind as having one hundred ergs of energy, and the average man uses fifty percent of his energy dealing with the everyday problems of the world—just general kinds of things—then he has fifty percent more to do creative kinds of things that he wants to do. Now that's a white person. Now a black person also has one hundred ergs; he uses fifty percent the same way a white man does, dealing with what the white man has [to deal with], so he has fifty percent left. But he uses twenty-five percent fighting being black, [with] all the problems being black and what it means. Which means he really only has twenty-five percent to do what the white man has fifty percent to do, and he's expected to do just as much as the white man with that twenty-five percent. ... So, that's kind of what happens. You just don't have as much energy left to do as much as you know you really could if you were free, [if] your mind were free. (Feagin 1991:115).

Right away, we see that a white privilege that results from the constant barrage of microaggressions people of color navigate daily is that whites have more energy left to face other things. As we have already seen, a common misunderstanding of the concept of "privilege" is that it suggests that everyone else's life is somehow easy if they have privilege, when that is not the case at all. Those who have race privilege may not have other forms of privilege—class, ability, sexual orientation, gender, religious, etc.—or they may indeed have all these forms of privilege yet still struggle in situations of abuse, violence, or political unrest. Every human needs a reserve of energy to deal with human conditions. However, the microaggression research demonstrates there is an added layer of consistent racism-related incidents sapping people's energy if they are perceived as not white—a depletion to which whites are not subjected.

This white privilege of extra energy to deal with life is clearly evident as an immediate/direct impact of microaggressions, but what about the cumulative/collective effects? The white privilege is not just that you don't have to deal with the stress of any particular microaggressive race-related event, but also that the climate of these events happening constantly does not form a fog cloud over your life, impacting your overall physical and mental health in the long term, as well as the overall well-being of your communities writ large. Take a particular event like the police killing of Oscar Grant III in California in 2009, or Michael Brown Jr. in Missouri or Eric Garner in New York in 2014, or the death of Sandra Bland in police custody in Texas in 2015. The authorities ruled these deaths as not race-related, even though ample evidence existed to challenge such assessments. We may begin with assuming that these events have an immediate effect on these individuals and their families, yet the research is telling us the impact does not end there. The medical science evidence is now mounting that these acts of microaggressive racism denial have "spillover effects" onto black Americans and other people of color who do not even know, live near, or are associated with such individual events (Bor et al. 2018; Eligon 2018; Feagin and McKinney 2005). This is because a message is clearly sent on the part of institutions that white determination of whether or not there was actually a racial issue at hand will take precedence over a person of color's experience.

Therefore, for their own families' and communities' protection, many African American parents and other people of color begin the arduous task of having to educate their children and other community members on racism and how to protect themselves from it. This emotional labor is of course dissonance producing because in most cases, there is nothing the target could have done to avoid the arbitrary attack. Much like the society that encourages women to take various protective measures to keep from being raped (when it is mostly men doing the raping), the oppressed group in society shoulders the burden of having to dodge bullets where efforts would be better spent on the (metaphorical and literal) shooter and gun. Therein lies the cumulative and collective impact of microaggressions—the white privilege is, as Peggy McIntosh put it on item #15 of her list: "I do not have to educate my children to be aware of systemic racism for their own daily physical protection" (McIntosh 1990). Sometimes referred to as "the talk" or "the conversation"—though it is more likely a series of ongoing conversations—analysts in the United States and Great Britain have studied how black parents navigate the challenges of having to convey the potentially devastating and trauma-inducing reality of racism to their children (Dunbar 2017; Rollock 2014; Rollock et al. 2014). These findings underscore the importance of not misunderstanding microaggressions as "individual" incidents or as on a merely psychological level alone. Not only do microaggressions have cumulative and community impact, but they are the foundation of what is often defined as institutional racism, a topic to which we now turn.

Institutional Racism and Microaggressions

Sociologists define **institutions** as *"established and organized systems of social behavior with a particular and recognized purpose"* (Andersen and Taylor 2006:4). Social institutions include health care, government, education, economy, families, religion, criminal justice, and the media. In this chapter, we plan to make a detailed investigation of economy, education, and criminal justice. In the following chapter, we devote an entire chapter to media and popular culture, mainly because media and social media are such pervasive influences on people's racial views and behaviors in the twenty-first century that they even shape how people come to understand and interact with all other institutions. Although focusing institutionally tends to invoke a large-scale, nameless, faceless bureaucratic understanding of human interaction, we must remember that institutions are created, maintained, and sustained by individuals. Without individuals, there are no institutions.

Typically, social scientists who study racism have distinguished between individual and institutional racism. (In the previous chapter, we also explored the difference between individual and institutional discrimination—noting it was a *somewhat* useful distinction.) The approach we want to introduce is one that *synthesizes* our understanding of both individual and institutional racism so that we can establish an analysis of how actions as seemingly minor as microaggressions have a direct impact on institutional racism and white privilege. In other words, something is altogether missing if we analyze one without the other. Although we feature three institutions in detail in this chapter, we cannot emphasize enough that the tools with which we analyze the white privilege in our three example institutions here can be applied to any institution. For instance, let us take one example related to health care. Non-Hispanic black women experience mortality and morbidity in childbirth at a rate of two to three times that of white women (Creanga et al. 2017; Howell et al. 2016). The white privilege here is surviving childbirth, or more broadly defined: white women (and white families) can place more faith in the medical institution to deliver them through routine procedures.

Because the dominant ideology is color-blindness, a typical reaction to this statistic might be to assume that institutions are race neutral. So the assumption goes, doctors take an oath to serve everyone equally, so the cultural racism frame may lead some to erroneously assume that these greater negative health and life consequences are somehow the fault of the mothers themselves—yet the data tell us otherwise. Even when statistically controlling for class, racial differences in health outcomes persist (Colen et al. 2018; Karlsen and Nazroo 2002). Put another way, the evidence shows us that even when African Americans have the same income and education background—i.e., the same access to resources such as food, sanitation, exercise, and other wellness practices shared in common by the middle class—their health still suffers more than whites'. These studies lead us to examining the health care institution itself with a more critical eye.

Bringing the above findings from the medical journals to life a bit more, sociologist Tressie McMillan Cottom poignantly and heartbreakingly shares her personal story of losing a child due to racist treatment within medical institutions in an essay published in *Time* magazine. Citing another important pattern—the fact that black babies are nearly twice as likely to die within the first year of their life as white babies—Cottom concludes: "When my daughter died, she and I became statistics" (Cottom 2019). A detailed read of her experience reveals that Cottom experienced some version of what we have identified here as microaggressions at the hands of medical professionals, over and over again with every cross-racial interaction in the system. She was assumed to be incompetent, marginalized, and not taken seriously. As Cottom puts it:

> I spoke in the way one might expect of someone with a lot of formal education. I had health insurance. I was married. All of my status characteristics screamed "competent," but nothing could shut down what my blackness screams when I walk into the room. (Cottom 2019)

When whites enter every social institution, whether they have socioeconomic resources or not, they can count on their perceived racial background not working against them in this way. Keep in mind, racism does not merely exist in outright refusal of service. In the above example, Cottom receives continuous treatment in one form or another, but her own description of her symptoms is discounted and not believed.

Had we visited this hospital and interviewed the various medical professionals that Cottom interacted with during her ordeal, it is quite likely that they would not view their own actions as racially biased or racist. They would be likely to recount their perception of what occurred in race-neutral terms. Whether it is health care, economy, education, criminal justice, or other institution, many of us still subscribe to the **legalistic fallacy**, which is *a way of thinking that erroneously assumes that racism is no longer a major problem in society because there are now laws against it* (Desmond and Emirbayer 2010). Cottom was not refused service; she was not turned away at the door; she was not charged a different rate for the same service—although such illegal actions do also still occur. But being admitted into previously segregated institutions without being on an equal footing once in the door does not result in equality. We often assume that the mere ability to be able to access quality health care (or to access any other social institution—a school, a job, etc.) means that racial equality has been achieved. Yet often the cross-racial interactions that occur within these institutions are where social inequalities are exacerbated (e.g., Ross et al. 2012; Spencer and Grace 2016; Yoo et al. 2009). In McIntosh's list of white privileges, she addresses several institutions, such as banks, schools, hospitals, criminal justice, workplace, noting that she can count on the color of her skin not "working against" how she is treated there, and whether or not she will be taken seriously therein (McIntosh 1990). In each and every institution, keep in mind it is whites who understand themselves as "not racist" who are nevertheless filtering their perceptions of interracial interactions through the lens of race. If they are not aware of white privilege and racism, it is all the more likely it is happening.

Cross-racial interactions were once thought to be the golden ticket toward racial equality. The **contact hypothesis** was originally proposed by Gordon Allport (cited in the previous chapter for his definition of prejudice), *predicting that the more cross-racial contact people had, the more their racial prejudice would decline.* While in general whites who have had more interracial contact tend to have lower racial prejudice than their white peers who have not, over the years the research has added many caveats to this pattern that tend to put a damper on the degree of optimism or faith we should place in interracial contact alone (Forbes 1997; Sigelman and Welch 1993). In particular, one token friend is not going to do it; repeated contact of *equal-status* peers while working toward a *common goal* is key, and the *institution* within which the contact occurs has to support and encourage it (Forbes 1997; Jackman and Crane 1986). Most of these conditions are not satisfied between doctor and patient, between employer and employee, between teacher and student, between police officer and citizen. All these interactions are characterized by a power imbalance, so if the only cross-racial interactions white people have with people of color in their lives are in a subservient role, the likelihood of white privilege being challenged is tenuous at best.

Moreover, to the extent to which these institutions have color-blindness as the dominant ideology from which to approach their interactions, the institutional support needed for directly addressing and challenging racism does not exist. Even at the micro level, some very close interracial relationships between friends do not produce a deeper understanding of racism and white privilege when the topic of race is avoided altogether and instead they focus only on what they have in common (O'Brien and Korgen 2007). Likewise, institutions whose only plan for racial equality is "we treat all people the same regardless of race" are not going to get very far in minimizing the white privilege that already exists in society (e.g., Byrd 2017; Lewis 2003). As we shall see when we review the economy, education, and criminal justice institutions, very often complaints about racism will be met with defensive color-blind rhetorical strategies like "anything but race" and "they are the racist ones"—projecting back onto the person of color for causing the problem by bringing up race at all (Bonilla-Silva 2017). As McIntosh writes, one white privilege is "If I declare there is a racial issue at hand, or there isn't a racial issue at hand, my race will lend me more credibility for either position than a person of color will have" (McIntosh 1990). And a hallmark of privilege is obliviousness. So if we put together the institutional context of colorblindness—a vague commitment to equality and fairness without an explicit commitment to minimize racism and white privilege in the institution—with lack of awareness and denial of privilege at the microaggression level, then racism and white privilege actually flourish as the norm, not as exception. This is because when racism is challenged, those who bring it up are not believed (and even blamed), and those who are accused of racism deploy race-neutral defenses.

These race-neutral defenses vary depending on the institution. In criminal justice, it can sound like a white shooter or police officer saying "I feared for my life" or "I felt threatened." In the economy, it can sound like an employer saying "she was just not a good fit" or "he violated a policy" (often referring to a policy that is rarely if ever enforced when it comes to the privileged). In education, it might sound like a teacher saying "I have to constantly police his behavior" (teachers), or children/peers saying "I don't think she would feel comfortable at our parties." Those who are committing microaggressions rarely interpret their own behaviors as racially motivated. It is unlikely that the health professionals serving Cottom in the above example would have been able to verbalize or admit to viewing Cottom, a black woman, as incompetent. In a society where whites are viewed as more likely to be the experts and the rational ones, when a person of color states they have been treated as incompetent and a white person says they were just acting in a rational, race-neutral manner, it is the white person who is more likely to be believed. So we must understand that white privilege is not just merely a result of individual unchecked prejudices or biases, or even microaggressions. In their analysis of inequality in health care, citing an intellectual debt to Bonilla-Silva, Spencer and Grace write: "racism is not just an implicit attitude that lives in the head of a single actor, but is an iterative, multilevel sociological accomplishment" (2016:113). It is not just that microaggressions happen, but that institutions are not set up to hear, believe, or intervene when white privilege occurs. Rather, they are set up to deny, deflect, and obfuscate in ways that ensure the persistence of white privilege systemically.

In the sections that follow, we present the specific evidence of how this interactive process carries out in each of the three example institutions. As Bonilla-Silva puts it, we have "racism without racists," or for the purposes of this book, we have white privilege without white awareness—the obliviousness that McIntosh so eloquently describes—and without that awareness, the work of dismantling privilege remains undone.

Institution #1: The Economy

One of the most fundamental ways a society can ensure its citizens have a right to life, liberty, and the pursuit of happiness is to make available the means for all people to be able to economically provide for themselves and their families. In this section, we will examine employment, income, and wealth as some basic measures of economic status, in order to analyze how white privilege functions in each of these areas. Let us begin with an overview of white privilege in these aspects of life: if you are what society considers white in the United States, you can expect, on average, to be nearly half as likely to experience unemployment (Bunker 2017; Cajner et al. 2017); to earn about 35 percent more income (Kochhar and Cilluffo 2018); and possess 86 times more wealth than African American families and 68 times more wealth than Latino families (Thompson 2018). And keep in mind that much of the research in these areas attempts to control for factors such as education level and other demographics, which means that even if you are a poor white person who comes from an economically disadvantaged background, there are still substantial advantages you will have over some others because of your perceived race. These advantages are a result of current as well as past/historical discrimination, especially in the case of wealth, so let us begin there.

In Chapter 1, we briefly mentioned when discussing racial formation the state's role in creating "affirmative action for whites." Recall that post–World War II suburbanization was subsidized by low-interest loans to whites that nonwhites could not benefit from in the same way due to government-sanctioned redlining practices, restricting the neighborhoods in which blacks could purchase homes (Desmond and Emirbayer 2010; Thompson 2018). As late as the 1960s, redlining was legal, so the African American families whose homes are worth $50,000 today, for example, include some veterans who fought alongside white families whose equivalent-sized homes are worth $300,000 because of the neighborhoods they were allowed to buy into, and the rates of mortgage interest and insurance banks required them to pay. In his book *White Like Me*, Tim Wise vividly illustrates how this dynamic then affects the next generation through his own family biography. He grew up living in an apartment with white parents of meager incomes, but his white grandmother actually owned her own home and had some equity in it, which would have been very unlikely for any African American family of that same generation due to the legal restrictions outlined above. Most everyday Americans' wealth is in their home ownership. This meant his family could borrow money for him to go to college, borrowing against the value of that home—again, virtually impossible for many African American families in the late twentieth century (Wise 2004). By this time, yes, many more African Americans are being admitted to college than ever before, but it takes a much different type of financial investment and sacrifice on the part of these families to make that happen due to the lack of historical accumulation of wealth possible as compared to white families.

Many families actually have negative wealth (more debt than income), and the racial discrepancy on this statistic is striking—whites are less than half as likely to have this problem as are black and Latino families:

> The proportion of all U.S. households with zero or "negative" wealth, meaning their debts exceed the value of their assets, has grown from 1 in 6 in 1983 to 1 in 5 households today. Families of color are much likelier to be in this precarious financial situation. Thirty-seven percent of Black families and 33 percent of Latino families have zero or negative wealth, compared to just 15.5 percent of White families. (Collins et al. 2019:3–4)

It is important to stress that multiple analyses have examined the "spending/savings behavior" argument and the evidence is clear on this point—it is not at all the case that individual/personal spending and saving behaviors, nor even education levels, can explain the racial wealth gap (Conley 2009; Oliver and Shapiro 2006). The racial wealth gap exists in large part because of historical and current racial inequities in the housing market and in banks and lending practices.

Because wealth, unlike income, is passed down from generation to generation, the history of racism and white privilege certainly plays a large role in these differences, but even after the US government passed the Fair Housing Act in 1968, lending practices continued to favor whites. In particular, the 2008 recession and foreclosure crisis hit blacks much harder than whites, both because of the racial segregation that already persisted in neighborhoods when the crisis hit and also because banks purposely targeted black families with subprime predatory loans with balloon payments that grew well beyond the overall value of their homes (Burd-Sharps and Rasch 2015; Rugh and Massey 2010; White 2015). Thus, it was indeed elite whites who caused the crisis to begin with. Writer Reniqua Allen shared her own poignant testimony in a 2019 *New York Times* editorial, as one of many black and Latino homeowners who were notified that they were party to a class action suit against the mortgage company with whom they financed their homes. Indeed, this mortgage company was one of many that was found to be engaging in these racist, discriminatory lending practices. The suit was settled, granting a few hundred dollars to each person, and meanwhile she had to sell her condo in 2018 for "far less" than what she paid for it in 2005 (Allen 2019). Certainly, whites were hit by this particular recession and deflation of housing values as well. However, economists have been pretty clear on the research on recovery from this Great Recession, and there remain striking differences by race:

> By 2050, a white household's home equity may be only 5 percent below what it would have been without the Great Recession, while a black household, with the same income and education levels, may have a home equity value 22 percent lower than it could have been without the effects of the Great Recession. (Burd-Sharps and Rasch 2015:23)

Again, this ability to recover has to do with the accumulated resources generations back that the family is able to tap into, as well as the different values of homes in housing markets that continue to be informally segregated by race. White privilege ensures thus not only will white families have more wealth than black, Latino, and Native American families, but that when economic crises hit, whites are not hit quite as hard and can bounce back substantially more easily than others.

Whereas home ownership is the primary source of wealth for most Americans, the racial wealth gap is also evident in patterns of ownership of labor and ownership of businesses/entrepreneurship. Perhaps one of the most highly visible patterns of this, which we shall also touch upon in the following chapter on media/pop culture, is ownership of professional sports teams like the National Basketball Association (NBA) and National Football Association (NFL). Famous black athletes who are highly paid for a short few years (provided they stay in optimal physical health) may obscure our view of the white privilege in these organizations. While players are 70 percent (NFL) to 75 percent (NBA) black in these leagues, as of 2017 there were zero black owners of any NFL teams, and only one black owner and two other nonwhite owners of 32 NBA teams (Lapchick 2015; Lapchick 2019). Wealth begets more wealth—most of these team owners are already wealthy from family investments, which is how they are able to buy the teams in the first place. Elite white men such as Steve Ballmer, owner of the Los Angeles Clippers, has a net worth of $38.4 billion, and Paul Allen, owner of both the Portland Trailblazers and the Seattle Seahawks, has a net worth of $21.7 billion—well surpassing any yearly salary a player will ever see (Badenhausen 2018). (As a quick comparison, the highest-ever paid athletes' salaries are in the $30 million range, not billion!) So there is white male privilege even in the highest tiers of society. We see the same patterns when women and people of color attempt to own their own businesses in other sectors of the economy as well. Women and minority-owned businesses typically make less than half of what they should, given their share of the market—for example, in 2012, 36.2 percent of businesses were owned by women, yet those businesses only accounted for 11.3 percent of the revenue; and for minority-owned businesses that were 28.6 percent of all businesses that year, they took in only 10.4 percent of the total revenue (Zarya 2015). In fact, just under 80 percent of all businesses were owned by whites that year, but they reaped over 90 percent of all revenue, leaving very little for everyone else (Zarya 2015). In their analyses of racial wealth gaps and the question of entrepreneurship, sociologists have found that one obstacle is that minority-owned businesses often find themselves selling to or serving a limited, segregated market (Conley 2009; Oliver and Shapiro 2006). That is, potential white clients and customers may be hesitant to try out a new company that is owned by a person of color, so minority owners are often left relying on the patronage of people of color only, who are a smaller percentage of the consumer market to begin with. As discussed previously, the skepticism of people of color as incompetent thus directly impacts the accumulation of capital in these areas. White male entrepreneurs are much more likely to have the benefit of outside investors for their startup than are female or black entrepreneurs (Zarya 2015).

Besides these glaring white privileges in wealth and net worth of homes and businesses, which are highly impacted by intergenerational transfer, one's personal income is influenced by white privilege also. A white man can expect to earn, on average, $5 to $6 per hour more than black and Hispanic men (Patten 2016). Even if we just compare college-educated white men over twenty-five to their peers with the same level of education, they still have the privilege of making $5–$10 more per hour than all women and most men of different racial groups (with the exception of Asian American men) with a college degree (Patten 2016). Though certainly white men experience racial privilege in earnings, white women still have some privilege as well. It is true that white men with the same level of education out-earn them, but when comparing white women to other women, white women have the privilege of earning 16 cents per dollar more than black women, 22 cents more per dollar than Latina women, and 25 cents more per dollar than Native American women (Connley 2018). There are three major reasons for this earnings gap: (1) the pay differential in the different types of jobs that white women and women of color go into (occupational segregation), especially the "**sticky floor**" *low-wage, low-benefit, poor working conditions jobs with no room for advancement that women of color are more concentrated in*; (2) white men are *more likely to be promoted and experience advancement* than are white women and especially women of color—this is often referred to as the **glass ceiling** for white women, and even the **concrete ceiling** for women of color, who experience a *small and seemingly impenetrable likelihood of advancing to top positions* as compared to their counterparts; and (3) various outright discrimination practices, especially in hiring (Thompson and Armato 2012). While all the evidence for the above is well documented, let us review some influential studies on these inequalities so we can home in on how white privilege works in the workplace.

Title VII of the Civil Rights Act of 1964 was seemingly a great victory, as it made it illegal to discriminate against someone on the basis of race, sex, national origin, color, or religion. However, many of the influential factors behind the pay gaps identified above are not brought to light under the current structure, where defendants must mount evidence to prove they have been discriminated against, since many times people may not even know they have been discriminated against. Moreover, an employer may likely frame their own actions in color-blind, race-neutral terms, making it difficult to prove in a court of law. Two influential studies (or series of studies) in the early 2000s both used innovative methodologies to investigate some of this behind-the-scenes racial discrimination in hiring. Bertrand and Mullainathan (2004) responded to over 1,300 employment ads in Chicago by sending out nearly 5,000 résumés, and these résumés represented applicants who had the same credentials and level of work experiences; the only difference was the first names of the applicants—they used "white-sounding" names like Emily and Greg along with "black-sounding" names like Lakisha and Jamal, so they could compare response rate based on perceived race. The results were striking. The "white-sounding" names were *50 percent more likely to get callbacks* for an interview than the "black-sounding" names. Economist Mullainathan notes that such biases exist despite the best of intentions, and indeed, similar patterns of white advantage have been uncovered with research in various other transactional spheres of social life—including doctors treating heart disease, car salespeople bargaining for a purchase price, landlords offering apartments for rent, and state legislators responding to contacts from constituents (Mullainathan 2015b). In all these cases, the white-sounding name was more likely to get better treatment and a more favorable outcome at rates much higher than just due to chance.

Likewise, Devah Pager and her colleagues (Pager 2003; Pager and Quillian 2005; Pager, Western, and Bonikowski 2009) have used this audit study methodology to send out hundreds of résumés in both Milwaukee and New York City. Pager was interested not only in the impact of race, but also a criminal record, on employers' willingness to hire. Across multiple studies, the striking and consistent pattern was that employers were more willing to hire a white man with a criminal record than a black man without one. Additionally, when coupling the field experiment (sending out the résumés) with a follow-up survey of the same employers (by phone), Pager and Quillian (2005) found that during the survey the employers indicated they would be just as likely to hire the black candidate as the white candidate, as well as those with and without the criminal record. Entitling their article "Walking the Talk?" these authors point out that the employers' talk (what they say) was quite different from their walk (who they actually called back when they got the résumés). Here, the white privilege is twofold—not only are white job seekers more likely to be considered for the job and thus potentially hired, but questionable aspects of their past (like a criminal record) are much more likely to be overlooked and not held against them. While that is white privilege at work for job seekers, the white privilege for the employers is that they are able to frame their decisions in race-neutral terms and come across as fair, and no one is the wiser. All of the above are serious obstacles as we go about attempting to address and solve these problems.

As Ta-Nehisi Coates has written: "Racism is not merely a simplistic hatred. It is, more often, broad sympathy toward some, and broader skepticism towards others" (Coates 2017:123–24). The sympathy that whites feel for each other when it comes to passing along resources and contacts necessary for securing jobs and promotions is sometimes just as influential if not more so than their skepticism about the abilities of people of color. In hundreds of interviews with white adults across several US states, DiTomaso, Parks-Yancy, and Post (2003) found that whites would simultaneously both admit to receiving "insider" information and assistance with securing employment through their own personal contacts and chastise people of color for not being hardworking enough. For example, one white man's cousin told him about a job opening and gave him a referral, and another white man's friend gave him answers to a test he would need to pass to get a job. Yet these same whites repeated the color-blind rhetoric about fairness and everyone having the same opportunities for success. They could not see the contradiction between their own advantages and their belief that there is a level playing field. They believed in the **myth of meritocracy**, or the **meritocratic ideology**—the *popular myth that everyone has an equal chance of making it to the top, which erroneously assumes that* *those at the top are the most deserving and those at the bottom thus must not be working hard enough.* This myth quite obviously ignores all the data we review in this book on white privilege. Meritocracy is an ideology that makes it difficult for many people to accept the evidence on white privilege when they are confronted with it, because it is an ideology indoctrinated into us our whole lives through institutions such as education, politics, and media. Clearly, the whites in the above interviews subscribed to this ideology even as they admitted to unequal advantages that they had in the job market. They definitely do not see these actions they took to get themselves ahead as having anything to do with race or white privilege.

The economic advantages that whites have in wealth, income and employment come from whites' behaviors to look out more for each other than for others, whites' greater distrust and skepticism of people of color and their credentials, and whites' denial of all this by seeing their actions as race neutral. Another vivid example of these factors at work can be seen in Deirdre Royster's (2003) study of working-class young men in Baltimore. Although both white and black students felt welcomed and treated well by the teachers at their vocational school, what the African American students did not realize is that whenever the white teachers found out about job openings through their personal networks, it was often a white student with whom these teachers identified most closely and thus would be the first one they thought of when asked for graduate referrals. Keep in mind that none of these positive referral behaviors are technically in violation of the Civil Rights Act described above. No official employment discrimination has occurred according to the law, because the black students' applications never even made it to the job site to be considered. Yet belief in the legalistic fallacy as well as the myth of meritocracy keep many from realizing that just because it is "illegal to discriminate" does not mean white privilege is not still in full swing. This *preference for others like oneself* is also known as **homosocial reproduction**, and with almost all of top corporate positions in the United States being held by white men, this homosocial reproduction has both race and gender implications. In 2018, only 6 percent of Fortune 500 companies had female CEOs; there were only three black male CEOs in 2018 when the American Express CEO departed; and there were zero African American female CEOs when Ursula Barnes stepped down from Xerox in 2018 (Warner and Corley 2017; White 2017). So when those at the top have a preference for those like themselves, we end up with white male privilege in leadership, exemplifying the glass ceiling. When a promotion comes up, those on top think first of those most like them.

Keeping the best opportunities reserved for white males is a pattern evident in the hiring and promotion evidence cited above, but it is also apparent in demotion and termination practices. In one detailed study of dismissals in a federal bureaucracy, after controlling for all the variables that would explain termination—disciplinary actions, absences, tenure on job, experience, and education among others—black employees were still 50 percent more likely to be fired than similar whites (Zwerling and Silver 1992). In another study of hundreds of EEOC racial discrimination claims, Light, Roscigno, and Kalev (2011) found that often employer accounts of termination of an employee will cite a policy violation and insist their actions were race neutral, while an employee points out that other white employees have violated similar policies but not been accordingly treated. Citing Vincent Roscigno's (2007) term **differential policing**, *as it pertains to employer practices, employers advance white privilege by giving whites a "free pass" to violate policies and procedures without formal sanction.* Such practices make legal discrimination claims difficult to enforce and remedy. The way that white employers perceive and interpret the workplace behaviors of their employees of color more critically goes back to the various micro-aggression examples we reviewed earlier in the chapter.

These differential hiring, firing, and promotion practices amount to opportunity hoarding of the best possible positions for elite white males. Income inequalities in the United States are rising to the point not seen since the Gilded Age when the Industrial Revolution first began (Mullan 2017), and as resources become more and more unequal between the top and the bottom, they become more scarce, resulting in **opportunity hoarding**—a term coined by Charles Tilly (1998) to describe *the process by which those who are already privileged seek to hold on to that advantage for their offspring and others like them.* This hoarding of the white elite is not only happening in the United States, but in places like Great Britain, where scholars Friedman and Laurison (2019) refer to it as the "class ceiling." Those whose parents were doctors were nearly 25 percent more likely to go on to become doctors themselves, and similar patterns were found for lawyers and other highly paid professions (Moore 2019). As we move into the next section on education, we shall see even more clearly how this process begins early in white children's lives, as their families seek to maximize their own advantages, all under the color-blind guise of wanting what's best for their children.

Institution #2: Education

Those who may become disenchanted by the racial economic inequality described above may attempt to turn more optimistically toward education as the supposed "great equalizer." Yet there are white privileges here as well. Whites can count on moving through their schooling with fewer obstacles, with higher achievement, and more resources and opportunities than students of color. Whites are 7 percent more likely than African Americans and 22 percent more likely than Hispanics to have graduated from high school; whites are also about 12 percent more likely to attend college and 14 percent more likely to graduate college than African Americans; and the disparity is even greater for advanced degrees, with whites nearly twice as likely to have an advanced degree as blacks (US Bureau of the Census 2017). There are also some sizable achievement gaps at the K–12 level—for example, in New York

City, for English and math skills tests for third through eighth grades, nearly double the percentage of white children pass these tests as African American children do (Beilock 2010). In some cases, even where schools have relatively equal numbers of black and white children, white children are two to three times more likely to get placed in advanced classes (Kohli and Quartz 201). School quality is a major factor behind many of the racial gaps, and the racial segregation in housing that we touched on in the previous section feeds directly into these educational differences.

A white privilege is access to better-quality schooling. Only 18 percent of white children attend high-poverty schools, as compared to 60 percent of black and Latino students who do so, and these schools tend to have lower scores on achievement tests and less trained/experienced teachers working there (Logan, Minca, and Adar 2012). Education is another institution where we have to question the legalistic fallacy, because although the 1954 *Brown v. Board of Education* decision legally "desegregated" public schools in the United States, the data show that most US schools are still highly segregated by race over 60 years later. The research is clear that programs like school choice, charter schools, and magnet schools that introduce this element of market dynamics into public schools in a "color-blind" manner almost always result in a more racially segregated environment in the school district than existed prior (Roda and Wells 2013; Saporito and Sohoni 2006). Furthermore, the rarer schools that actually do have racially mixed/balanced populations often experience **resegregation** within the schools—*the process by which curricular placement or "tracking" creates a segregated environment by classroom within the school walls.* Even where African American and Latino students have similar ability levels as whites, often they are nevertheless placed into lower-level classes than their white peers, and sometimes cross-racial interaction would not even occur during the course of a school day because these classes are in totally different parts of the building (Bush et al. 2001; Mickelson 2001). And this separate education is not equal. The higher-ability, advanced placement courses which have mostly white students in them tend to have better teachers and give students more college-prep anticipatory socialization and critical thinking opportunities that prepare them better for college.

Why does this separate-but-equal education system continue to exist, despite the laws that were aimed to end it? There are so many reasons, but in the brief space we have here, we focus on two that relate most closely to white privilege: opportunity hoarding on the part of white parents and families, and teacher/administrator bias, fueled by microaggressive assumptions about students of color that block/slow their progress and thus advantage whites. In the previous section, we discussed how opportunity hoarding affects preserving job opportunities for whites, and it is especially salient when examining educational resources as well. White parents maneuver themselves not only to create white isolation in school districts, but even within schools to access better opportunities and exert power and influence over teachers and administrators to proffer better outcomes for their children. In an interesting doublespeak, white parents will even say they desire a racially diverse environment for their children but then place their children in predominantly white schools using color-blind language about school quality (Hagerman 2018). In their research in a New York City school district, Roda and Wells (2013) refer to this as a "fractured habitus," as there is a breakdown between what parents *say* they value and the self-interested behavior they actually *do*. White parents actually function as an interest group as they wield their cultural capital and political power to hoard educational resources away from people of color (Lyken-Segosebe and Hinz 2015). Even when and if they do attend racially diverse schools, as compared to parents of color, white parents are more likely to exert undue pressure on teachers and administrators to avoid negative sanctions and consequences for their children (Lewis and Diamond 2015). It is important to note that the favored treatment whites are able to secure as a result of their lobbying and hoarding does not mean that black and Latino parents are not also fierce advocates for their children. Yet institutional gatekeepers consistently respond more favorably to the way white parents advocate and to the relatively more politically powerful position of whites in communities—even in suburban areas where families of color come from educated backgrounds (Rollock et al. 2015). Although they may not be intentionally setting out to perpetuate racism and white privilege, what they tell themselves is good parenting (being advocates for their children) does indeed result in white advantage. This is not inevitable, as there are some more anti-racist ways for white parents to behave—becoming advocates for all children in the community, not just their own—that we will outline in our closing chapter. But practicing these strategies requires abandoning the color-blind approach that remains all too common.

Color-blind racism remains the ideological underpinning keeping white privilege alive both with white families' opportunity-hoarding behaviors and with the behaviors of faculty, staff, and administrators within the schools. Many teachers and educational administrators will not only tell you that they do not see race, or race is not an issue, but they may also even tell you that they celebrate diversity and have a multicultural environment in their schools (Lewis 2001; 2003). Yet research on actual patterns of inequality in education shows otherwise. Institutions of learning often use diversity-positive slogans but in practice fall short of equitable treatment. Extensive studies, using ethnographic methods (going inside schools, observing and interviewing students, teachers, and administrators) in the United States as well as Canada demonstrate that stakeholders often confuse cultural food and holiday celebrations, and/or brief history lessons, with anti-racism (Lewis 2003; Randolph 2012; Ryan 2003). They engage in what Randolph (2012) terms a color-blind multiculturalism—they pay lip service to being pro-diversity, but when it comes time to actually implementing programs that would potentially close achievement gaps, such as bilingual education, actions often do not follow willingly. This general pattern continues in higher education—nearly every college website boasts a pretty picture of "diverse" faces (who may or may not actually attend the school), but Historically White Colleges and Universities (HWCUs) continue to be spaces that privilege whiteness and make students of color feel isolated and unwelcomed (Byrd 2017; Feagin et al. 1996; Houts Picca and Feagin 2007). Indeed, evidence from a study of over 500 university admissions counselors demonstrates that HWCUs are actually quite selective about what kind of African American student they admit—if they show signs of having been actively challenging inequality in their communities while in high school (i.e., involved with civil rights organizations), universities are less likely to admit them (Thornhill 2018). These findings underscore the primary concern with diversity as window dressing rather than as an actual impetus for changing the structure of the organization. We must not confuse slogans or even diversity of curricular content with structural inequality in terms of quality of educational experience for every student.

In order to challenge the white privilege in education, just having a diverse student body alone does not do much. Even in suburban, racially integrated high schools, there still exist racial disparities that advantage whites. There are multiple factors adding up to cumulative disadvantage for black and Hispanic students and relative advantages for whites. The already-mentioned lower net worth of homes in racially segregated housing makes it harder for black suburban families to afford tutoring and other extra resources which advantage whites. Then, the white students in these schools are more likely to be recommended for advanced-placement classes, even with similar ability levels to students of color who don't get placed in these upper classes. Having not been exposed to the more advanced skills and vocabulary that appear on achievement tests and SAT/ACT exams thus further disadvantages students of color and advantages whites (Diamond 2006). As a result, the unexamined, unchecked racial biases that teachers and administrators bring to their assessments of students further contribute to these inequalities. Evidence shows that both implicit and explicit bias on the part of white instructors negatively affects students' performance on assessments (Jacoby-Senghor, Sinclair, and Shelton 2016), and teacher bias against African American cultural expressions impacts the likelihood of these students getting recommended for special education (Neal et al. 2003), as well as less likely to be recommended for gifted education even when the ability is there (Howard 2013). Educational researchers have identified an ideology that harms students of color, known as the "deficit model," with which teachers and administrators may approach African American and Latino students, without even realizing it—mistakenly assuming that they have not been taught to value education, or that they do not have the same potential for success as white students (Howard 2013; Valencia 2002). Under this model, the privilege for white students (and their families) is that they do not have to work to prove the teacher wrong.

The fact that most teachers in the United States are white and female (Loewus 2017), coupled with the fact that over half of all public school children in the nation are now nonwhite (Geiger 2018), creates a situation of the increased likelihood of black and Latino disadvantage, particularly for young boys of color (Delpit 2006; Howard 2013). And although the numbers of black and brown boys that the educational system is shortchanging seems striking, the challenges that girls of color face are equally as problematic (Crenshaw et al. 2015; Wun 2016). In both cases, although the specific content of the stereotyping varies by gender, the end result is similar—white children are often assumed to be smarter and well behaved, and their behavior is held to age-appropriate standards, while black and Latino children all too often face criminalization of their behavior in the schools, interfering with their educational experience (Bernstein 2017).

We would be remiss in concluding this section on education and moving onto the next section on criminal justice without emphasizing that the existence of the **school-to-prison pipeline** (STPP) results in a major white privilege for white children and families. The school-to-prison pipeline is a relatively new term, invented in the twenty-first century, to describe a particular relationship between the institutions of education and criminal justice that has a deeply rooted and much longer history than the date of the invention of the term would suggest (Crawley and Hirschfield 2018). While criminalizing everyday black behavior as a form of social control and repression has a long history, the postindustrial economy and disappearance of work from the inner city, coupled with reduced funding for public schools and privatization of criminal justice services, have led to a situation where zero-tolerance discipline policies and police officers in schools have become increasingly common (Brent 2016). This increase in using criminal-justice resources, policies, and practices within the schools to handle classroom management and discipline matters once left solely to the schools has resulted in some striking racial disparities. A US Department of Education study found in a nationwide sample of schools where 18 percent of the students were African American, African Americans accounted for almost half of all suspensions, making them three and a half times more likely to be suspended than their white classmates (Wilf 2012). The study also found that the very presence of a police officer in a school increased the number of behavioral incidents reported, which then increased the young people's criminal records. As we have already seen above, teacher biases from predominantly white teachers confound this unequal and unfair pattern—observational research in classrooms has discovered that white teachers disproportionately target black students for subjective and minor disciplinary complaints (Bryan 2017). Teachers are often unaware that their behaviors are this disproportionately unequal and justify their actions with race-neutral explanations. In just one of many such examples, in January 2019, four twelve-year-old girls at a New York middle school were strip-searched for drugs at school with the justification that they exhibited "giddy" behavior (Herreria 2019). Many such incidents never make it to the public eye.

An educational white privilege thus includes the ability for children to make minor behavioral mistakes and have them never impact their schooling progress or result in a criminal record. White children are assumed innocent until proven guilty, whereas in practice, the process often works the opposite for children of color—the first assumption is that they are up to no good and not to be trusted, and that is how many teachers and education administrators end up treating them, even when they perceive themselves as just responding to a race-neutral behavior standard. While certainly schooling can be challenging for students in many other ways—learning disabilities, family structure changes, financial hardships, frequent moving, peer pressures, test anxieties—the evidence shows that there is still an unearned advantage in being white, even while experiencing such difficulties. And students of color may very well be experiencing all of this *plus* facing the racism perpetuated by the educational institution and those who comprise it—one less hurdle for whites to clear. We encourage you to research on your own how white privilege also impacts one's access to college and universities, as well as one's progress to graduating and actually receiving a college degree.

Institution #3: Criminal Justice

There is no shortage of poorly educated, poorly paid whites experiencing pain and suffering in these times of increasing social inequality, so perhaps the most vivid white privilege left to identify in this context is one's likelihood of surviving an encounter with police. This is but one of many unearned advantages whites can expect when interacting with (and even in avoiding altogether) interactions with the criminal justice system. Whites are much less likely (less than half as likely) to be stopped by police than blacks are, and when whites are (rarely) stopped, they are much less likely to be searched (Quigley 2010). And even though whites are no more likely to use or sell drugs than blacks, whites are much less likely to be arrested or imprisoned for drugs than blacks (Rosenberg, Groves, and Blankenship 2017; Quigley 2010). Whites are much more likely to either get treatment or never have to go to prison or have the drug issue appear on their records (Alexander 2010; Rosenberg et al. 2017). A white privilege is being much less likely to spend time in prison—black men are five times as likely, and Latino men nearly three times as likely, than white men to ever be incarcerated (Quigley 2010). Since the vast majority of people in prison are there today for drug-related offenses, and drug use rates are similar across racial groups, it is evident that the racial discrepancy in prison is not due to the fact that whites are not committing any less crime, but rather that they are not having to do the time. Whites are not getting caught because they are not being watched enough. This results in two important consequences: (1) whites are much less likely to die during an encounter with police; and (2) whites are less likely to be scarred by the mark of a criminal record. As with our other institutional analyses, these white privileges are a result of both how racism is structured into the system and the daily microaggressions practiced by those individuals within the system.

Sadly, in the United States, an average of three men per day are killed by police officers, and those men are more likely to be black or Latino than white—in fact, Latino men are killed by police at about one and a half times more often than whites, and black men are killed by police twice as often as white men (Crist 2018; Edwards, Esposito, and Lee 2018). Although many studies focus on men, the research also shows us that the press may not be focusing as much on women—indeed, when examining police killings of unarmed citizens, black women were killed by police more than any other demographic group (Johnson Jr., Gilbert, and Ibrahim 2018; Lisenby 2018). So whether male or female, whites are more likely to survive police encounters than any other group. There are both structural and individual level factors creating this disparity.

At the structural level, police are much more likely to patrol predominantly black and Latino neighborhoods than majority-white areas (Mullainathan 2015a). Thus, a white privilege is not being subjected to police **hypersurveillance**—*excessive critical attention and monitoring of one's everyday behaviors and environs.* Unfortunately, circular arguments are often used to justify hypersurveillance—police departments say they have a heavier presence in these areas because crime happens more in these areas, but of course the more their efforts are focused there, the more crime they will find. Again, we know from drug use data that these laws are being violated in all races and classes of society. However, an organizational decision is being made where to primarily focus the resources of time and energy of law enforcement activities, and this is going to result in racial disparities, whether or not there is any racial bias on the part of individual officers (Scott 2017; Tomaskovic-Devey, Mason, and Zingraff 2004). In some police departments, a further motivator for hypersurveillance of poor communities of color is a reward structure for officers' "collars"—that is, arrests that result in convictions. As we shall discuss in more depth shortly, due to an overreliance on public defenders and plea bargaining, poor and nonwhite defendants are more likely to be convicted of charges, whether or not they are any more guilty, so it actually pays for police officers to hedge their bets on an arrest of a person with fewer resources, if they are rewarded most for arrests that lead to convictions (Chambliss 2000). This is why it is so important to focus beyond just individual officers' biases and intents. We must also focus on how the criminal justice system is organized and arranged in its policies and practices, which goes well beyond individual officers' racial backgrounds and biases.

Police killings of unarmed civilians, which disproportionately happen to African Americans, also are more likely to occur in areas with high racial segregation, high unemployment, and low educational attainment. Even when controlling for crime and arrest rates, it is clear that police not only use hypersurveillance in poor, black communities, but they are more likely to shoot first and ask questions later under these conditions (Mesic et al. 2018; Mock 2018). As social media has increasingly brought police killings of unarmed African Americans to public attention, some observers have raised an astute question about white privilege—how is it that so many white *armed* mass shooters are captured into police custody, alive, without incident (Harriot 2016)? Racial bias notwithstanding, the institutional consequences are clear—there are very few cases of a police officer actually facing any charges for killing unarmed African Americans, and in the rare cases when the charges are pursued in court, it is even rarer that the charges result in an actual conviction for the officer (Park 2018). It is more common for the city or state to have to pay civil damages to the family of the deceased than it is for an officer to be held accountable. A study in the United Kingdom found similar patterns—a disproportionately higher number of black and Caribbean-descent Britons died due to excessive force while in police custody than whites—and even though the total number of deaths was far smaller than in the United States, the officers likewise never faced convictions (Gayle 2018). These structural supports allow racism to continue as the *typical* way the institution functions—devaluation of black victims, coupled with the benefit of the doubt given to white criminals as well as police officers. We cannot reduce these unjust killings at the hands of the state to isolated exceptions of "bad apples" or merely the result of individual biases, when so much structural support clearly maintains these patterns.

Now that we have reviewed the structural underpinnings that allow the disproportionate police killing of unarmed African Americans to continue, let us examine the practice of racial profiling by individual officers as well as entire departments. **Racial profiling** occurs when *race, ethnicity or skin color is used as a proxy for suspicion—often to justify a traffic stop or other police surveillance activity.* This practice is another reason why many people of color have more frequent interactions with police than whites and why more whites are able to evade police surveillance without being detected or harmed. Police continue to practice this method, even when research says it is not actually the most efficient way of catching crime (Warren et al. 2006). One white privilege is that one's race usually does not "fit the profile," and thus one is able to avoid police hypersurveillance. Police departments are beginning to acknowledge that implicit bias influences their use of racial profiling, and some have implemented cultural sensitivity training and other programs to try to reduce the problem (Spencer, Charbonneau, and Glaser 2016). However, it is not merely individual biases that fuel this practice. Institutional supports exist, such as police officers subscribing to an informal code of silence where they protect each other's transgressions, and even the practice of a retaliatory type of hypersurveillance in a community immediately following events where police officers have been harmed (Legewie 2016). For these and many other reasons, when whites commit crimes, they are less likely to even result in arrests in the first place.

Once arrested, whites are less likely to have to wait in jail for their trial, which then puts them in a highly advantageous position for getting the best possible outcome for the charges they are facing. Research shows that black and Hispanic defendants get consistently higher bail amounts than white defendants and thus are less likely than whites to get pretrial release (Demuth and Steffensmeier 2004; Schlesinger 2005). Having to wait in jail while facing charges makes defendants highly vulnerable to plea bargains. Over 95 percent of criminal cases are plea bargained and do not go to trial (Quigley 2010). Thus, it is not surprising that African Americans are more likely than whites to have been wrongly convicted of crimes they did not commit; additionally, they also have to wait longer than whites for their names to be cleared (Chokshi 2017; Gross, Possley, and Stephens 2017). Although whites are less likely to be convicted and sentenced, when they are sentenced, their sentences tend to be shorter than those for blacks and Hispanics—in fact, somewhere between 67 to 83 percent of life sentences are being served by African Americans (Quigley 2010). At every stage of the criminal justice process, there is substantive data revealing white advantage—resulting in more African Americans under criminal control now than there were during slavery, leading analyst Michelle Alexander (2010) to call mass incarceration "the new Jim Crow." Alexander's extensive research reveals how there are all kinds of alternative-to-sentencing programs that whites access more, such that even when whites do come into contact with the criminal justice system, they are more often able to avoid the mark of a criminal record altogether than are people of color.

The fact is that even with federal sentencing guidelines and other policies and procedures that attempt to require uniform standards of the criminal justice system, every step in the process involves a sizable amount of **selective enforcement/discretion**—*human decisions whether or not to follow a standard policy or to show mercy/leniency.* Judges show discretion often during their decision-making processes, but so do prosecutors, lawyers, probation officers, police officers, and every other stakeholder in the institution. Again, we have an interaction between the institution whose structure permits discretion, and humans, whose implicit biases are known to lean toward whites. In areas like prosecutorial discretion, it has been acknowledged that implicit biases can play a role in deciding whether or not to charge someone with a crime, as well as the severity of the charge (Smith and Levinson 2011). A white privilege is that at any step of the process, whites can count on a stakeholder's use of discretion not working against them.

We have already reviewed earlier in this chapter the evidence showing how a criminal record does not seem to impact whites nearly as negatively in their life after being convicted (and possibly serving time) as it does people of color. Whites are more likely to be considered favorably for job prospects even after having a criminal record (Alexander 2010; Pager 2003). Through the pretrial negotiations mentioned above, whites are also more likely to avoid the felony convictions which could effectively disenfranchise them, even after time served is completed. Nearly half of all Americans ineligible to vote due to felony convictions are African American (even though they make up less than 15 percent of the population overall), making this seemingly color-blind policy highly problematic (Schaefer and Kraska 2012). There are so many ways that hypersurveillance make interaction with the criminal justice system nearly inevitable if you are not white, and this impacts families and communities in many ripple-effect ways.

We also mentioned previously how police killings of unarmed African Americans have mental health consequences on African Americans, even when they did not personally know or live in the same community as the victim (Eligon 2018). The knowledge that one is susceptible to this sort of unchecked killing, particularly when no indictments or convictions usually result for the officers, is ever-present in a way that incites fear and impedes freedom of movement. A white privilege for not only police officers, but even everyday white citizens who have killed African Americans, is that using Stand Your Ground laws or other justifications such as "I feared for my life" can often result in avoiding legal consequences altogether. Families of color live every day with this uneasy knowledge, while whites do not have to educate their children about surviving a police encounter, making no sudden movements when they are pulled over by police, and so forth. Also, let us point out that whenever there is significant media exposure in a trial of a white person killing an unarmed black American, there is an elevated stress level for African Americans, particularly when there is an acquittal, which happens more often than not (McDougal and Jayawardene 2013). This comes not only with a reminder that their lives matter less, but many outside observers like to weigh in with their opinions, which can be hostile and critical of the entire African American community, as opposed to just dealing with the parties involved in the trial. For example, during the trial of George Zimmerman, who was acquitted for the killing of unarmed black teenager Trayvon Martin in 2013 while acting as a neighborhood watch patrolman, many whites spoke out negatively about African Americans in public venues such as media outlets while the trial was going on (O'Brien and Prince 2015). Intensified media exposure can often re-traumatize the community.

In the following chapter on the media, we will discuss more how stereotypes about black and Latino criminality privilege whites, as they are assumed innocent until proven guilty. Perhaps the most vivid examples of this are situations in which *white people have actually committed crimes and then made up stories about unnamed African Americans in order to get the heat of the investigation away from themselves.* Law professor Katheryn Russell-Brown (2008) terms these **racial hoaxes** in her book *The Color of Crime* and counted close to 70 examples of these reported in one decade between 1987 and 1996. Sometimes these white hoaxes have been so convincing that law enforcement has actually coerced an innocent African American person into confessing to the crime, as in the case of Charles Stuart's murder of his wife in 1989. A white privilege here is that as a witness to a crime, your testimony is more likely to be believed—even when it should not be. Thankfully, in our closing chapter, we will review how more voices than ever are starting to speak out against white privilege in the criminal justice system—calling for reform, mainly because of race and class inequalities. Social media has helped with social movement building, but as the above evidence makes clear, much more is still to be done.

White Privilege: Quantitative/Qualitative, Micro/Macro, Explicit/Complicit

In our three example institutions, we offer a framework within which to analyze white privilege that we encourage you to apply to other institutions of which you are part—health care, government, military, religion, etc. For any institution you examine (and which we do for media/pop culture in the following chapter), here are some guiding questions:

- By the numbers, what quantitative advantages can whites expect to experience in this institution? Examine what the resources are, what the highest positions of power are, and how they are distributed. (For example, in economy, we looked at how much more income, wealth, and the likelihood of being hired/fired whites had; in education, we saw how many more years of education, how much more likely to get higher placements, less likely to get disciplined; in criminal justice, we looked at how much more likely whites are to survive a police encounter and less likely to be arrested/imprisoned.) Also, think about what historical (and current) structural factors have led to these quantitative advantages.

- Due to the above structural (relatively) advantageous positioning within these institutions that whites typically experience, how are the interpersonal interactions qualitatively different for whites? What kinds of suspicions are whites less likely to confront, what assumptions of competence, virtue, and innocence can whites expect (and might they even take for granted) within this particular institution? What kinds of mundane human errors are whites permitted to make without much notice or negative impact on their future? (This is the microaggressions piece.)

- What are the *explicit*/obvious pro-white biases that tend to come out in this institution? (For example, there may have been lawsuits won by plaintiffs that exposed racial discrimination and disparities within this institution that unfairly advantaged whites and excluded others.) How do gatekeepers and everyday members of the institution remain *complicit* in white privilege by using *color-blind* interpretations/justifications for racial disparities?

We have addressed the above questions for each of our three example institutions, and we will address these questions of media and pop culture in the following chapter. Finally, in our closing chapter, we discuss concrete strategies for disrupting the complicity described above.

Although there was not nearly enough space here to review each of these institutions thoroughly, this was not our aim, and there are plenty of textbooks that provide a more detailed review of the evidence of the discrimination that African Americans, Latinos, Asian Americans, Native Americans, and other people of color face in every social institution. Instead, we emphasized that white privilege is not an aberration or a fluke of bias within otherwise neutral social systems; rather, these institutions are structured at every turn to unfairly advantage whiteness (Bonilla-Silva 2017; Feagin and Ducey 2017; Ray 2019). White privilege in their functioning is the norm, not the exception, and a crucial component of normative operations is to justify racial unequal outcomes with race-neutral explanations. This process is accomplished at both the structural and individual levels, and each feeds into the other. Our purpose behind this approach is to not bombard you with statistics about racial inequality, but rather to understand what racial inequality and white privilege feel like in everyday lived experience. Often white privilege is not something overt like some guardian angel swooping up a white person and giving them a VIP private entrance into the institution, where they float effortlessly through and never have any difficulties. Indeed, it is as mundane and as basic as whites approaching an institution and taking for granted that it is going to do what it is supposed to do (e.g., educate them, keep them safe), and that it will treat them with respect and assumed competence until proven otherwise. Yet also, when confronted with charges of racism, whites can also count on the institution backing them when they say they are not racist—even when a person of color is experiencing real undeniable harm at this institution's hands. By the close of this book, though, we hope you have some concrete strategies for how to disrupt these patterns and help to rebuild institutions that offer equal treatment to all, not just some.

Real-Life Example

Getting a "Pass"

We live in what some have referred to as a post-civil rights era—laws say racial discrimination is illegal, but racial inequality and white privilege still pervade every social institution. None of the examples below are actually "illegal" according to current US law but are clearly racist, unequal, and result in white privilege. Be thinking about what in society allows these things to happen and what might be able to be changed to reduce their continued occurrence:

(A) Tyrone is a black man who holds an administrative/leadership position in a higher education institution with a racially diverse student body, but highest leadership remains predominantly white. Like others in his role, he is responsible for hosting events that involve food. Once, when removing the food at the end of the event (cleaning up after an event), he was confronted as if he was stealing it. His every minor spelling error is picked apart by supervisors, while errors by white colleagues in equal or similar roles are overlooked. A predecessor in his position (white male) received assistance with doctoral program tuition through an informal/discretionary policy (not an official HR benefit), but when Tyrone asked for the same assistance, he was told the funds were no longer available. As a result of this "chilly climate," Tyrone retains a professional, cordial relationship with his supervisor, but does not overly share personal chit-chat with her like other whites at the institution. Tyrone was ultimately fired for violating a relatively minor university policy: not responding to e-mail within 48 hours. Employment law does not ask whether others have not violated the policy and been similarly punished, but certainly many others have done so and not been fired. There was little Tyrone could do but admit to human error, even though he watched many of his white colleagues make many more serious errors and continue to be employed there.

(B) Michael is a fourth-grade African American boy who attends a racially mixed but majority white school whose teachers and principal are mostly white females. His ability level is above average (according to standardized test assessments), but grades and behavior continue to be challenges with his teachers. His parents receive not infrequent calls from the principal about his behavior—usually relatively minor incidents involving multiple children teasing, using a bad word, or not making a good choice. In speaking with Michael, his parents learn that other white (and also some nonwhite female) students may be engaging in similar behavior but not getting called out or disciplined similarly. However, Michael is admittedly involved in some of these activities too. Michael's teacher's perception of him as a troublemaker seems to be affecting his grades on everyday assignments—he is not given the benefit of the doubt, for example, when he leaves the back of a page blank because he does not see it, instead getting a 50 percent for the assignment, when he does know the material. Other children may be prompted or reminded in a more empathetic fashion by the teacher. Michael may have to repeat a grade or incur disciplinary action, which will affect his chances of continuing onto the advanced programs offered in his school district that more clearly/truly reflect his abilities, impacting his chances for college, etc.

(C) Sally is the white parent of two racially mixed children—Lisa and Lamont. She expects to keep them in the same schools when she moves to a new residence but does not realize she has moved into a different school district. The school secretary informs her that the policy is she must change schools, but when Sally asks to speak with the principal, the principal is sympathetic to her situation and tells her about an out-of-zone request form that allows the kids to stay where they are. This allows Lisa to be where she can access a highly prestigious magnet high school program that will position her well for college. Meanwhile, Lamont gets caught in the wrong place at the wrong time, and Sally is headed to juvenile court with him. However, when she calls the clerk of the court, she is told about an alternatives-to-punishment program that allows Lamont to bypass a mark on his record by completing 100 hours of community service. These hours will help him on college applications too. Sally is grateful because she would have never known about either of these "workarounds" for her children without another (white) person telling her—but she can't help but wonder if everyone is afforded this same information.

Racial Bias and Health Care: The Case of Maternal Mortality

According to the Centers for Disease Control and Prevention, black women have a risk for pregnancy-related deaths that is three to four times higher than that for white women. This striking statistic is in large part due to systemic inequities, including decreased access to healthy food, safe neighborhoods, quality schools, adequate employment opportunities, and reliable transportation for black women. Coupled with chronic conditions such as high blood pressure, obesity, and diabetes that black women experience at higher rates, delivering a child in a hospital of lower quality than where white mothers deliver children make giving birth more dangerous.

Sadly, the United States has become the developed country with the highest rates of maternal mortality rates. Many studies highlight that race is not solely the factor at play, as higher education levels and socioeconomic status does not seem to lessen this disparity. For instance, in a study conducted by the New York City Department of Health and Mental Hygiene, higher rates of severe pregnancy complications were found in black women with a college degree compared to white women who had not graduated high school. The story of the sudden death of Dr. Shalon Irving, a black epidemiologist at the Centers for Disease Control and Prevention, provides a striking representation of the state of maternal mortality in America. She focused her career on research that analyzed how limited health care options led to poor health outcomes. Although she was employed by one the most distinguished health agencies, earning multiple master's degrees and a dual-subject PhD, Dr. Irving died of complications just weeks after giving birth to her newborn. Here, we see that factors like social advantages such as higher levels of education, prestige, and income do not form a shield against racial disparity in health care. Black expectant and new mothers also frequently report that nurses and doctors do not take their reports of pain seriously, reflecting a broader phenomenon shown in various studies that pain is more likely undertreated in black patients when compared to white patients.

Still other studies point to the unceasing discrimination that black women experience via the powerful combination of race and gender that could be a major cause of poor maternal outcomes. The stress of existing as a black woman in American society can take a substantial physical cost, especially during pregnancy and childbirth. The term *weathering* was devised by Arline Geronimus, a professor at the University of Michigan School of Public Health. It describes how continuous discrimination distresses the body and speeds up aging at the cellular level, increasing the susceptibility of blacks to diseases like diabetes and hypertension at much younger ages then whites. As one can imagine, weathering may have significant effects, as stress causes the most common pregnancy complication, premature labor. Not surprisingly, black women are 49 percent more likely than white women to give birth preterm.

In August 2018, Senator Kamala Harris introduced a maternal mortality bill in hopes to address this health crisis. Among other goals, the bill would seek to tackle implicit bias in medicine and would introduce two grant programs: one to screen pregnant women for risk factors and another to fund professional training programs in health care that include bias training.

Things to Consider: In what ways could more diversity in the health care system alleviate racial disparities in medicine? Other than legislative means, what are other avenues that could be utilized in order to decrease racial disparity in health care? How could social media campaigns and the media fuel change? Think of actions on the community, state, and federal levels that could help to lower maternal mortality.

CHAPTER 4

Pop Culture and Media Representation

I N MANY WAYS, media has a profound effect on our lives, as it influences the ways in which we perceive people, how we think about ourselves, and the way we live daily. In fact, the more media that we consume, the greater the tendency to believe that what we are seeing is normal. It is a reflection of who we are, for better or worse. Americans increasingly turn to social media as a source for news, activism, and political information. Also, social media may be used as space to contribute to a social cause or catalyze a social movement. Social media also can serve as an important venue where groups with common interests come together to share ideas and information. At times, Twitter, Facebook, and other social media sites can help users bring greater attention to issues through their collective voice and in recent years has been an outlet to expose racial inequities.

Media can also be a source of entertainment. Likewise, sports have been described as the opiate of the masses, for its ability to soothe us and give us some relief from the rigors of everyday lives. We often see sports as a place where rule-following of a given game appears to take precedence over such aspects like race and gender identity. However, on closer inspection, we see that sports can be a microcosm of race relations in America. This is especially true in football, which has become a cornerstone in American culture and carries huge influence through merchandising, ticket sales, and endorsements for athletes. Another powerhouse in media is the music industry. Music videos receive millions of views a week from all over the world (now increasingly online versus music television). As a result, the music that is created and the artists who create content can be perceived as culturally significant because the messages they display are contemporary representations of multiple identities. Performances by artists can also inform society about conceptions of race and gender through lyrics, dress, and comments made by artists when off stage. In these different facets of American popular culture, it is important to consider the following: How does media serve to reinforce racial stereotypes? How does is it become a catalyst for changing them? How does racial privilege present itself in popular culture? How does media serve as a window into racial dynamics in society at large?

Film, Television, and Controlling Images

Beginning in its infancy, some may argue that Hollywood served as an avenue to forward white privilege. In 1915, a three-hour saga entitled *The Birth of a Nation*, directed by D.W. Griffith, became the first major motion picture. The film was screened at the White House weeks after its release for President Woodrow Wilson and became a propaganda tool which reinvigorated the Ku Klux Klan, which had a robust following through Jim Crow (Muhammad 2019). This film cost a whopping $110,000 to make at the time but grossed over $20 million and (by some estimates as much as $100 million), illuminating what a monetary powerhouse the Hollywood movie industry would be in subsequent decades (Stokes 2007). The film depicted stereotypical tropes of African Americans via white actors in black-face (popularized first in the 1830s in minstrel shows) and highlighted the menace African Americans posed to white America. These minstrel shows representing black people as simple-minded, lazy buffoons reached their height during the 1830s and 1840s, the first dramatic form that was uniquely American (Lott 1993). This tradition of white actors playing nonwhite roles would continue as a commonplace practice in the twentieth century and to a lesser extent in the twenty-first century. In *Breakfast at Tiffany's* (1961), Mickey Rooney played the role of a buffoon-like Japanese landlord with an exaggerated accent, prosthetic buck teeth, and thick glasses (Moreno and Arthur 2016). In 1965's *The Face of Fu Manchu*, Christopher Lee donned overstated facial hair and slanted eyes to play Fu Manchu, a sinister and scheming Chinese man (Simons 2016). Both portrayals of Asian men play into stereotypical tropes of Asian men as clumsy idiots or "yellow perils," hell-bent on bringing destruction to the Western world. Cultural icon Elvis Presley, who was white, played Joe Lightcloud, a Native American character in *Stay Away Joe* (1968). *The House of the Spirits* in 1993 starred Meryl Streep, Vanessa Redgrave, Winona Ryder, and Glenn Close in a film taking place in Chile with characters who came from Latin American ancestry. In an ultimate irony, the only minorities featured in the movie depicted a prostitute, a rape victim, and a nanny. Well into to the twenty-first century, white actors continue to play roles that were based on characters who are people of color. *A Mighty Heart*, released in 2007, starred Angelina Jolie as Mariane Pearl, who is of Afro-Cuban ancestry. Jolie darkened her skin for the role and appeared to also alter her hair texture for this part (Moreno and Arthur 2016). For *Ghost in the Shell* in 2017, Scarlett Johansson played Motoko Kusanagi, who is Japanese (Simons 2016). In each of the aforementioned films, casting white actors took precedence over finding minority actors who would more accurately portray the characters they were representing on screen. This implies that white actors have superior talent, while minority actors lack the talent and the proper know-how to fully capture their roles.

When we witness a lack of racial diversity in visual media, it can be extremely problematic as we have consumed images from television and film for the entirety of our lives, and they become a significant source of how we view the world. Media is an important force in our lives as it gives us the basis for controlling images that direct individuals how to categorize and analyze the images they see daily. Controlling images go further than stereotypes, as they have been so entrenched in our minds that they control individuals who are stereotyped and also substantiate the attitudes of the people engaging in stereotyping. These images have a cumulative effect and become more and more powerful because we are shown the same narrative over and over again until we adopt them and believe them to be fact. These particular images guide behavior to and from those persons represented, confine what is viewed and understood about them, and when internalized, deeply influence the self-perceptions of the marginalized (Beauboeuf-Lafontant 2009). Sociologist Patricia Hill Collins explains that **controlling images** are *"images [that] are designed to make racism, sexism, poverty, and other forms of social injustice appear to be natural, normal, and inevitable parts of everyday life"* (Collins 2005:69). Because we are shown that oppression of certain communities is normal, we believe that is just the manner in which reality operates without questioning the problematic nature of this viewpoint. Hill Collins also explores the concept of controlling images in her book, *Black Sexual Politics*, where she investigates a variety of tropes associated with African American women. She notes that "portraying African American women as stereotypical mammies, matriarchs, welfare recipients, and hot mommas has been essential to the political economy of domination fostering Black women's oppression" (Collins 2000:142). Although each trope is unique, they all share a commonality of having sexuality that is outside the norm, either too sexualized (e.g., hot momma) or not sexual enough (e.g., mammy). Because they fall outside of what is "normal," they are considered other, and this gives those who have created this trope power in normalizing the marginalization of African American women in such ways as in terms of beauty, political and economic equality, and cultural values (Collins 2000). Similarly, in her examination of Latinos and their choices in selecting marriage partners, Jessica Vasquez-Tokos notes that controlling images of Latinos help perpetuate racial inequality by training people on how to observe and treat racial groups, and as a result create a racial order (Vasquez-Tokos 2017).

The damage caused by the absence or stifling of a multitude of narratives in media is further explained through the model of symbolic annihilation. **Symbolic annihilation** is a term first used by Gerbner and Gross in 1976 to label *the exclusion or underrepresentation of particular groups in media as a tactic to sustain social inequality*. According to them, "representation in the fictional world signifies social existence; absence means symbolic annihilation" and serves as a tool to perpetuate inequality in society (Gerbner and Gross 1976:182). Pierre Bourdieu's idea of symbolic violence dovetails on the concept as an understated violence, which gives media consumers a template on how to treat minority groups through confirmed social norms. This violence may be wielded across different social axes, including sexual orientation, gender, and ethnicity. This symbolic annihilation can discount the validity of an identity through negative depictions or the exclusion of marginalized groups in media (Bourdieu and Passeron 2014).

Generally, the stories we see on film and television tend to marginalize women and people of color. However, there has been a push in recent years to increase the diversity of casts and also those behind the scenes. Although there have been gains in the film and television industries in recent years, minorities still remain underrepresented in these entertainment sectors. In their 2019 study of inclusion of people of color and women in film and television, Darnell Hunt, Ana-Christina Ramón, and Michael Tran examined nearly 200 of the top theatrical film releases of 2017 and over 1,300 cable, broadcast, and digital platform television shows from the 2016–2017 season (Hunt, Ramon, and Tran 2019). The study found that although minorities make up about 40 percent of the American population, people of color comprised only 19.8 percent of lead actors in theatrical films, 12.6 percent of film writers, and 7.8 percent of directors. Among broadcast scripted leads, people of color comprised 21.5 percent of roles, while 21.3 percent of cable scripted leads were played by minority actors (Hunt et al. 2019). In another intersectional look at film, Smith et al. examined 48,757 characters in over 1,000 of the highest-grossing films from between 2007 and 2017. These researchers discovered that female characters with speaking roles held only about 30.6 percent of all roles. For the top 100 movies of 2017, 29.3 percent of roles were from racial/ethnic minority groups, while 2.5 percent were disabled characters, and less than 1 percent of all characters were identified as LGBT (Smith et al. 2018). The overall trend seen in both studies is that both TV and film content remain platforms that sideline communities that are already marginalized. In this way, television and film simultaneously reflect a trend of marginalization in society for these groups, but also reinforce it through lack of adequate representation. In a study by the Geena Davis Institute on Gender in Media that examined the top-grossing family films from 2007–2017, white leads outnumbered minority leads fourfold in films during this decade. Among leads of color, 74.0 percent are male, while 26.0 percent are female, and although films with white leads have grossed more than films with leads of color for most of the past decade, this pattern changed in the past two years. Case in point: films with leads of color grossed $81.8 million compared to $70.3 million for films with white leads. The majority of leading characters of color are black (60.4 percent), followed by Latinx (15.4 percent), Asian American/Southeast Asian (14.2 percent), Middle Eastern (3.6 percent), Native American/Hawaiian/Asian Pacific Islander (2.4 percent), and "Other" (4.1 percent) (Geena Davis Institute on Gender in Media 2019). These more recent surprises posed a major challenge to the dominant, white male privilege narrative that women leads and/or leads of color would not bring in enough profits and show some promise of future anti-racism, which we discuss more in the closing chapter.

Another recent change is the expansion of web-based content. Distributors such as Amazon, Hulu, and Netflix have changed the way in which viewers receive content. Now, Netflix has more original content than any one channel or cable channel to date. The audience viewing habits command content creation, which is a paradigm shift from the traditions of network or studio executives determining what we as consumers see on the screen. Netflix, Amazon, and Hulu do not need to play by the traditional rules because each has their own means of broadcasting chosen programming to a massive number of viewers (Boboltz and Williams 2016). This being the case, digital content providers could have the potential to lead the charge in combating inequality in media representation. However, so far, the statistics of minority roles on streaming platforms appear to be very strikingly similar to network television. For example, racial/ethnic minorities account for 21.3 percent of digital scripted leads and about 17.6 percent of digital reality and other leads, and minority creators comprise about 16.5 percent of digital scripted shows (Hunt et al. 2019). Digital content has more promising numbers for minority representation; however, it remains to be seen how and if digital streaming services can achieve an elevated level of inclusion and diversity in their content. Undoubtedly, white privilege exists on the screen and in the decision-making involved in making choices to the talent who creates every facet on content creation in Hollywood. So, this must mean that audiences favor white talent, but is this really the case?

Although these statistics reflect a slow progression to increasing diversity and inclusion in TV and film, it appears that audiences would gladly welcome casts more representative of what American society looks like in reality in regard to race representation. Increasingly diverse audiences also mean a need for more diversity on the screen that echoes this actuality. For instance, films with casts that were from 31 to 40 percent minority enjoyed the highest median global box office revenues, and those with majority-minority casts boasted the highest median return on investment. By contrast, films with the most racially and ethnically homogeneous casts were the poorest performers (Hunt et al. 2019). Minorities were responsible for the majority of ticket revenue for five of the top-grossing ten films in 2017. Films with casts of 31 to 40 percent people of color were released, on average, in most international markets in 2017. On an interesting note, films with black and Latino leads and majority-minority casts were released, on average, in the fewest international markets in 2017 (Hunt et al. 2019). This finding seems to illuminate that white privilege reigns supreme as diversity is viewed as welcome, only to the extent that minority actors do not comprise a majority of the actors or take on key lead roles.

In an effort to underscore a lack of racial inclusion in Hollywood, social media has been utilized as a tool to raise awareness of this lack of diversity. Most notably, the #OscarsSoWhite movement in 2016 emphasized the lack of racial diversity in Hollywood by spotlighting that all actors nominated in the leading and supporting categories were white. This campaign was spearheaded by April Reign and led to a critical look at not only who was being nominated, but the Academy membership as a whole. With concerns mounting over the Academy of Motion Picture Arts and Sciences membership, which was 94 percent white in 2016, sweeping changes were made in response. In 2017, the Academy extended invitations to 774 new voting members, 39 percent of whom were female and 39 percent who were non-white (Reign 2018). There was a pledge to double the number of people of color and women in the Academy's membership by 2020 made by former Academy of Motion Picture Arts and Sciences president Cheryl Boone Isaacs, which indicates a concerted effort to increase diversity. In addition, members who have not been active in the past ten years cannot vote on nominees, in hopes of making way for those who have less time in their film career to effect change in the Academy (Reign 2018). These tangible changes seem promising for the future of Hollywood cou-pled with a series of movies in the recent past with casts starring minority leads, including *BlacKkKlansman*, *Get Out*, *Hidden Figures*, and *Black Panther* (all were also successes at the box office and received award nominations). These films por-trayed African Americans as intelligent, witty, complicated, dignified, and robust, a far cry from the stereotypical two-dimensional roles usually given to African Amer-icans in film.

The 2017 Oscars ceremony thrust racial politics into the forefront yet again when Faye Dunaway and Warren Beatty mistakenly announced *La La Land* as Best Picture of the year. *Moonlight*, the movie that follows the upbringing of a queer man in Miami, was the true victor, with Barry Jenkins, a gay black man, at the helm as its director (Moore 2017). The stark contrast between the two films was glaring. Many criticized *La La Land* for its lack of diversity in its cast although it takes place in modern-day Los Angeles, while *Moonlight* centered on an intersec-tional look at masculinity, sexuality, economic deprivation, and family dynamics in the black community (Cooper 2017). Honest oversight or not, the flub did take away from the monumental nature of the win. This was the first LGBTQ film to win the Best Picture prize and also the first film in this category to focus on the lives of black people, rather than the degradation of them by white people (e.g., *12 Years a Slave*) (Cooper 2017). To be slighted in this way, at such a special moment as the whole world watches on, parallels the ways in which black achievement goes uncel-ebrated far too often. Activist April Reign warns that some positive changes that came from #OscarsSoWhite should not deflect us from the great deal of work that still stands to be done in the Hollywood community. In a tweet in 2018, she pro-claimed, "Until we are no longer lauding 'firsts' after a 90-year history, until we can no longer count a traditionally underrepresented community's number of nomi-nations in a particular category on our fingers, #OscarsSoWhite remains relevant"

(Reign 2018). Although progress is ongoing, it reminds us that we must remain vigilant in order to ensure that it continues. One promising road to inclusivity is through the idea of inclusion riders, which would increase diversity on sets through contractual means. A frenzy around this term ignited at the 2018 Oscars ceremony, when Frances McDormand won in the Best Actress category for *Three Billboards Outside Ebbing, Missouri*, concluding her acceptance with, "I have two words to leave with you tonight, ladies and gentlemen: inclusion rider" (Dwyer 2018). Although this familiarized popular culture with this concept, the term was first introduced by Dr. Stacy Smith from USC Annenberg's Media, Diversity & Social Change Initiative in 2014 as an equity rider, as a way to combat gender inequality in Hollywood. Dr. Smith envisioned inclusion riders as a parallel to the Rooney Rule in the National Football League (which will be discussed at greater length in this chapter and Chapter 5), which stipulated that teams must consider minority candidates for head coaching positions (Smith 2014). Although initially meant to apply to gender inequity, **inclusion riders** refer *to contractual requirements that would stipulate an assured level of diversity in a production's cast and crew*, reflecting a more realistic representation of societal demographics (Dwyer 2018). In 2016, Smith teamed up with Kalpana Kotagal, a civil rights attorney, and Fanshen Cox DiGiovanni, who led strategic outreach at Pearl Street Films, Ben Affleck and Matt Damon's production company. These three women merged their expertise in order to devise an inclusion rider template for those interested in adopting a commitment to diversity on the basis of ability, race, gender, sexual orientation, and other axes of inequity (Lee 2019). As a result, there have been tangible changes exhibited in various aspects of the television and film world. Notably, Warner Bros. implemented a diversity policy that will also track progress and shortcomings in terms of inclusion via an annual report. Along with Amazon Studios, both companies have pledged to employ inclusion riders for all upcoming productions. Creative Artists Agency has recently fostered programs for diverse talent, including a database of television writers who are racial minorities, a training program for aspiring writers from diverse backgrounds, and also multiple networking and leadership events (Lee 2019). In an effort to fight for diversity among film critics, the Sundance Film Festival, Toronto Film Festival, and SXSW have vowed to present accreditation to journalists of marginalized backgrounds.

Sports and White Privilege

The National Football League (NFL) and the National Basketball Association (NBA) draw in millions of viewers yearly to watch their favorite athletes compete, but sports also have much to tell us about racial dynamics in America. Observing sports is often viewed as a popular culture staple that brings people together through shared aims to relax, be entertained, and revel in the excitement of the crowd and the action in the arena. In 2015, the NBA was compromised of 23.3 percent white players, 74.4 percent black players, 1.8 percent Latino players, and .2 percent Asian players. This league holds the greatest proportion of black athletes in any major professional sports league in Canada or the United States. A majority of viewers of the league are also people of color, with 47 percent black viewers, 34 percent white viewers, 11 percent Hispanic viewers, and 8 percent Asian viewers (Lapchick 2015). The unique combination of the racial diversity of players, as well as the racial diversity of audiences for the NBA and NFL, often leads observers to assume that these sports arenas are the "great equalizer" and assume these are areas where white privilege no longer exists. In actuality, this is not at all the case. As we reviewed in Chapter 3, with any institution, we need to examine who holds the top positions, who makes the decisions, and whether race continues to play a role in participants' ability to move up the ranks and experience longevity with the organization. Although we do not have enough space here to apply this kind of analysis to every sports league, we encourage you to especially ask this of both the NBA and the NFL as you do your own research. As an example of how to do this, for the remainder of this section, we will focus on the NFL as a case study in white privilege.

The NFL's player composition is mostly nonwhite; however, this only tells a small piece of the story as key leadership roles remain in the control of whites. For example, in the 2017 NFL season, only 9 out 32 quarterbacks were nonwhite, leaving whites to fill 82 percent of the center position (Bembry 2017). How could this be the case when the racial composition of the NFL would suggest that most quarterbacks should be black? In his book *Playing While White: Privilege and Power on and off the Field*, David Leonard argues that white privilege is at play here, as white athletes are promoted as smart leads, hardworking, and exemplary. By celebrating such white quarterbacks as Tom Brady to Aaron Rodgers to Tim Tebow as role models who are self-disciplined and industrious, collectively we are also championing whiteness. This is ever apparent when in comparison, black athletes are viewed as either "ungrateful millionaires" or "natural athletes," marking racial distinction (Leonard 2017). Leonard also points out that Bill Belichick, the coach of the New England Patriots, is often associated with wearing a hoodie on the sidelines, although young, black men are pegged as gangsters or criminal when sporting this apparel (like the representation of Trayvon Martin being a thug because he wore a hoodie the night he was murdered) (Leonard 2017). This stark difference in treatment demonstrates that race matters in the ways in which we look at individuals and how we maintain racial hierarchy, even in unassuming places like sport.

Discrimination in coaching has been an ongoing issue in the NFL, but the implementation of the Rooney Rule at the very least displayed a desire to take the league in a direction to become more inclusive of minority representation off the field. The Rooney Rule is named for Dan Rooney, a former chairman of the

NFL's diversity committee and also a former owner of the Pittsburgh Steelers. This rule emerged in 2003 as an affirmative action policy that mandated teams to consider and interview nonwhite candidates for head coaching positions (Freedman 2014). In 2009, the rule was enlarged to include player personnel positions and senior management roles also. The rule came about as a response to two firings of black head coaches, Dennis Green of the Minnesota Vikings and Tony Dungy of the Tampa Bay Buccaneers, which appeared to be unwarranted. At the time, Green experienced his first losing season in a decade, and Dungy had a winning track record with the Buccaneers. Soon after, Johnnie Cochran and Cyrus Mehri, both civil rights lawyers, issued a study that concluded that black head coaches were more often fired and less often hired than their white peers, even as they won a higher proportion of games, which sparked the campaign for more equitable policy in hiring (Freedman 2014). The Rooney Rule was of vital importance because until the Raiders hired Tom Flores in 1979, Fritz Pollard was the only head coach who was a person of color, who served as a coach back in the 1920s (Sonnad 2018). John Wooten and Kellen Winslow, both past NFL players, created an alliance of minority coaches, scouts, and front-office staff to serve as an "institutional conscience" for the purpose of bringing about more equity in NFL hiring (Freedman 2014). The rule showed promise, as there were only seven head coaches who were minorities at the onset of the Rooney Rule, and by 2014, there were fourteen head coaches of color. Although some strides have been made, there is so much more to be done. Speaking to this point, 2018 statistics highlight that 75 percent of head coaches are white, and nearly 72 percent of office personnel and 100 percent of CEOs/presidents are still white in the league (Sonnad, 2018). This data demonstrates the true state of reality—white privilege is systematically entrenched in major positions of power in the league. As long as this remains the case, it will be extremely difficult to make inroads to allow for people of color to wield any significant source of power.

A key figure in the National Football League who brought attention to issues of racial marginalization and white privilege to the forefront in the recent past is former San Francisco 49ers quarterback Colin Kaepernick. His stand against racial injustice first began in 2016 when he remained seated during the national anthem instead of following the tradition of standing during the anthem. In the following weeks, he would kneel instead of sitting during regular-season games (Abdul-Jabbar 2018). Colin Kaepernick describes his actions as a protest against racial injustice and notes, "I am not going to stand up to show pride in a flag for a country that oppresses black people and people of color. To me, this is bigger than football and it would be selfish on my part to look the other way. There are bodies in the street and people getting paid leave and getting away with murder" (Wyche 2016). It is important to note two powerful points about this statement by Kaepernick: his connection of sport to its great influence on society at large and that standing for the flag represented much more than just adhering to tradition, but also accepting the oppression of people of color that the country engages in systematically. This scenario conjures up the question, could this truly be the "land of the free" when institutional racism and discrimination seemingly seep into every social institution and people of color must pay the price, sometimes at the cost of their lives?

This nonviolent protest fueled a media firestorm that both brought intense scrutiny and criticism for being unpatriotic while simultaneously inspiring similar forms of protest and praise from others. One of Kaepernick's strongest opponents was President Donald Trump, who had taken a keen interest in Kaepernick's kneeling during the national anthem. During a rally in Alabama in September 2017, Donald Trump exclaimed, "Get that son of a bitch off the field right now. He's fired. He's fired!" in response to Kaepernick's protests on the field (Hill 2019). Trump further expressed his distaste for the quarterback with the comment "I don't like what Nike did. I don't think it's appropriate," he said. "I honor the flag. I honor our national anthem" in September 2018 (Gleeson 2018). This came after Nike announced Colin Kaepernick would be the face of the thirtieth anniversary celebration of the "Just Do It" campaign. Trump's comments equated a peaceful protest against injustice to something unpatriotic. Trump voiced a popular opinion: to question a system of power that reinforces white privilege is un-American, and these athletes should just be happy making millions of dollars and play the game. Also, Kaepernick's career was undoubtedly affected by his protests over the national anthem. After the 2016–2017 season, Kaepernick did not renew his contract with the San Francisco 49ers and became a free agent; however, no team signed him (Barrabi 2019). Kaepernick filed a complaint against the NFL in November 2017 asserting the NFL and team owners conspired together to not hire him. In 2018, Kaepernick rescinded this grievance after coming to an agreement with the National Football League and team owners for an undisclosed sum. But in a twist, an arbiter ruled that the NFL could not dismiss the complaint, as it breaks a bargaining agreement between the NFL and NFLPA (the union), leaving the door open for future legal action (Vera 2018). President Trump had boasted in the past about being the reason why NFL teams did not pick up Kaepernick out of fear they would receive public criticism from Trump. These boastful comments may have provided key evidence in validating Kaepernick's claim of collusion among the NFL to keep him off the field and could prove to be extremely costly for the NFL (Hill 2019).

Kaepernick is just one example of several athletes of color over the past few decades to use their popular platform to shine a light on racial injustice, dating back to at least an iconic moment in 1968, when Tommie Smith and John Carlos raised their fists in a Black Power gesture as they received their medals for the 200-meter race at the Summer Olympic Games in Mexico City. As Kareem Abdul-Jabbar, a legendary former professional NBA basketball player, states:

> Right now, sports may be the best hope for change regarding racial disparity because it has the best chance of informing white Americans of that disparity and motivating them to act. The problem is that this is not the message that those who profit from disparity want the public to hear. They attempt to silence voices of dissent in sports today just as they have throughout my lifetime and before. And that attempt is always disguised as an appeal to patriotism. (Abdul-Jabbar 2018)

This quote perfectly sums up the dynamics involved in Kaepernick's kneeling protest against injustice. Abdul-Jabbar illustrates the potential of sports to shine a spotlight on the serious issues of racial injustice in an unlikely setting, usually reserved for the entertainment of the masses. Sadly, it is not enough just to have awareness of these issues, but a willingness to alter harmful behavior is necessary if any change is to come in the future. If it is a message that causes discomfort among whites because they feel attacked because of their racial background, it becomes uncomfortable and an immediate reaction is to silence it. Not only does it cause a sense of uneasiness, but it also elicits a fear that the privilege that rises out of this disparity will disappear. If whites do not acknowledge their privilege, the problem can be swept under the rug and racial power dynamics at play can continue to benefit those individuals who benefit most from the silencing of people of color, in this case team owners and NFL executives.

Social Media and White Privilege

Both Hollywood and sports existed well before social media, but social media has only amplified their cultural reach. As we turn our attention next to social media, which is often seen as a new and modern development, we must first emphasize how any form of new media is merely a reflection of the culture that produces it. From the beginning of this text, we have explored how race was invented as a pseudoscientific idea that not only became rule through laws and politics, but then became embedded in how we see each other as human beings and the way we relate to each other. In Chapter 2, we defined prejudice, discrimination, and racism—focusing on racism as a system of advantage that privileges whites—but let us now examine cultural racism specifically. **Cultural racism** *is the belief in society that one culture holds superiority over another culture and may incorporate stereotypes of those from distinctive ethnic or racial groups than the majority race.* Cultural racism replaced the biological race theories of the past commonly held between the 1600s to the end of World War II, claiming that there were scientific bases for the superiority of "the white race." For instance, Darwin argued that western European societies far exceeded those civilizations of their savage counterparts (Darwin 1871). In America, Madison Grant contended those with Nordic ancestry possessed racial superiority but were committing "race suicide" due to interracial marriage and procreation in his 1916 book *The Passing of the Great Race* (Grant 1916). Hitler personally thanked Grant for his publication, and it would go on to deeply influence Nazi propaganda in the coming years (Kühl 2002). These types of theories fell out of favor in 1950 with "The Race Question" published by the United Nations Educational, Scientific and Cultural Organization (UNESCO), which noted, "For all practical social purposes 'race' is not so much a biological phenomenon as a social myth. The myth of 'race' has created an enormous amount of human and social damage. In recent years, it has taken a heavy toll in human lives, and caused untold suffering" (UNESCO, 1950). After the atrocities during World War II, especially the Holocaust, this type of stand showed a desire for the harassment, discrimination, and senseless murders of people based on racial inferiority to cease. Millions of people died, were held captive, and were injured for meaningless reasons based on their ethnic, religious, and racial background.

Now that the belief that biological differences based on racial difference was widely unacceptable, cultural difference became the foundation for arguments of superiority. Cultural racism was first theorized by scholars from western Europe during the 1980s and 1990s. These theorists found guidance in Critical Race Theory, which posits that society sustains white supremacy over time, the law has a significant role in this maintenance, and investigates ways in which to lessen racial suppression (Crenshaw et al. 1995). During this time, the concept of cultural racism had been called different names like "new racism" by Barker and "neo-racism" by Balibar (Barker 1981 and Balibar and Wallerstein 1991). Balibar saw the emergence of new racism as linked to decolonization and the increasing numbers of non-European immigrants in Europe beginning after World War II. This perspective substituted colonizers employing biological explanations to validate conquering other societies around the globe. Neo-racism generated a racism without the idea of race as immigration or immigrants replaced this category. The power of this type of racism lies in the illusion that cultural difference is unbeatable, and crossing cultural boundaries of different customs and lifestyles would prove detrimental to society (Balibar and Wallerstein 1991). This notion masks the inherent belief that Western culture, and therein whiteness, is supreme and should not be tainted by the influence of foreign culture. If we see anything that deviates from white culture as way too different (whether it may be the case or not), then societies that privilege whiteness will never have to undergo the perceived difficulty of integrating new cultures. White privilege allows people to never have to go out of their way to embrace a culture that is not "theirs," all the while expecting other cultures to embrace mainstream, white culture wholeheartedly. Additionally, by failing to engage in efforts to understand other cultures from the start, we risk not benefiting from the advantages of cultural exchange. Another theorist, Karen Wren, focuses on the idea of nationalism as the main basis for cultural racism. Culture should be unique to a given territory or nation, which becomes a closed community, where foreigners should not enjoy the resources of that nation. Under cultural racism, culture is static, cross-cultural exchange does not happen, and ethnic groups have attached stereotypes (Wren 2001).

Other theorists like Henry Giroux and Rebecca Powell specifically concentrate on the cultural racism featured in the United States political system. In the 1990s, Giroux examined how American political conservatives used culturally racist beliefs in their political narratives. He uses the presidency of George H.W. Bush as an example, where the president acknowledged ethnic and racial diversity, but at the same time understood it as a hazard to national unity (Giroux 1993). Here again, we see nationalism used as a tool of harmony while seemingly advocating for divisions between racial and ethnic groups. Giroux urged teachers to use critical approaches in educating students so they can recognize how various types of media bolster ethnocentric standards and practices, and how to confront these depictions. For Rebecca Powell, both liberal and conservative politics maintain cultural racism by normalizing white American culture. Although white liberals in the United States recognize systematic racism in the country, they also support cultural assimilation for nonwhites, which also connotes a viewpoint that white culture is superior (Powell 2000). Like Giroux, Powell sees the power in education in diminishing cultural racism and how popular media perpetuates its existence. She offers a few practical suggestions for curriculum for students like investigating how media images exemplify ideals of cultural racism or recounting historical events from diverse cultural viewpoints (Powell 2000). Both approaches ensure that we not only discuss antiracist tactics, but also reflect on behaviors and the practices of our cultural institutions that reinforce cultural racism both intentionally and unintentionally.

As we turn toward exploring the power of social media to either perpetuate or challenge white privilege, we urge you to consider how the cultural racism of white superiority—whether blatant or subtle—influences these narratives. To the extent that social media is a more democratized and decentralized form of expression than mass media, is it thus exempt from cultural racism? Let us explore some possible answers to this question in the remaining sections of this chapter.

Black Lives Matter

The #BlackLivesMatter (BLM) movement emerged on social media in 2013 after George Zimmerman was acquitted in the murder of Trayvon Martin, an African American teen, in 2012. Alicia Garza, Patrisse Cullors, and Opal Tometi coined the hashtag, but the movement lacks an official hierarchy and is comprised of a dispersed network. The movement held demonstrations against the murders of two other unarmed black men by police, Eric Garner in New York City and Michael Brown in Ferguson, Missouri, and continue to protest against other deaths of African Americans who continue to die as a result of police actions. According to their website, "The Black Lives Matter Global Network is a chapter-based, member-led organization whose mission is to build local power and to intervene in violence inflicted on Black communities by the state and vigilantes" and centers on "those who have been marginalized within Black liberation movements" (Black Lives Matter 2019). The fact that this movement was founded by three black women with no fixed organizational structure makes it truly unique through its commitment to welcome all who may have felt marginalized by black liberation movements. It distinguishes itself from movements in the past that favored leadership at the hands of heterosexual, black males. Its guiding principles include diversity, restorative justice, intergenerational, globalism, queer affirming, transgender affirming, black women, unapologetically black, collective value, loving engagement, empathy, black villages and black families (Black Lives Matter 2019). This strong commitment to be inclusive of factors such as location, age, gender, sexual orientation, and generation makes it a community committed to appreciating intersectionality in its base.

In criticism of BLM, the phrase "All Lives Matter" spread through Internet and social media presence, claiming that every life has the same value as we are all human beings. This type of rationalization reinforces a color-blind ideology that acknowledging race is the problem, not the systematic oppression of people of color in this country for centuries. Simply ignoring a problem is not a viable solution for problem solving. It reduces racism from an institutional problem to an issue that concerns individual racists, who are few and far between. This is the ultimate manifestation of white privilege: to disregard the marginalization of people of color based on race, just because it is not an issue for whites. In this way, it can just perpetuate the idea that blacks are angry instigators, dredging up old issues, while whites have progressed forward to "not see color."

In 2014, "Blue Lives Matter" began in the wake of the shooting death of two New York Police Department officers, calling for those who are convicted of killing police officers to be sentenced under hate crime laws. The movement consists of active-duty and retired law enforcement officers (Blue Lives Matter 2019). Some have argued that this movement is misguided, as law enforcement officers move around society with respect and honor and are not often considered inferior, diametrically opposed to the reality of black life in America (Russell 2016). These backlash movements further prove exactly why groups like Black Lives Matter exist. When people of color bring awareness to the injustices they live through daily, it is often silenced or seen as exaggeration, dismissing the lived experience of minorities and downplaying just how cultural racism has woven itself through the fabric of all American institutions.

Cultural racism ran especially rampant during the US presidency of Donald Trump. Trump applied racist rhetoric throughout his presidential campaign and presidency, in addition to demeaning the disabled, veterans, women, immigrants, and many other marginalized groups. For instance, in July 2019, Trump tweeted that four Democratic minority, female members of Congress (Rashida Tlaib, Ilhan Omar, Ayana Pressley, and Alexandria Ocasio-Cortez) should "go back" where they came from (Mathis 2019). It appears to be no coincidence that this argument targeted this group of women of color, who include immigrants and children of immigrants to this country. With this statement, Trump emphasized that cultural racism is based on national identity, casting people of color aside as a threat to national unity and judging them as not quite American, although all four women are American citizens. Prior to his foray into presidential campaigning, Trump also led the charge to claim that President Barack Obama was not a US citizen. By pandering to the xenophobic tendencies of his base, Trump played on the fears of some white Americans that people of color are threatening their white privilege. This group of women did pose a threat, but this threat came in causing more difficulty in GOP reelection efforts (Yglesias 2019). The Unite the Right rally, a gathering of white supremacists in Charlottesville, Virginia, occurred in 2017 and ended with a white supremacist, James Alex Fields Jr., mowing down a crowd of people with his car and murdering Heather Heyer. After this tragedy, Trump soon claimed that there were "very fine people on both sides," implying that he considered white supremacists to be good people, too (Shafer 2019).

Nationalist politics like Trump's experienced a resurgence across many parts of the Western globe during the early twenty-first century. Immigration reform has been emphasized thoroughly in several European countries as well as during Trump's campaign and presidency, through the guise of border security and a plan to build a wall along the US border with Mexico. Trump's border wall was put on hold when a lower court froze $2.5 billion in funding and later an appeals court affirmed this decision. After asking the US Supreme Court to review this monetary freeze, the Supreme Court ruled in favor of the administration in July 2019. A lower court had initially frozen the $2.5 billion in funds, and an appeals court had agreed. But the administration then asked the Supreme Court to review the freeze, and in a 5–4 decision, the high court granted the Trump administration the military funds to build sections of the wall, even though Trump has always claimed that Mexico would pay for it (Taylor 2019). In his racist actions against nonwhite immigrants, Trump called Mexican migrants rapists, suggested immigrants from "shithole" countries (like Haiti and African nations) should stop immigrating to America, called in troops to stop the "invasion" of Central Americans into the country, separated children from their parents at the border and kept them in cages, and halted temporary protected status for Haitians, Salvadorans, Hondurans, and Nicaraguans fleeing wars and natural catastrophes. Trump's ire for immigrants was less about his genuine concern for national security but more to do with limiting access for immigrants of color to resources earned by "hardworking" white Americans. Trump did not focus on immigration from predominantly white countries, but rather it was immigrants who are nonwhite that he posited as the main problem. His inhumane treatment of detained immigrants at the Mexican border, his disdain for those fleeing life-threatening life circumstances, and his characterizations of predominantly black countries as "shitholes" demonstrated a rising tide of nationalist concern among Western powers that foreigners would increase the already growing minority population in "their" country. These concerns and fear about immigration among supporters of Trump and other nationalist rulers like him may very well also stem from a faulty perception that immigration could threaten the white privilege they enjoy every day. This line of thinking circles back to the notion of cultural racism, where America represents a shining beacon of civility, superiority, and whiteness, and anything that would threaten these needs to be stopped sooner rather than later.

Whites Calling Police on Black People for Doing Normal Activities

In the age of social media, cultural racism has revealed itself very clearly through a host of incidents where police were called on black people by white individuals as they engaged in everyday, typical activities. Although such hypersurveillance behaviors privileging whites existed long before cell phones, with the advent of video cameras on cell phones, such incidents have gained significant media attention on the Internet and through social media. For example, in April of 2018, employees at a Starbucks location in Philadelphia called the police on two black men because they asked to use the restrooms, although they had not purchased any items. The two men, Rashon Nelson and Donte Robinson, refused to leave when asked to do so and asserted they were waiting on the arrival of an associate to discuss a real estate opportunity (Neuman 2018). After the video went viral and protests ensued, Starbucks apologized for the company's actions and closed 8,000 stores to hold racial bias training for its nearly 175,000 workers. About one month later, the men came to a settlement with Starbucks for an unknown sum and the opportunity to complete bachelor's degrees through an online program offered by Arizona State University free of charge (Neuman 2018). The negative media attention received by Starbucks held them accountable for the biased action of their employees, but hopefully the racial bias training will aid in decreasing these kinds of incidents.

Also in April 2018, in Oakland, California, a white woman, Jennifer Schulte, called the cops on a black family for "illegally" using a charcoal grill in a park. She made two separate calls to the dispatcher about her concern that the men were grilling in a non-designated grilling area (they were in fact in a designated area) and "that coals don't burn more children and we don't have to pay more taxes." And in her second call, she indicated that "I'm really scared! You gotta come quick!" Schulte was named "BBQ Becky" and the video of her on the phone with the dispatcher went viral (Zhao 2018). Her hysteria over a situation that was not even a cause for concern brings about a feeling that if blacks do something that upsets a white person (even if that act is normal), they should stop doing it immediately. Her bizarre comments about taxpayer money going to injured children and blacks engaging in "illegal" activity only goes to confirm widespread stereotypes about blacks being supported by the state financially and as people who engage in criminal activities. This scene also exemplifies how white privilege allows whites to believe that they can control black bodies—the space they occupy, their activities, etc., and if they cannot, the threat of control through the state is always an option.

Yet another incident occurred when a white woman called the police on an eight-year-old black girl for "illegally selling water without a permit" as she raised money for a Disneyland trip after her mother lost her job. This woman, Alison Ettel, later claimed she responded out of frustration from the noise made by Jordan Rodgers and her mom, Erin Austin, not out of racial bias. Ettel also is seen on tape claiming that they were selling the water on her property, although they were on a public sidewalk. Erin Austin refutes these claims and asserts that complaints over noise were never mentioned in the confrontation. After the video went viral, Ettel was nicknamed "Permit Patty," and she lost many ties with cannabis-related companies, who had once conducted business with TreatWell, a medical marijuana business that makes products for pets founded by Ettel (Chokshi 2018). This occurrence proved that even children of color cannot hide from the informal policing of black bodies. By maintaining that Austin and Rodgers were on "private property," "Permit Patty" lets them know where and where they may not go. Because Ettel was bothered by their presence, she believed she had the right to remove them out of her space.

Although catchy nicknames such as "Permit Patty" and "BBQ Becky" have helped to quickly spread occurrences of racial profiling through social media, some warn that these names minimize harmful situations for people of color. By giving these women cute nicknames, it is argued that white women who call the police on blacks doing ordinary activities are absolved from their racially charged actions (Wright 2018). Individuals on social media assert that we should be using their real names in order to let them be accountable for their wrongdoings. Because people of color have a history of being harmed or killed because of their racial background, especially at the hands of law enforcement, it is no joking matter. These nicknames could disguise white privilege at play and also forward the idea that white women should be protected from harm, especially at the hands of minorities.

At one of the most prestigious institutions in the world, Yale University, a white student, Sarah Braasch, called the police on a black student, Lolade Siyonbola, for napping in a common room in university housing in 2018, telling police that there was somebody who looked like they were not where they were supposed to be. This was not Braasch's first time calling the police on a black student; three months prior, she allegedly called the police on a black student after he asked for directions. In this incident, when the police arrived, Siyonbola unlocked the door of her room in front of police to show that she actually lived there, but seemingly unsatisfied, they still asked for her ID. Only after she verified her identity did the police chide Braasch for her actions (Yan 2018). These actions show a record on the part of Braasch to willfully engage in racial profiling in at least two cases. Braasch used her white privilege to show Siyonbola that she did not belong at a school like Yale, and a black presence on campus was somehow suspicious. The police in this incident also appear to have racially profiled Siyonbola when they continued to question her identity even after she opened her doom room.

In a most bizarre incident, a black man, Shaquille Dukes, was arrested for disorderly conduct in 2019 after walking outside a hospital with an IV in his arm, wheeling around an IV machine, and wearing a hospital gown. Dukes had been admitted to Freeport Hospital in Illinois for treatment of asthma and pneumonia when doctors suggested he walked around outside for a while. A white security guard stopped Dukes after he accused him of stealing the equipment to sell on eBay. Police were called for backup and arrested Dukes and two other men who were with him. Dukes said he suffered an asthma attack while being taken to the police department and was held in the back of the police car until paramedics arrived. According to Dukes, he was taken back to the hospital in handcuffs (Fieldstadt 2019). This preposterous series of events really displays the power of white privilege. Even under the care of a hospital, attached to medical equipment that is pumping medication into their veins, minorities may be entangled in suspicious and criminal activity. At the most vulnerable moment, people of color cannot take solace in being in a safe place, where they can receive the care they need and deserve. Racial disparity never sleeps, and because of this, people of color must guard themselves against discrimination and prejudice at their weakest moments. In addition to the aforementioned incidents described here, black people reported to CNN having the cops called on them in 2018 for such reasons as: golfing too slowly, campaigning door to door, driving in a car with a white grandmother, swimming in a pool, working as a firefighter, redeeming a coupon, babysitting two white children, moving into an apartment, wearing a backpack that brushed against a woman, delivering newspapers, working out at a gym, and driving with leaves on their car (Griggs 2018). Such a laundry list further underscores the absurdity of white privilege in comparison to the hypersurveillance of people of color. When they make these calls to police, their white entitlement leads them to assume their interpretation of a setting must be the only correct one. We see this normalization of white interpretations of "other" cultures in the music industry as well, a topic to which we now turn.

Cultural Appropriation and the Music Industry

Music is another media-based cultural product which may sometimes be interpreted as a "great equalizer" space, as there are several mega-superstars in the business who are not white. However, as we have seen with sports and other arenas, sometimes we have to look more closely to see who has the power to write the paychecks and make the decisions. **Cultural appropriation** *occurs when members of a dominant culture utilize elements of a minority culture outside of their original cultural context*. These elements can include styles of dress, music, language, and religious customs (Rogers 2006). It can also pertain to the use of symbols, ideas, and relics or other facets of human-made visual or nonvisual culture (Schneider 2003). Susan Scafidi characterizes cultural appropriation as "taking intellectual property, traditional knowledge, cultural expressions, or artifacts from someone else's culture without permission. This can include unauthorized use of another culture's dance, dress, music, language, folklore, cuisine, traditional medicine, religious symbols, etc." (Scafidi 2005).

Cultural appropriation emerged as a term in academia during the 1980s, even though the general concept had been studied before this time. Race scholar George Lipsitz defines the term *strategic anti-essentialism* to mean the deliberate use of a cultural form that is external to your own culture to define yourself or your group. According to Lipsitz, this phenomenon occurs in majority and minority cultures. Nonetheless, the majority culture must make a great effort to acknowledge the importance and societal context of these culture forms in order not to further progress the already unequal power dynamics of the majority and minority cultures (Lipsitz 1994). For instance, in 2015, #reclaimthebindi was created by people of South Asian ancestry in opposition to those outside the culture who wear it. A bindi is a colored dot worn between the eyebrows. Traditionally, the area between the eyebrows (where the bindi is placed) is said to be the *ajna*, or "seat of concealed wisdom." The bindi is said to capture energy and increase concentration (Pintchman 2007). The impetus of this movement came off the heels of the bindi being worn at music festivals like the Coachella Valley Music and Arts Festival in California as a fashion statement without understanding its importance to Hindu and Southeast Asian culture (Hellyer 2015). This movement pushed to empower Southeast Asian women and illuminates the importance of social media campaigns in bringing to light issues for communities of color. This hashtag created a community that could rally around this issue, connecting those who may be dispersed otherwise.

Especially in the forum of the music industry, cultural appropriation has been a cause for concern, as accusations of white artists stealing aspects of minority culture have come up frequently. For example, as black music gained favor in white music circles in the 1950s, record companies made a choice to record black music performed by white musicians. As a result, musical genres such as the blues, jazz, and rock 'n' roll were associated with white artists, although black artists pioneered these genres (Nittle 2009). These black musicians did not receive the financial compensation they deserved for their artistic contributions. The result of this type of appropriation not only leaves black artists stripped of their creativity and craft, but also allows white performers to benefit financially from something they did not create. This example illuminates the ability of whites to cherry-pick what they want from a given culture to use for their advantage without acknowledgment of the financial and psychological damage done. Elvis Presley is an artist often criticized as a cultural appropriator of black music. In hip-hop duo Public Enemy's song "Fight the Power," Chuck D states that "Elvis was a hero to most, but he never meant shit to me," this lyric expressing his frustration with what he sees as the concept of white artists profiting off the hard work and dedication of black artists (Genius 2009). Years later after the release of the song, Chuck D noted that although he respected Elvis as an artist, his rise to icon status downplayed all others who were also contributing to the genre and stated that "my heroes came from someone else. My heroes came before him. My heroes were probably his heroes" (Genius 2019). In a *Jet* article in 1957, Elvis told the magazine that he acknowledged that rock 'n' roll had existed long before his career and claimed that nobody could perform the music quite in the way black artists could (Williams 2017). Although this was his perspective, it does not excuse the fact that the white-led entertainment industry groomed Elvis to become an international superstar through his film and music career. It cannot be ignored that especially at this time, his whiteness made black music palpable for white audiences and propelled his meteoric rise to fame.

Questions of cultural appropriation by white musical artists continued well into the twenty-first century, sparking controversy and spanning musical genres. In hip-hop, Iggy Azalea, a female Australian-born rapper, has come under fire for assuming the signature rap flow of African Americans associated with the hip-hop scene in the South United States. What makes her success more problematic is the difference between her speaking voice versus the "blackcent" she employs when performing her tracks. On the heels of her smash success "Fancy" featuring Charli XCX, she became the female rapper with the longest-running top single on the Billboard Hot 100 in 2014 with Grammy nominations to follow (Zimmerman 2017). The complete altering of her voice when rapping calls into question if she is simply mocking what she believes a rapper should sound like. This scenario also appears to be one where she can capitalize off her white femininity and when convenient choose aspects of black culture that are self-serving. The blurred line between admiration and appropriation can occur subtly, but artists should take care to reflect on the difference between these two selections. Macklemore, a white male hip-hop artist from Seattle, has also recently drawn attention for his mainstream success and Grammy nomination for Best Rap Album in 2014. Macklemore ultimately won the category over acclaimed African American Compton-raised artist Kendrick Lamar, and media coverage went into overdrive. To further add fuel to the fire, Macklemore posted a text he sent to Kendrick Lamar about how he should have won the Grammy and that he had robbed Kendrick of the award. Speaking to the situation on a radio show, Macklemore states that "this is not a culture that white people started. So I do believe, as much as I have honed my craft, as much as I have put in years of dedication into the music that I love, I do believe that I need to know my place, and that comes from me listening" (Leight 2014). Here, the acknowledgment of the black roots of hip-hop grounds his participation in the genre. As a white person engaged in a predominantly black art form, it is important for people to give credit where credit is due and to point out the origins of a given cultural component.

In pop music, other complaints of cultural appropriation have arisen when American white artists flaunt fashion and other cultural aspects of cultures not their own. In 2013, Miley Cyrus completely transformed herself from an unassuming pop star into an over-the-top persona, with an unapologetic in-your-face sexuality for her album *Bangerz*. Cyrus uploaded a video twerking to a song called "Wop" by J. Dash in that same year. Twerking originated out of the New Orleans bounce scene in the late 1980s and consists of an individual shaking their buttocks in a squatted position. It is a dance associated with black, urban culture but first went viral in the mainstream in 2011 (Blaec 2017). At the height of the album's success, Cyrus could be seen wearing gold grills on her teeth and collaborating with hip-hop stars like rapper Juicy J and producer Mike WiLL Made-It. Her record producers also noted that she desired music that sounded "black." Soon, there was backlash from black people who argued that she was using this newfound black identity in order to gain more fame. Within the past few years, the singer has distanced herself from hip-hop culture and claims that she is not into the misogynistic and materialistic nature of hip-hop. This seems like a blatant denial of her white privilege and cultural appropriation of African American culture, when useful for an image overhaul. Now, making sweeping generalizations of most hip-hop being sexually demeaning to women and covetous, she is proving herself to be out of touch from her actions in the recent past that appeared to put value on these very aspects. Cyrus flaunts her white privilege by now distancing herself from hip-hop, then demeaning it before she tosses it aside as her career goes in another musical direction.

In this chapter, we discussed the power of media in forwarding messages that privilege whites, even at the cost of oppressing racial and ethnic minorities. Popular culture is often dismissed as low culture, lacking depth and meaning with only value for entertaining us. Because most people see popular culture in this way, it is that much easier to introduce images that reinforce the inequality in society. If we can brush it aside as solely entertainment, its strength and tendency to reinforce white privilege can be undermined or even ignored completely. Social media is a force of the recent past, however, has revolutionized how we connect and share information in the digital age. In the next chapter, we will reflect on the power of white privilege and tangible ways to combat the systematic elevation of white culture in America.

Real-Life Example

Social Media and Social Movements

In 2013, this movement began with the introduction of the hashtag **#BlackLives-Matter** on social media after the acquittal of George Zimmerman in the shooting death of African American teenager Trayvon Martin in Sanford, Florida. The movement gained more notoriety after protests in 2014 following the deaths of Michael Brown and Eric Garner, two African American men killed by police officers. The movement has demonstrated against the deaths of numerous other African Americans by police actions or while in police custody. All three founders of the movement are women and two identify as gay. The hashtag #Black Lives Matter has been tweeted more than 30 million times as of September 2016. The phrase "All Lives Matter" and #bluelivesmatter (a pro-police movement) have sprung up in criticism against the Black Lives Matter movement. Additionally, leaders in the black community criticize the movement and there have been allegations of sexism and racism against the group.

1. How can social media serve as a springboard for social change and activism in society? Do you think that social media will be the main way that people organize movements in the future?

2. What are some of the advantages of using social media as a way of bringing a voice to certain issues? How can social media create a platform for social justice?

3. In your experience, how has social media provided spaces for social activism for civil rights movements? Have these movements been successful?

4. How does social media help to reinforce the status quo of white racial privilege? How does it promote racial diversity and inclusion?

For this real-life example box, research your own examples of social media posts that exemplify white privilege as it relates to the Black Lives Matter movement (#BLM). If someone were to post such comments/views to your own page, how would you respond? Make note of how members of other racial/ethnic groups besides black and white relate to #BLM and how other social statuses besides race (e.g., class, sexuality, gender) inform it.

How Do We Navigate Cultural Appropriation?

In 2016, Chris Martin of the British band Coldplay and Beyoncé came under scrutiny for their video of "Hymn for the Weekend," filmed in the streets of Mumbai during the Hindu festival of Holi. Beyoncé plays a Bollywood starlet donning henna tattoos, saris, and traditional Indian jewelry. Chris Martin roams the streets singing and dancing with Mumbai locals as they welcome him with open arms into the Holi celebrations. Much of the controversy revolves around the stereotypical portrayals of Indian people and Indian culture overall. India is presented as a two-dimensional world that emphasizes the stereotypical notions of India through poverty, vibrant color, and mysticism/spirituality. For example, Chris Martin rides a rickshaw to a cinema to see the Bollywood film in which Beyoncé stars. Some people find Beyoncé's portrayal of a Bollywood actress as unnecessary when an authentic Bollywood star could fill that the role.

Asian Americans have also come under criticism for their participation in hip-hop culture, as it has operated as a predominantly black cultural art form. Mainstream hip-hop can tend to be characterized by appropriation—both of black culture by non-blacks, but also African American artists' appropriation of Asian and South Asian styles. Although Asian American artists in mainstream hip-hop are nearly invisible, borrowing parts of Asian culture such as martial arts themes or beats with Asian instruments are perceived as acceptable by black artists. Some may wonder if non-blacks who participate in hip-hop are engaging in cultural appropriation, or mimicking a culture whose context they do not fully appreciate or comprehend, when they engage in and create hip-hop themselves.

Things to consider:

Where is the distinction drawn between admiration for culture and appropriation? How does Martin's actions in "Hymn for the Weekend" differ from Beyoncé's role in the video, given the cultural context of British colonialism in India? What impact does their racial difference make?

Can one minority culture appropriate another minority culture? How does gender identity affect the ways in which cultural facets are appropriated? In what ways can people be harmed when their culture is appropriated? In what ways can we engage in cultural appropriation through fashion? Religious customs? Cultural tradition?

Issues of White Privilege and Racial Insensitivity in College Life

(A) College Dean G: College Dean G is a dean of a newly built college in the Southwest. The issue of the school mascot comes up at the university board meeting. Some members of the board and donors to the school considered using a Native American mascot to represent the college. They believe that it would be a suitable way to honor the Native American tribe that lives in various regions of the state. Other residents of the city believe that this is an offensive act, as the tribe was not consulted about the plan and that the mascot will not accurately represent the tribe. The dean is not sure how she will resolve the issue. Are there ways that the dean can both honor the tribe without the use of a Native American mascot?

(B) College Student B: College Student B is a white, male college student at one of the most prestigious colleges in America. He received a full athletic scholarship from the school as a member of the tennis team. The summer after his freshman year, a few of his teammates walk in on him at a party where he is sexually assaulting another student. He is charged and convicted of rape after a trial. In this jurisdiction, a rape conviction carries a minimum two-year sentence. Although this is the case, the judge decides that B should only serve a six-month sentence for the crime because too much jail time could ruin a potentially promising future for College Student B. The judge is a white male as well and also graduated from the university College Student B attends. In what ways could the race of the judge and College Student B affect the student's sentence?

(C) Sorority Member Z: Sorority Member Z is a junior in college and is of Korean and Mexican ancestry. She is excited to go to a few Halloween parties this weekend. She is invited to a multicultural event at a fraternity, and she thought it might be nice to go to a party that celebrates multiculturalism in their predominantly white school, especially being a biracial student herself. When she arrives at the party, there is a huge banner that reads "Straight Outta Mexico." She notices many students in oversized sombreros, ponchos, and mustaches, and some have darkened their skin with makeup. How are these costumes racially insensitive? How do they reinforce stereotypes of Mexican Americans in the media? Is this an instance of cultural appropriation?

CHAPTER 5

Anti-racism

M R. FREDERICK DOUGLASS, escaped slave, abolitionist, writer, speaker, and activist, famously noted: "Power concedes nothing without a demand. It never has and it never will" (Douglass 2000 [1857]:457). Given the many substantial white privileges we have outlined here, whites are clearly in an advantageous position, so why would they want anything to change? Is it only up to the work of people of color to fight for racial justice and equality? The good news is that people of color have been freedom fighters attacking racial oppression and white privilege since its inception, and at any point in history, one can often find a small handful of whites—sometimes even more than a small handful—joining in that struggle. In this chapter, although we will still clarify key terms and concepts to frame our discussion, the main focus will be actual practices. What kinds of everyday practices can individuals take to combat white privilege in the world around them? Our aim is to provide a variety of answers to this question, at both the micro and macro levels of action. We also analyze here how important it is to stay critical and vigilant about one's own role in anti-racist practice. To be blunt, no matter how "woke" a person is or becomes, they will still make mistakes upon committing to living an anti-racist life. Here we therefore review anti-racist actions that are effective, as well as those that may have proved counterproductive, and how anti-racists can work through their mistakes to continue to evolve on this lifelong path.

From Non-racist to Anti-racist

In Chapter 2, we defined anti-racism by contrasting it with non-racism. Non-racists are those who profess to be "not racist," which may take the form of statements such as "I don't have a racist bone in my body" or "I am the least racist person I know." In contrast, anti-racists will first and foremost acknowledge the continued existence of racism, not only surrounding them, but also within their own lives, coupled with a resolution to do something about it. As of this writing, multiple studies lead us to deduce that the proportion of whites who may actually be anti-racist is still a small minority of US whites. For example, an NPR poll in 2017 found that a majority of whites (55 percent) actually believe that discrimination against whites exists (even though many could not describe a particular example or believe it happened to them personally) (Gonyea 2017). Another Pew Research Center study in 2019 found that even though a majority (53 percent) thought race relations had gotten worse in the United States since the Trump election, it is still a majority (54 percent) of those surveyed who either think we have done enough or have gone too far in giving black people rights equal to whites (Brown 2019). Eduardo Bonilla-Silva's (2017) study found that only about 12 to 15 percent of white subjects could be categorized as racial progressives—that is, they supported affirmative action and intermarriage, had significant relationships with people of color in their lives, and agreed that antiblack racism is still a factor in everyday life. We believe the lower percentage yield from Bonilla-Silva's work is more accurate than the survey/closed-ended-question-only methodology, since Bonilla-Silva actually made use of both quantitative and in-depth interview/qualitative data, reducing the validity challenges of social desirability bias that often affects polls about race. And keep in mind, even this percentage is only identifying people who <u>believe</u> that something needs to be done about racism, not necessarily those who are actually <u>doing</u> anything about it, which would make them anti-racist. Thus, we think the best estimate is likely about 10 percent of whites or fewer who actively practice anti-racism.

Since the 1990s, social scientists have been studying racial identity development, including the typical processes by which whites come to be aware of racism (if at all), and if and when they reach that point, how they develop a commitment to anti-racism. Although identity development theories are often based on stages, it is important to note that most stage theorists agree that individuals do not always proceed in a linear fashion through the stages, nor do they even inhabit all the stages at all. These caveats notwithstanding, this body of work on racial identity development is helpful in emphasizing that becoming anti-racist is a *process* that does not happen overnight and that being *anti-racist* is not to be confused with some "earlier"/different levels of awareness about race. Janet Helms (1990) is considered one of the earliest racial identity development scholars, and she developed six stages, not just for whites, but also for African Americans and other people of color who look slightly different from the white stages. Because there are so few numbers of white anti-racists—and we are concerning ourselves here with the structural position of white privilege—we will focus here on the white racial identity development stages, which are: Contact, Disintegration, Reintegration, Pseudo-Independence, Immersion, and Autonomy. The first three stages involve various levels of becoming unsettled and disturbed about racial identity, and since we have already discussed how race is a relational category, it should not be a surprise that some of the first steps of developing a racial identity involve the realization that one's racialized experiences may be different from others'. Early stages of awareness about this can sometimes involve feelings of anger, guilt, and defensiveness (Tatum 1994)—emotions not unlike those expressed by a typical "non-racist." Many of the statements we examined in our discussion of color-blind racism would be typically espoused by white individuals in these stages, such as "they are the racist ones" (projection); they are "playing the race card" (minimization); or "a black man took my job" (appeals to abstract liberalism). In this chapter on anti-racism, though, we want to concern ourselves more with the latter three stages: Pseudo-Independence, Immersion, and Autonomy. It is in these stages that whites show a potential movement toward anti-racism. But again, it is a process, and some may not ever get fully there.

According to racial identity theorists, when whites hit Pseudo-Independence, they begin to accept the reality of racism and want to potentially do something about it, but they may continue to do so in color-blind ways (i.e., "stop hate," "we are all the same"), or they may be more interested in allying themselves with people of color than examining their own whiteness (O'Brien 2001). In other words, they may seek to form interracial relationships, but do so in a way that "ignore[s] difference" (Jones and Carter 1996:16). Tatum (1994), Wise (2004), and many others have argued that a key action that can help whites move out of this seemingly paralytic state and into a more self-aware form of anti-racism is to learn more about the history of white anti-racists. According to the racial identity development model, the process of studying white anti-racist role models (past and current) is what occurs during the fifth stage of Immersion. Because one of many stumbling blocks for whites is "white guilt," the Immersion process can help move one out of this guilt-ridden place, as they learn that some other whites have also been associated with anti-racist work. The sixth and final stage in this theory is the Autonomy stage, whereby a more secure white anti-racist identity occurs—although not ever without stumbling blocks or making mistakes, which can be expected to be lifelong (O'Brien 2001; O'Brien 2003).

More recently, mirroring the work of these academics but expanding it, a group of activists has developed a "racism scale" to visually represent this progression through steps of racial awareness (Demnowicz 2017). Based on a Twitter post that went viral and was then treated as a public product for people to comment on and add to, this racism scale can be found at https://racismscale.weebly.com/. The scale begins with terrorism and overt racism, moves through subconscious racism and indifference, to defensiveness, justification, and denial before it goes to its second half, which focuses more on anti-racism. On the anti-racist side, it begins with the "white savior," "woke justification," and "performative ally"—noting that all three of these spots on the continuum can be affected by "white guilt." So it is not until the latter and final three positions on the racism scale that we can see some more effective anti-racist positions: awareness, allyship, and abolitionist. What is helpful is that the typical questions and statements made by persons at each point on the continuum are also provided. For example, "woke justification" includes statements like "we are one race, the human race," while "performative ally" includes statements like "if they want our help, they should be more respectful" and "being involved with this will help my reputation." These are what we might call green or novice/beginner anti-racist statements that are indicative of whites who may have good intentions of wanting to be anti-racist but have not yet fully examined their privilege and how it manifests itself in anti-racist work. As we move to the final three points on the continuum (awareness, allyship, and abolitionist), we see statements like "Yes, my life as a poor white person was hard, but not the same as being a person of color," and "I will put my safety, health, and freedom on the line to fight for people of color. I will let them lead and not try to be at the center" (Demnowicz 2017). What the racial identity development theorists and the racism scale activists both demonstrate is that simply acknowledging that *racism exists* and agreeing *something should be done to end it* is not the end point for effective anti-racism. Even when what we already know is a minority of whites even agree to these two statements, actually doing something about racism that is effective and not counterproductive is a distinctly different, and further, next step.

Here, then, we might distinguish between non-racism, **anti-racism in theory**, and **anti-racism in conscious practice**. An excellent first step is *acknowledging white privilege exists and agreeing something should be done about it*, which would make one an **anti-racist in theory**. Bonilla-Silva (2017) refers to these as racial progressives in his study. However, in order to be an **anti-racist in practice**, one would have to be *committing to some actions*—actions consist of everything from simple everyday conversations to confronting institutions and making institutional change. And then, to have a **conscious practice of anti-racism**, *one's actions would need to be grounded in a reflexive, ongoing process of examining and interrogating one's own position in the social structure and how that position affects the consequences of one's anti-racist practices*. We cannot overstate the case that simply a move from non-racist to anti-racist, even in theory, is a monumental step. Campt's (2018a) White Ally Toolkit program, for example, has as its goal to flip the percentage of whites who think racism is just as bad against whites as against blacks from 55/45 to 45/55. The method is to encourage whites to have the difficult conversations with each other that sometimes do not go over as well with people of color in the room. Later on in this chapter, we will discuss specific action strategies, of which this is one. But for now, we want to focus on this percentage split. Campt's hope is not that 55 percent of whites will become anti-racist in practice, but rather that they will simply become anti-racist in theory—that is, that they will merely acknowledge the structural reality of white privilege as the foundation of racism. And he acknowledges that this "in theory" shift alone will take a tremendous amount of work but will still be beneficial. It can indirectly impact social policy in terms of voting, political participation, and other areas. So we do not want to minimize this shift. However, for the remainder of the chapter, we will focus more directly on anti-racist *practice*. Let us begin with how one develops a *conscious* anti-racist practice—because white privilege is at the heart of the answer.

Anti-racists of Color and Anti-racist Whites: White Privilege

From the beginning of anti-racist efforts, which we know now were not until after the invention of "race" as a dividing tool of colonialism, activists of color were clear about challenging white privilege. When Sojourner Truth asked "Ain't I a Woman?" in 1851, she was asking why "woman" was defined as a *white* woman and did not include women of color (hooks 1981). When W.E.B. Du Bois wrote about double consciousness and the veil in 1903, he was asking why "human" and "American" were assumed to be white, and anyone else was a "problem" (Du Bois 1996[1903]). And from the onset of whites' involvement with anti-racist struggles, their relatively privileged position vis-à-vis their counterparts of color in the movement has been a source of tension. Even the abolitionist movements were not free from racism. Indeed, many white abolitionists opposed slavery on moral and/or religious grounds but still affirmed white superiority (Aptheker 1992). Frederick Douglass reports that as an abolitionist speaker, he was not only paid less than white abolitionist speakers but was even at times introduced with terms like *thing* or *it* in ways that designated him as less than human (Mathias 2017). Whites getting involved in anti-racist struggles have often meant well but both intentionally and unintentionally perpetuated white privilege, even while professing to want to end forms of racism.

Both Martin Luther King Jr. and Malcolm X, among others, spoke and wrote on the trouble with "white moderates" and "white liberals." These would be rough equivalents to what we described above as anti-racists in theory. These are whites who are already in the minority by acknowledging racism is a problem needing to be addressed, but all too often have critiques for how anti-racists of color choose to address racism. As Dr. King put it in his Letter from the Birmingham Jail in 1963:

> First, I must confess that over the past few years I have been gravely
> disappointed with the white moderate. I have almost reached the
> regrettable conclusion that the Negro's great stumbling block in his stride
> toward freedom is not the White Citizen's Counciler or the Ku Klux
> Klanner, but the white moderate, who is more devoted to "order" than
> to justice; who prefers a negative peace which is the absence of tension to
> a positive peace which is the presence of justice; who constantly says: "I
> agree with you in the goal you seek, but I cannot agree with your methods
> of direct action"; who paternalistically believes he can set the timetable
> for another man's freedom; who lives by a mythical concept of time and

who constantly advises the Negro to wait for a "more convenient season." Shallow understanding from people of good will is more frustrating than absolute misunderstanding from people of ill will. Lukewarm acceptance is much more bewildering than outright rejection. (King 1963: 9–10)

In this excerpt, one concept Dr. King raises is **paternalism**—in anti-racism, paternalism amounts to a *patronizing attitude on the part of whites that they know better than people of color what should be done and how it should be done*. This kind of white paternalism has historically fostered distrust between anti-racists of color and white anti-racists, and is not new. Many anti-racists of color have written and spoken about this particular way that white privilege manifests itself in anti-racist work.

Note King's position that paternalism from whites who want to help is actually "more frustrating" than those whites who are overtly not interested in being anti-racist at all. This challenges the continuum/stage theories we discussed in the previous section, where overt racists are considered less developed in their anti-racist journey than a pseudo-independent or performative ally, who at least acknowledges racism exists and wants to help fight it. Indeed, King describes the frustration and distrust as stronger because these so-called white allies are in closer contact and more is expected from them, yet still they fail and fall short. And hurting someone at close range can be more damaging than someone you never expected to trust in the first place. Malcolm X took a similar position when he used the wolf/fox analogy to discuss the difference between white racists and white liberals:

> "Conservatism" in America's politics means "Let's keep the niggers in their place." And "liberalism" means "Let's keep the knee-grows in their place—but tell them we'll treat them a little better; let's fool them more, with more promises." With these choices, I felt that the American black man only needed to choose, which one to be eaten by, the "liberal" fox or the "conservative" wolf—because both of them would eat him. [At least] in a wolf's den, I'd always known exactly where I stood; I'd watch the dangerous wolf closer than I would the smooth, sly fox. The wolf's very growling would keep me alert and fighting him to survive, whereas I might be lulled and fooled by the tricky fox (X 1992[1964]:380).

These types of concerns about the damages that well-intentioned whites could do while working as activists in the civil rights movement came to a head in 1966 when one of the key organizations, the Student Nonviolent Coordinating Committee (SNCC) recommended that whites exit their group and focus their efforts on educating each other. They too noted paternalism as well as notions of black inferiority that made it difficult to continue effective interracial anti-racist practice (Farmer 2017). So it is not just anti-racists in theory, but also anti-racists in practice, that have continued to perpetuate white privilege even while doing anti-racist work.

Critical race scholar Richard Delgado (1996) has coined the term **false empathy**, which can help illuminate the potential damages of an anti-racist practice that is not conscious or critically reflexive of white privilege. False empathy is basically *an ill-informed form of empathy whereby one envisions oneself in another's shoes but is still bringing one's own perspective without a clear understanding of the other's*. Echoing the above sentiments of Dr. King and Malcolm X, Delgado too warns that false empathy can be more damaging than those who are not bothering to empathize at all:

> False empathy is worse than none at all, worse than indifference. It makes you overconfident, so that you can easily harm the intended beneficiary. You are apt to be paternalistic, thinking you know what the other really wants or needs. You can easily substitute your own goal for his. You visualize what you would want if you were he, when your experiences and needs are radically different. (Delgado 1996:31)

Note that paternalism is a common thread across all these critiques of white involvement in anti-racism. Across multiple analyses of white anti-racists, there is a pattern of whites lacking humility and not always being willing to submit themselves to people of color setting the agenda, even though they are seemingly unified in their desires to work to end racism together. In fact, as media becomes increasingly digitized, there is no shortage of Op-Eds, memes, YouTube public service announcements, and more, aimed at white anti-racists who mean well but are nevertheless carrying white privilege into their anti-racist work in potentially harmful ways.

Although the term "ally" or "white ally" is sometimes used as a synonym for white anti-racists, since the Black Lives Matter movement began in 2013, some activists of color have called into question this terminology for unwittingly perpetuating white privilege as well. For example, an activist named Feminista Jones attending a Harlem, New York, Black Lives Matter demonstration explained that an ally to her meant equal support both ways, and as a person of color she does not feel equally obligated to support whites' need to survive because the needs are not comparable. She also noted how "ally" could connote a type of cheerleader or support-from-afar role instead of getting into the trenches and "rolling up my sleeves"—in other words, it may connote a lack of willingness to make equal sacrifices as an anti-racist of color (Hackman 2015). Another critique of white allyship is delineated by writer Gyasi Lake:

> As a system, whiteness acts as an invisible elevator that lifts white voices floors above the Black voices that are most marginalized.

This is the most harmful aspect of "white allyship." In the white supremacist society we inhabit, it has the effect of de-prioritizing and de-centering the Black voices that are most affected in order to champion white voices that are deemed more palpable. (Lake 2019)

In other words, by emphasizing their whiteness as part of the anti-racist movement, they nevertheless still cash in on their white privilege, as their public stances become elevated and celebrated over and above their colleagues of color. Lake uses the compare/contrast of the power of the voices of comedian Mo'Nique and actress Ellen Pompeo as they both spoke out about pay inequity in Hollywood, yet Pompeo was more widely heralded as a white woman. As Lake writes: "The bar for white 'allies' is absurdly low and I'm tired of watching them be praised for reaching it" (Lake 2019). This discussion is instructive because even when one may be personally reflective and humble about one's own role, the racist society at large will nevertheless elevate white voices above those of color because of whites' structural position. Thus, being an anti-racist in conscious practice requires navigating the delicate balance of knowing when white voices of conscience are urgently needed and when whites need to pass the mic to voices of color that have far too often been marginalized.

Two practices that a group called the People's Institute for Survival and Beyond (PISB) teaches in its Undoing Racism workshops that can be helpful to a conscious practice of anti-racism are **authentic relationships** (with people of color) and **maintaining relationships** (with non-practicing whites) (O'Brien 2001). Research on interracial friendships and relationships reveals that all too often these personal connections rely on color-blind ways of relating to each other that do not critically examine the role of racism and white privilege in each partner or friend's life (Childs 2005; Korgen 2002). So when PISB advises whites to build **authentic relationships** with people of color to keep them accountable, what they mean is *not* the typical color-blind interracial relationship, but rather a *connection where the person of color feels free to speak frankly about times when racism and white privilege may be impacting the white friend's anti-racist practice*. In order to be able to speak freely, the white friend must be consciously reflexive about not allowing denial, defensiveness, or other manifestations of white fragility to interfere with deep listening to such critiques. There is a fine line here as well. Mutual accountability requires white anti-racists to not become over-reliant on expecting people of color to educate them about racism, and rather expects white anti-racists to be active agents in their own ongoing education and awareness. All too often, the **entitlement** that comes along with white socialization trains whites to expect to be taught about racism by people of color, which puts an undue burden on an already-stressed population.

The second practice of **maintaining relationships** refers to a request that anti-racists of color often make of whites. As we saw in the above historic event of 1966, when the SNCC directed whites to work with each other, anti-racists of color have identified a crucial need in the movement for racial justice where whites can play a role more uniquely suited for them—reaching out to other whites, in attempting to bring them to greater awareness about racism and white privilege, where anti-racists of color are not able to get through. In other words, many whites can tend to see other white people as "more objective" sources of information and can likewise tend to minimize people of color as "playing the race card" or otherwise exaggerating the reality of racism. Acknowledging this *unfortunate reality and unjust double standard in white perception of race-related information* which O'Brien (2001) has referred to as **privileged polemics**, anti-racists of color have a history of strongly encouraging white anti-racists to do their work with other whites, where people of color may not be able to be believed or trusted as well. White anti-racists historically have had to be constantly reminded of the importance of this work with other whites because they can tend to want to gravitate more toward people of color and avoid the whites with whom they have race-related disagreements. As the PISB organization states, white people can have a tendency to view relationships as disposable, and people of color do not have that luxury (O'Brien 2001). Rather than breaking off relationships with other whites who are not anti-racist like them, the practice of **maintaining relationships** *encourages whites to stay in relationships with other whites and make having ongoing conversations with them about race part of their conscious anti-racist practice.*

Many anti-racists of color across history have repeatedly implored this request of well-meaning whites. This is a powerful indictment of one of the many ways white privilege impacts anti-racist work. As Michael Eric Dyson put it in his "Brief but Spectacular Challenge to White America,"

> You're going to get into circles that I will never get into. You're going to go home to Thanksgiving. Go home and talk to granny, not before you eat the turkey or the stuffing or the pumpkin pie. But after, then say to her, you know what, I have got black and brown and red and yellow friends, and it's not what you say. Or say to your cousin and your uncle, this is not how it goes down. And when we do that, we can get rid of the amnesia that has blocked a white grappling with its own problems and issues, and tell the truth about race in America. (Dyson 2017a)

Anti-racists of color like Dyson give instructive advice here that the conversations with "granny" are exactly the work white anti-racists are structurally positioned to do. Yet all too often they may avoid the uncomfortable work and show up to a Black Lives Matter march instead, where everyone may be already in agreement with them. It is not that one action is better or more effective than another, but that addressing racism and white privilege from as many angles as possible is key. Similarly, David Campt, an African American founder of the White Ally Toolkit uses humor to drive the point home: "I have never been around white people when there wasn't a black person there" (Campt 2018b). Campt's method, which we discuss more in the next section, encourages whites to have the difficult conversations with each other using empathic listening and storytelling. Direct confrontation may appear righteous, but it is often discouraged by veteran anti-racists who encourage this maintaining relationships idea.

While there is not space enough here to cover all the critiques and various ways white anti-racists make mistakes and inadvertently perpetuate white privilege through their anti-racist work, suffice it to say that a key component of a conscious practice of anti-racism is an ongoing awareness of the different structural positions of whites and people of color and how this impacts one's own practice. If becoming aware about racism and white privilege means eschewing color-blindness, then it should be no different once embarking upon anti-racist work. One of the key pieces of advice for white anti-racists that recurs across multiple sources is remaining humble—this kind of humility requires being adaptable and amenable, open to critique, as opposed to shutting down and giving up when one is challenged (DiAngelo 2011; Dyson 2017b; Campt 2018a; Farmer 2017; Mallott et al. 2019; O'Brien 2001; O'Brien 2003). There is no shortage of places to start, or ways to act—just a sampling of which we shall outline in the next section.

Cultivating a Conscious Anti-racist Practice

The approach we have stressed throughout this text is the interdependence of the macro/institutional and the micro/individual aspects of racism and white privilege. We have illustrated with evidence how interpersonal relationships and everyday interactions create the conditions through which whites are advantaged in institutional spaces. As such, the anti-racist practices we outline here necessarily implicate both everyday interactions in relationships with others as well as structural policy changes that anti-racists can impact through direct action.

A well-rounded list of anti-racist practices typically includes the more visible things one might traditionally consider activism, alongside the less visible everyday relationship-building activities. One example list of actions is provided by Dyson (2017), including the proposal of people practicing individual-level reparations. This kind of practice means intentionally seeking out accountants, doctors, contracting companies of various sorts that are owned by people of color and compensating them justly (or even more) for their services. Dyson also advocates educating oneself and others about racism, as well as participating in marches, protests, and rallies. This comprehensive list is not unlike the findings of Mallott et al. (2019), who interviewed several white anti-racists and found that their practices fell into one of four categories—educating others about racism (in workshops, classes, groups, online forums, etc.); participating in leadership practices (marches, rallies, protests, and other forms of direct action); cultivating interracial personal relationships; and continuing to educate themselves.

Everyday interpersonal interactions can be a fruitful site of anti-racist practice. In the 1990s, a group called the Race Traitors or New Abolitionists advocated the practice of interrupting white privilege—such as when a police officer pulls you over and only gives you a warning, or when someone gives you an opportunity because "people like you" are the kind we want here—by calling into question the very assumption that one is "white" in the first place. Whites often tell racist jokes to another white person assuming they will either laugh or at least go along with it, so the new abolitionists suggested challenging that person with something like, "you must think I'm white" (Ignatiev and Garvey 1996). Such acts of individually refusing white privilege when it is extended to you are daring indeed, but many argue it is that kind of daring that is necessary to disrupt the system.

O'Brien (2001) developed a continuum of four types of anti-racist individual action strategies based on interviews with thirty white anti-racists. Type 1 is direct, angry confrontation and is typically reserved for situations where there is a limited time and space to address something blatant. Type 2 can be either direct or delayed and involves engaging the speaker in dialogue, trying to explain to them in a teacher role, or using analogies, why something they've said or done is racist. Type 3 is sometimes direct but often slightly delayed and involves not addressing the speaker's racist comment directly, but rather coming back shortly thereafter with contrasting positive feedback about people of color. For example, when a white woman at church welcomes a newcomer by saying, "We're so glad you're here because you can save the church, the blacks are taking over," the white newcomer waits until after the sermon to reestablish contact with the woman and tell her that one of the reasons she sought that particular church was because of its racial diversity. Another example of this Type 3 strategy was shared with O'Brien during a Confronting Racism workshop she led based on the research about these four types. An African American workshop participant recalled that her supervisor constantly brought in newspaper articles from the crime section of the paper, asking her did she know the person, so as a counteractive strategy, she began collecting newspaper articles about various amazing humanitarian deeds and inventions that African Americans had done, and every time the supervisor asked her, "Do you know this person?" she counteracted him with, "No, but do you know this person?" (showing the positive image of African Americans).

The fourth and final strategy was only delayed, and not unlike the first strategy, had inconsistent effectiveness. The anti-racist decides not to confront the speaker at all and instead decides to form a relationship with them that establishes trust so that only later they can broach the subject of racism together. The middle two strategies (Types 2 and 3) were considered the ones with the highest likelihood of being effective. This is because the direct, angry confrontation (Type 1) was likely to turn off the person and provoke defensiveness and/or counterattack, while the "build a trusting relationship" strategy (Type 4) may end up being a "cop-out" where the anti-racist actually never ends up challenging the speaker at all (O'Brien 2001). Campt's (2018a) white ally toolkit method is not unlike these latter strategies on the continuum that reject confrontational actions. Campt presents a variety of psychological research to bolster his position that people who are argumentatively challenged are only likely to double down on their original position. If true attitude/behavior change is the goal, Campt maintains that a combination of active listening, empathy, and personal storytelling is a more effective way to challenge racist beliefs than direct confrontation.

The challenge of using interpersonal interactions as a primary site of anti-racist practice is, of course, that one never knows when they are going to occur. One has to be "at the ready" and commit to anti-racism as a life practice as opposed to a job or role one plays only in one certain location. African American poet Claudia Rankin (2019) wrote about a series of airport and airplane interactions with various white men who were strangers to her, analyzing the different reactions she got, depending on the person, as she selected from various conversational strategies with which to challenge them as they took advantage of white privilege. These were incidents such as cutting in line, assuming she was not first class, and getting better flight attendant service and responsiveness. Not unlike Campt's strategies discussed above, Rankin used a combination of tactics that included trying to forge common ground with the actors on race-neutral topics as well as asking them pointed questions about their own behavior and taken-for-granted assumptions. Not surprisingly, the various white men's responses ranged from defensiveness and indignation to, on rare occasion, self-reflection, humility, and remorse, coupled with a resolve to do better (Rankin 2019). Such practices of everyday anti-racism can thus be expected to be uncomfortable more often than not, and one should not be surprised when failure is more common than success. However, one never knows when one might be able to make a distinct difference.

In various ways, the above actions are challenging microaggressions and are likely seen as attitude-changing projects. However, everyday anti-racist interactions can also add up to institutional change. Asking critical questions about the organizational practices of the various institutions of which one is a part can be important first steps to creating institutional change. The PISB group we mentioned earlier that leads Undoing Racism workshops encourages participants to think about how they might be a gatekeeper in certain institutions, and then reflect on how they might be able to use their gatekeeper position to challenge institutional racism from within (O'Brien 2001). Crossroads Antiracism Organizing & Training, a national organization, has developed a "Continuum on Becoming an Anti-Racist Multicultural Institution" (Table 5.1) that is instructive in a number of ways. Reading from left to right, one can see how an organization can move from being completely

Table 5.1 Continuum on Becoming an Anti-Racist Multicultural Institution

MONOCULTURAL ==> MULTICULTURAL ==> ANTIRACIST ==> ANTI-RACIST MULTICULTURAL					
Racial and Cultural Differences Seen as Deficits ==> Tolerant of Racial and Cultural Differences ==> Racial and Cultural Differences Seen as Assets					
1. EXCLUSIVE **A Segregated Institution**	**2. PASSIVE** **A "Club" Institution**	**3. SYMBOLIC CHANGE** **A Multicultural Organization**	**4. IDENTITY CHANGE** **An Antiracist Institution**	**5. STRUCTURAL CHANGE** **A Transforming Institution**	**6. FULLY INCLUSIVE** **A Transformed Institution in a Transformed Society**
• Intentionally and publicly excludes or segregates African Americans, Arab Americans, Native Americans, Latinos and Asian Americans	• Tolerant of a limited number of People of Color with "proper" perspective and credentials	• Makes official policy pronouncements regarding multicultural diversity	• Growing understanding of racism as barrier to effective diversity	• Commits to process of intentional institutional restructuring, based upon antiracist analysis and identity	• Future vision of an institution and wider community that has overcome systemic racism
• Intentionally and publicly enforces the racist status quo throughout institution	• May still secretly limit or exclude People of Color in contradiction to public policies	• Sees itself as "non-racist" institution with open doors to People of Color	• Develops analysis of systemic racism	• Audits and restructures all aspects of institutional life to ensure full participation of People of Color, including their worldview, culture and lifestyles	• Institution's life reflects full participation and shared power with diverse racial, cultural, and economic groups in determining its mission, structure, constituency, policies and practices
• Institutionalization of racism includes formal policies and practices, teachings, and decision making on all levels	• Continues to intentionally maintain white power and privilege through its formal policies and practices, teachings, and decision making on all levels of institutional life	• Carries out intentional inclusiveness efforts, recruiting "someone of color" on committees or office staff	• Sponsors programs of antiracism training	• Implements structures, policies and practices with inclusive decision making and other forms of power sharing on all levels of the institution's life and work	• Full participation in decisions that shape the institution, and inclusion of diverse cultures, lifestyles, and interests
	• Often declares, "We don't have a problem."	• Expanding view of diversity includes other socially oppressed groups such as women, disabled, elderly and children, LGBTQ, citizens of developing nations, etc.	• New consciousness of institutionalized white power and privilege		• A sense of restored community and mutual caring
			• Develops intentional identity as an "anti-racist" institution		
			• Develops intentional identity as an "antiracist institution"		
			• Begins to develop accountability to racially oppressed communities		

(Continued)

Chapter 5 — Anti-racism | 117

Table 5.1 Continuum on Becoming an Anti-Racist Multicultural Institution (*Continued*)

	MONOCULTURAL ==> MULTICULTURAL ==> ANTIRACIST ==> ANTI-RACIST MULTICULTURAL				
	Racial and Cultural Differences Seen as Deficits ==> Tolerant of Racial and Cultural Differences ==> Racial and Cultural Differences Seen as Assets				
1. EXCLUSIVE A Segregated Institution	**2. PASSIVE** A "Club" Institution	**3. SYMBOLIC CHANGE** A Multicultural Organization	**4. IDENTITY CHANGE** An Antiracist Institution	**5. STRUCTURAL CHANGE** A Transforming Institution	**6. FULLY INCLUSIVE** A Transformed Institution in a Transformed Society
• Usually has similar intentional policies and practices toward other socially oppressed groups such as women, disabled, elderly and children, LGBTQ, citizens of developing nations, etc.		*But...* • "Not those who make waves" • Little or no contextual change in culture, policies, and decisionmaking • Is still relatively unaware of continuing patterns of privilege, paternalism and control	• Increasing commitment to dismantle racism and eliminate inherent white advantage *But...* • Institutional structures and culture that maintain white power and privilege still intact and relatively untouched	• Commits to struggle to dismantle racism in the wider community, and builds clear lines of accountability to racially oppressed communities • Antiracist multicultural diversity becomes an institutionalized asset • Redefines and rebuilds all relationships and activities in society, based on antiracist commitments • Allies with others in combating all forms of social oppression.	

Bailey Jackson, et al., "Continuum on Becoming Antiracist Multicultural Institution." Copyright © by Crossroads Anti-Racism Organizing and Training. Reprinted with permission.

segregated and exclusive, to only token inclusion, to ways that are largely symbolic and do not fundamentally alter the white-advantaging structure of the institution. It is not until one moves to the latter half on the right side of the continuum that anti-racism begins to impact the organization in meaningful ways, such that it is more fully inclusive and equitable (Crossroads 2017). This continuum gives anti-racists who are interested in creating anti-racism within the institutions of which they are a part some ideas of where to start working with other allies in their own organizations.

Note that both the terms *anti-racist* and *multicultural* are used here. We have titled this concluding chapter "Anti-racism" quite deliberately. Particularly in the education community, but also in other fields, some critique has been leveled at terms like *diversity* and *multiculturalism* for failing to reduce white privilege; instead perpetuating structural racism with an "add diversity and stir" approach (Kailin 2002; Pincus 2011; Randolph 2012). Certainly an all-white organization is indicative of racism and white privilege, and racial diversity in terms of membership is one step toward becoming more inclusive. However, what research demonstrates is when accompanying changes do not occur to the culture and structure of the organization, it can still remain just as hostile and unwelcoming to the new members of the previously underrepresented groups. This pattern is consistent across nearly any majority/minority group setting, whether it is women entering previously all-male corporations (Kanter 1993), African Americans at predominantly white colleges and universities (Byrd 2017; Feagin, Vera, and Imani 1996), suburban school districts (Lewis 2003) and many other institutional arrangements. Token celebrations of diversity that do not deal with the difficult and often uncomfortable reality of inequality and power imbalances inevitably fail and fall flat. So the continuum purposefully places the word "anti-racist" first in the title, to indicate that once an organization has truly undergone the difficult work of confronting marginalization, exclusion, and privilege in its past and present, then a more inclusive multiculturalism can occur. However, anti-racism itself necessitates interrogating white privilege in a way "diversity" and "multiculturalism" often do not.

Changing the processes by which people are "let in" to institutions, from the lowest to the highest levels, is an important way to confront institutional racism and privilege. As we have already established, while overt exclusion is certainly still happening, simply going through "the usual" channels of nepotism and homosocial reproduction without intent to exclude is a major culprit in perpetuating white privilege. Recall from Chapter 4, there are two notable examples of countering these dynamics and attempting to level the playing field in the sports and entertainment industries—the Rooney Rule and inclusion riders. The Rooney Rule began in the National Football League (NFL) in 2003, named after the then-owner of the Pittsburgh Steelers (Dan Rooney), who was tasked with examining the League's dismal effort at hiring and retaining minority coaches. Considered a "soft" form of affirmative action because it does not require any candidate to be hired, it directs hiring processes to include at least one minority candidate in the interview process (DuBois 2016). Although as of 2018 there were zero black owners and only seven black head coaches in the NFL—an organization where the players are 70 percent black—the NFL has actually earned an "A-" grade for its improvement in racial diversity in hiring for the past nine years from the Institute for Diversity and Ethics in Sport, which shows how far it has come since the Rooney Rule first began in 2003 (Lapchick 2019). Other businesses and industries have taken note, and this is something that any individual who is part of a hiring committee in any organization can certainly suggest as a method of procedure. Whether it is your student club or fraternity or sorority, your religious organization, or your full-time job, when it is time to select someone for a new position or leadership role, you can ask yourselves whether your final pool is all white, and if it is, you can practice a version of the Rooney Rule by at least adding a name into the ring as part of the selection process.

The inclusion rider is something that got a good amount of press after Frances McDormand used part of her Golden Globe acceptance speech in 2018 to mention this term (Dwyer 2018; Neville and Anastasio 2019). Unlike the Rooney Rule, which basically has to be implemented by those in hiring positions, the inclusion rider is an attempt by those who are being hired to use their "star power" to refuse to work for a particular project unless it includes adequate representation across the team—both in front of and behind the camera. Michael B. Jordan was one of the first actors known to insist on this after the announcement, and the inclusion rider for his project referred not only to racial diversity, but also gender and sexual orientation (Levin 2018). The idea for inclusion riders was originally developed to focus on gender representation by Stacy Smith at the Annenberg Inclusion Initiative at the University of Southern California, and civil rights attorney Kalpana Kotogal drafted the language to be used in contracts (Dwyer 2018). Although Hollywood is where the conversation began, it has extended to the scientific community, where persons of privilege are beginning to "use their privilege" when they are invited to speak on a panel, by refusing the invitation to speak unless the panel includes diversity, and/or declining the invitation and suggesting alternative colleagues who are not white men (Belluck 2019; Cannon 2018). A conscious practice of anti-racism, then, could potentially include some practice of an inclusion rider no matter where one is invited or included. This would be another way to impact institutional racism even as one individual.

Then, even when an organization becomes more inclusive, a conscious practice of anti-racism means continuing to be an advocate, and on the lookout for people using seemingly race-neutral explanations to force people of color out for no longer being a "good fit." Sometimes referred to as **passive racism**, *doing nothing in the face of race-neutral language that privileges whiteness and marginalizes others* is not consistent with a conscious practice of anti-racism. Not only attaining, but maintaining, a diverse organization requires constant attention to the way white privilege works. Speaking out when these kinds of dynamics occur requires constantly educating oneself and paying attention (Beetham 2017). Having the support of an anti-racist organization can be helpful here, a topic to which we now turn.

Anti-racist Organizations

Although there is not enough space here to list every anti-racist organization in existence (and also the frequency with which organizations are born and evolve), which precludes our ability to provide such a comprehensive list here, this section will provide an overview of some possibilities to get readers started. We want to pay particular attention to the three example institutions we reviewed in Chapter 3—economy, education, and criminal justice—as there is a great deal of anti-racist work going on aimed at making change in these institutions, among others.

One of the oldest anti-racist organizations in the United States is the National Association of the Advancement of Colored People (NAACP), which was cofounded in 1909 by whites and African Americans. Some who are unfamiliar with this history and the activities of the organization may erroneously assume from the title/name that this is not an organization white people can join, but this is an assumption formed from ignorance. Most anyone can become a card-carrying member, and many local chapters even have officers who identify as white or some other race. The organization does have a commitment to having people of color in leadership roles and to advancing the education and political empowerment of those who have been historically marginalized and disadvantaged. There are over 2,000 local chapters nationwide, and there is a statewide organization in all fifty states. According to a 2019 version of the website, there are seven key areas where the NAACP does its work—federal advocacy, environmental and climate justice, health, media diversity, education, economic opportunity, and criminal justice. With respect to education, the NAACP offers scholarships as well as webinars and training on how to advance equity in education and better serve underserved students. They have a position against charter schools on their website and do federal advocacy around this position as well as many others. With respect to economics, the website mentions focusing on unemployment, wealth, lack of jobs, lack of affordable housing, and foreclosures. With respect to criminal justice, the organization offers educational tools for training about racial profiling and takes stands on sentencing reform and the difficulty of reentering the workforce after incarceration. You can find out more at (www.naacp.org).

Although not nearly as old as the NAACP, another organization with about a half century of longevity is the Southern Poverty Law Center (SPLC), whose Teaching Tolerance and Hatewatch programs may be more recognizable than the organization's name itself. The SPLC was founded in 1971 by two white civil rights lawyers (the NAACP was also founded largely by lawyers). According to their web-site: "The SPLC is dedicated to fighting hate and bigotry and to seeking justice for the most vulnerable members of our society. Using litigation, education, and other forms of advocacy, the SPLC works toward the day when the ideals of equal justice and equal opportunity will be a reality" (www.splcenter.org). Their Hate-watch program monitors white supremacist groups and takes legal action when possible. Their Teaching Tolerance program was founded in 1991 and provides lesson plans and other free resources to teachers and educators who want to add anti-bias, social justice–oriented material to their curricula. In addition to these programs, the legal advocacy SPLC focuses on immigrant rights, injustice in the criminal justice system, and economic injustice, such as predatory lending and the cash bail system. Although their state offices are in the US south (Alabama, Flor-ida, Mississippi, and Louisiana), anyone can join and contribute. The SPLC is also responsible for the Civil Rights Memorial that opened in 1989 in Montgomery, Alabama (www.splcenter.org).

While the above two organizations were anchored in the civil rights movement and continue their work today, some newer organizations founded in the age of the Internet and social media in the aftermath of racist events that captured national and international attention have been doing highly effective work more recently. Two such groups are Color of Change (founded in 2005 after Hurricane Katrina) and Black Lives Matter (founded in 2013 after the killing of Trayvon Martin). By using tactics such as e-mail and social media petitions and protest marches in local communities, these groups have shamed officials in various local communities and even major global corporations into taking action to correct racist injustices that have occurred on their watch.

Color of Change uses media as its primary mode of communication, and its online presence is its strength. It is an organization that finds out about instances of racism from its members and then starts petition campaigns and press releases to draw attention to these injustices. Color of Change has gotten national and international attention for many occurrences that the mainstream media at first did not cover. On its website, anyone can sign up and start a campaign. Guidestar, a database that indexes all the nonprofit organizations in the United States, lists Color of Change as "the nation's largest online racial justice organization" with 1.4 million members (www.guidestar.org). On Color of Change's website, they list several of their victories including getting Fox News to cancel Bill O'Reilly's show (O'Reilly is a news personality whose show was a "platform for antiblack vitriol and misogyny"); getting a new legal team and justice for the Jena 6 (a small group of black students who were harassed for sitting under the "white tree" in Louisiana and then unfairly targeted by local school officials and the district attorney); and getting over 100 corporate sponsors to stop funding ALEC (a "secretive right-wing policy promoter" that is featured in the documentary *13* as a primary driver of private for-profit prisons, stand-your-ground laws, and other damaging criminal justice practices). Color of Change has also pressured Facebook and Twitter into reevaluating its policies on hate speech and other unjust practices. The sheer range of the scope of this organization's campaigns is pretty phenomenal. From advocating for just a few little black and Latinx girls in an elementary school, to challenging a ban on hijabs in high school athletics, to challenging global corporate conglomerates, Color of Change leverages its membership to get lesser-told stories into the mainstream media and makes public outcry about injustice its weapon for getting powerful corporations and politicians to act. This kind of anti-racism is something one can participate in without ever leaving home and boasts an impressive list of results (www.colorofchange.org).

The Black Lives Matter organization (BLM) is a bit newer, and has a combination of online, media, and on-ground presence. It lists twenty-four chapter locations across North America and also includes statements of solidarity with BLM-related movements in places globally, including Great Britain and Brazil. Racist events of 2013–2014, including the shooting of Trayvon Martin by George Zimmerman in Sanford, Florida, and the shooting of Michael Brown by police officer Darren Wilson and subsequent riots in Ferguson, Missouri, are two pivotal events that galvanized Black Lives Matter. It was founded by three black women—Patrisse Cullors, Alicia Garza, and Opal Tomett. The organization's slogan and organizing tactics were so successful that it actually broadened to become more than an organization, but also a movement so impactful that scholars have begun writing and studying about its cultural significance. New York University professor Frank Leon Roberts, who created the Black Lives Matter syllabus, explains that there are really two different BLMs—the Black Lives Matter organization with the twenty-four chapters, and then the broader Black Lives Matter movement that is a coalition of a variety of human rights organizations, including the Black Youth Project 100, the Dream Defenders, Assata's Daughters, the St. Louis Action council, Millennial Activists United, and the Organization for Black Struggle (Roberts 2018). Roberts maintains that BLM laid the groundwork that made the success of other movements possible, such as #MeToo and #TimesUp. BLM counts many successes, including exposing police corruption in cities like Baltimore, Chicago, Ferguson, and Cleveland, as well as bringing attention to human rights violations in the enforcement of immigration laws. By signing up for the BLM's e-mail list and/or following them on social media, you can find out when actions and campaigns are happening (https://blacklivesmatter.com).

As we previously addressed false assumptions about whites being unwelcome in NAACP, it is no surprise that similar misinformation abounds regarding the relationship of whiteness to Black Lives Matter. Whites have countered with "all lives matter," not understanding their privileged position, and perhaps blinded by entitlement, assuming that "black lives matter" excludes them. But on the contrary:

a quick Google image search for white allies of Black Lives Matter reveals that any BLM protest march often includes white participants as allies. Alicia Garza, one of the cofounders of BLM, says she is excited to see white allies raising Black Lives Matter flags in front of mostly white schools in Vermont, for example (Yang 2018). While white allies are certainly welcomed in BLM, as discussed in the previous section, it is important that whites participate with humility and with critical reflexivity. All too often, whites have been observed exhibiting duplicitous behavior, which breeds mistrust. For instance, writer Michael Harriot (2017) describes whites who participate in a BLM march or rally, but then fight to defend white privilege in segregated school districts or call the police on black youth who look "suspicious." Some whites may not view their own behavior as duplicitous; they may instead view these as two totally different situations and may have developed a rationale for themselves that explains away the perceived discrepancy. However, such justifications are not consistent with the type of conscious anti-racist practice we outlined in the prior section. Thus, it is whiteness without critical consciousness that is not desired—it is not whiteness wholesale that is rejected.

The twenty-first century organizations like Color of Change and BLM are also much more explicit about the importance of having leadership roles in the hands of people of color than the older organizations like the NAACP and SPLC that have included substantial white leadership. In black-led organizations, whites are expected to humble themselves to that leadership, and they are also expected to step up as leaders, especially in predominantly white settings and communities. In other words, as Harriot outlines, the ideal combination of conscious anti-racist practice would be, if we considered the march/rally space as a "field," whites would walk the walk and talk the talk both on and off the field—but much more so off the field, in spaces where people of color may not be present or heard.

While the four organizations we have covered above are some of the most expansive and best known, there are many other groups working on anti-racist projects and policies. We will discuss three more examples related to education, economy, and criminal justice, respectively, but we encourage you to research the many more options we do not have enough space to comprehensively review here. With respect to education, the Advancement Project is a racial justice organization founded in 1999 that works not only on voting rights, immigration, and criminal justice, but also on "education justice" and the school-to-prison pipeline. Several of the campaigns listed on the website deal with fighting for police-free schools, especially taking the position that having police and guns in schools will not make kids safer and instead will only further target the most vulnerable. The organization also takes a strong stance that having police in schools further contributes to the school-to-prison pipeline for brown and black youth. They also oppose immigration policy enforcement of ICE in schools. The Advancement Project has offices in both Los Angeles and Washington, DC, and uses a combination of lawyers and litigation with social media and direct action campaigns (https://advancementproject.org). This is just one example organization, and there are many other ways to get involved if education is your focus, particularly at your own university and/or your local community.

In terms of economic racial justice, one organization that has existed almost as long as the NAACP is the National Urban League (NUL), founded in 1910. As stated on its website, its mission is to promote "economic empowerment through education and job training, housing and community development, workforce development, entrepreneurship, health, and quality of life" (https://nul.org). The National Urban League's vision is that every person has a job with a living wage and good benefits. Recall in Chapter 3, we reviewed evidence of racial discrimination in employment and how white privilege and homosocial reproduction keeps the best and top positions in the hands of whites. The NUL's job bank system and entrepreneur training attempts to counter that pattern of white privilege by supporting African Americans in their search for employment. In Chapter 3 we also discussed the racial wealth gap, and examined the evidence of how white privilege in home ownership is a major barrier to equality, including discriminatory lending practices. The NUL addresses some of these barriers with this notable goal: "Every American lives in safe, decent, affordable and energy efficient housing on fair terms" (https://nul.org/housing). The NUL cites some of the research we already reviewed in Chapter 3, that the 2008 recession hit African Americans the hardest, especially in terms of home foreclosures, and so it also provides resources to support families trying to stay afloat amidst these inequities. You can support the NUL's work by donating and/or contacting one of its hundreds of local branches and offices because many of the local chapters provide some kind of employment and leadership networking events and opportunities.

The third and final example institution we focus on is criminal justice, and as we have already seen, many of the premier national organizations such as BLM and Color of Change often expose the white privilege and the deadly injustices that happen far too often in this institution. Color of Change has another project called Winning Justice, which lists six demands: ending the cash bail system; stopping kids from being treated as adults; avoiding over-criminalizing low-level offenses; ending secrecy and increasing transparency for prosecutors; stopping the separation of families and criminalization of immigrants; and increasing police accountability (https://www.winningjustice.org). Many times, websites such as these will be running a particular campaign targeting petitions toward a particular jurisdiction, a particular case within that jurisdiction, or even a particular state/governor, encouraging them to act. But also, you can keep track of where your local representatives and candidates stand on these issues and work to support candidates who will champion some of these policies aimed at increasing equality and decreasing white privilege in this institution.

Another criminal justice area to focus on is reentry into society after prison. Recall that a major contention of the "new Jim Crow" argument is that the mark of a criminal record now serves the same "color-blind" function as race once did overtly during legal segregation—such that even after one's sentence has been served, the ability to secure housing, get a job, vote, and many other basic rights continue to be denied. The "Ban the Box" campaign, founded in 2004, is one project aimed at addressing this injustice (http://bantheboxcampaign.org/), and it was organized by a group called All of Us or None, which is a project of the Legal Services for Prisoners with Children organization (https://www.prisonerswithchildren.org/our-projects/allofus-or-none/). Ban the Box refers to removing the question about criminal records from job applications. The National Employment Law Project has published a guide on its website of all the states and municipalities that have passed some version of such laws—they vary in how extensive they are and whether they apply to public and/or private employers (Avery 2019). As far as restoring voting rights, one organization to consider as a resource is the Brennan Center for Justice (https://www.brennancenter.org/issues/restoring-voting-rights). Although these organizations are not primarily defined by racial justice, they are clear that their criminal justice reform advocacy areas are policies that historically and currently have a disproportionately negative impact on racial minorities. The Brennan Center's website provides a state-by-state guide on where the laws stand, as well as how you can get involved in a particular state's efforts to restore rights if they have not already.

Although not always driven by a particular organization, lawmakers will occasionally propose legislation attempting to address white privilege and inequity in criminal justice and other institutions. We have already discussed ending the cash bail system, and ban the box, for example. You can always keep your eye out for federal, state, and local level proposed legislation that impacts these issues and contact your legislators to show your support. Interestingly, the excessive 911 calls discussed in our previous chapter (Chapter 4) have been met with some innovative legislative responses in selected regions of the United States. For example, in June 2019, the Oregon state senate voted by a sizable majority to make it a crime punishable by a $250 fine for callers who make complaints to 911 on people doing everyday tasks, for wasting state resources on the bogus calls. One of the lawmakers who helped introduce the legislation had some personal experience with this—she was an African American candidate knocking on doors and campaigning when white citizens reported her to the police for just doing her job (Associated Press 2019). A similar bill was in consideration by the Grand Rapids, Michigan, city council that would be a human rights ordinance, punishable by a $500 fine for those who "racially profile people of color for participating in their lives" (Holcombe 2019). Measures like these at the very least call attention to how costly and inefficient racism can be, when race is used as an ineffective proxy for actual suspicious behavior. Remember that even everyday citizens can suggest legislation to their elected representatives. You can also enlist some of the organizations listed above, such as Color of Change, to help you start a petition, supporting a policy like this, or any other related measure.

There are many more areas of criminal justice racism to be addressed and many more organizations working on them, and with some research, you can locate more. Likewise, there are other institutions we have not covered as extensively in this chapter where white privilege abounds—such as health care, politics, media—and more anti-racist organizations exist that are also addressing these problems. We hope our brief sampling of some organizations here in this section inspires you to find more and to see there is no shortage of ways to get involved.

Moreover, as this text draws to a close, our aim is that the evidence we have presented here has made it plain that unfortunately, there are few areas of social life not impacted by white privilege. As a construct that has no basis in biology or chemistry, but was constructed by law to serve an economic and political purpose, whiteness has been imbued with a morally outrageous degree of social power. Until that imbalance of power is attacked from every angle by people of conscience, it is likely to continue to exist. Although assembling this preponderance of evidence has been a sobering task, it is our shared belief that our society can do better than it has been doing to ensure racial justice. We hold out the hope that readers like yourself will join in that struggle and encourage others to do likewise.

Real-Life Example

When Good Intentions Aren't Enough

Most analysts of racism agree that anti-racists are in the minority in a continuingly racist society. Those who take the step to walk against that moving walkway of white privilege are rare indeed. Yet white privilege persists even in anti-racist work. Think about how you might interrupt or break the cycle of white privilege if you witnessed each of these situations, or if you were to lead an anti-racist organization, how you might guard against such incidents happening in the first place:

(A) Church XYZ: After clergy of color exit leadership roles due to the denomination's ongoing struggles with racism and white privilege (inability to make diverse hires at high levels), this church that is known in the community (and the nation) for its progressive social justice identity designates an international day of teach-ins during Sunday services about white privilege. Adam attends and notices interesting patterns during an open-mic portion of the service: members of the congregation are patting themselves on the back about one or two things they have done to challenge racism in their own lives and expressing frustration with racism "out there"; others are speaking much more about black disadvantage than they are about white privilege (and with it the assumption that most folks of color are poor/disadvantaged); and still others are bringing up examples of when they felt discriminated against as whites in rare environments such as HBCUs. What might Adam say to lead the congregation to a more reflective examination of its own white privilege when it is his turn to take the mic at this forum?

(B) Carrie is a white, middle-class empty nester, downsized from her suburban home to a small condo after being widowed. A Latina neighbor's young son Tony has been assisting her with various tasks spontaneously in her yard and on her car when she comes outside, so she has begun paying him. As she has gotten to know him, she can't help but notice he does not have the summer camp and extracurricular activities that her now-grown, successful children had when they were his age. So Carrie begins taking him on small "field trips" to the local art museum, planetarium, and zoo with the approval of his mother, who does not have the time or finances to take him herself. These actions make Carrie feel good about the difference she is making in Tony's life. If Carrie were also building authentic relationships in her life with anti-racists of color, what might such a true friend have to say to her about her activities?

(C) Kendall has been quietly and diligently working as an organizer on several race/multicultural-related boards and community groups for many years. Kendall gains credibility in the community and becomes one of several NAACP life-time members in the town, regularly attending meetings. When an opening for NAACP secretary comes up, Kendall becomes one of the NAACP's first white officeholders in the town. Having served as a secretary for several other community groups, Kendall is shocked to find that the local NAACP still hand-writes its minutes and snail mails to members. It does not have a website, e-mail list, or way to file-share information and comment/edit before public release—except by old-fashioned paper means. Kendall gets excited to be able to make a contribution by showing them how to modernize everything—however, to Kendall's surprise, the suggestions are not well taken. What might be going on here? What are some alternative ways to proceed that might gain more traction?

Intersectionality

Micro-affirmations as Anti-racist Practice

Micro-affirmations are defined as small acts in the workplace fostering listening, comfort, support, and inclusion for people who may feel unseen or unwelcome in a given environment (Rowe 2008). These often seemingly small acts can encourage notable differences in institutional environments like the workplace and educational institutions.

Powell, Demetriou, and Fisher (2013) produce a set of tangible actions of distilled micro-affirmations that could be used to challenge and affirm experiences. Some of the actions include affirming emotional reactions and using them to heal and empower and to use active listening through such means as asking clarifying questions, eye contact, and open body positioning. Recognizing and validating experiences is another palpable action which incorporates verbalizing care about the consequence of an event and a readiness to contemplate a fruitful path forward.

As many combat micro-aggressions, micro-insults, micro-assaults and micro-invalidations on a daily basis, how might micro-affirmations be utilized to bring about positive change?

Things to Consider: How can students and educators use micro-affirmations to promote inclusive classrooms through curriculum, inclusive language, and reducing bias against those from minority or disadvantaged groups based on gender, sexual orientation, ability, or religious affiliation? How can employers foster mentoring training that brings awareness and encourages micro-affirmations to counter the difficulties people of color face in their place of employment? Think of three micro-aggressions that may occur in the classroom or work environments and micro-affirmations that could be expressed to provide more compassionate and mindful institutional settings.

Glossary

Active racism: Engaging in active prejudice and/or discrimination in a way that favors whites

Anti-racism in conscious practice: Acknowledging white privilege exists, agrees something should be done about it, and commits to some action(s) working against it. Those actions are also grounded in a reflexive, ongoing process of examining and interrogating one's own position in the social structure and how that position affects the consequences of one's anti-racist practices.

Anti-racism in practice: Acknowledging white privilege exists, agrees something should be done about it, and commits to some action(s) working against it

Anti-racism in theory: Acknowledging white privilege exists and agrees something should be done about it

Anti-racism: Deliberately challenging and working against white advantage

Anti-racist: One who engages in anti-racism as defined above

Assimilation: The process by which a minority group becomes absorbed into the dominant culture and is eventually virtually indistinguishable—melting into the metaphorical melting pot

Authentic relationships: A component of anti-racism in conscious practice—an interracial friendship where the person of color feels free to speak frankly about times when racism and white privilege may be impacting the white friend's anti-racist practice

Aversive racism: Racism without awareness; when individuals state that they are not racially prejudiced but then exhibit racially biased nonverbal and implicit biases in interracial interactions

Color-blind racism: An ideology that "explains contemporary racial inequality as a result of nonracial dynamics" and thus reproduces inequality by way of "practices that are subtle, institutional, and apparently nonracial" (Bonilla-Silva 2014:2–3)

Colorism: The favoring of lighter skin tone over darker skin tone among communities of color; cannot be understood without taking into account the ubiquitous influence of the European colonialist elevation of whiteness and lightness as the preferred and most-prized standard

Concrete ceiling: A small and seemingly impenetrable likelihood of advancing to top positions as compared to their counterparts, even as compared to white women, experienced by people of color

Contact hypothesis: Proposes that individuals' prejudices about a group can decrease with actual contact with members of the group about whom they hold prejudices

Controlling images: Images designed to make racism, sexism, poverty, and other forms of social injustice appear to be natural, normal, and inevitable parts of everyday life

Cultural appropriation: Occurs when members of a dominant culture utilize elements of a minority culture outside of their original cultural context

Cultural racism: The belief in society that one culture holds superiority over another culture and may incorporate stereotypes of those from distinctive ethnic or racial groups than the majority race

Differential policing: As it pertains to employer practices, employers advance white privilege by giving whites a "free pass" to violate policies and procedures without formal sanction

Discrimination: An action that excludes individuals based on perceived racial group membership; it should be noted that the exclusion does not have to include ill will or even prejudice

Dominant group: The group that controls a disproportionately larger share of power and resources and greater life chances (as compared to the subordinated group)

Double consciousness: Refers to how people of color must be keenly aware at all times, for their very survival, of both how they see themselves and how whites view them (Du Bois 1996[1903])

Entitlement: A barrier to anti-racism in conscious practice—white socialization that trains whites to expect to be taught about racism by people of color, which puts an undue burden on an already-stressed population

Ethnicity (or ethnic group): A group that shares a common ancestry and/or cultural practices and heritage

False empathy: An ill-informed form of empathy whereby one envisions oneself in another's shoes but is still bringing one's own perspective without a clear understanding of the other's

Glass ceiling: A small and seemingly impenetrable likelihood of advancing to top positions as compared to their counterparts, experienced by white women, and men and women of color

Homosocial reproduction: preference for others like oneself, especially in socializing and organization forming

Hypersurveillance: Excessive critical attention and monitoring of one's everyday behaviors and environs

Ideology: A belief system aimed at rationalizing and justifying existing social arrangements

Individual discrimination: Acts of discrimination carried out against others as part of individual choices and actions

Inclusion riders: Contractual requirements that would stipulate an assured level of diversity in a production's cast and crew

Institutional discrimination: Discrimination carried out by agents of institutions and/or as implemented by policies that have discriminatory effects

Institutions: "Established and organized systems of social behavior with a particular and recognized purpose" (Andersen and Taylor 2006:4)

Interethnic prejudice: Members of a same "race" making assumptions about an individual of a different ethnicity based on his/her ethnic group membership

Internalized racism: Internalizing wider society's ideology that whiteness is the preferred norm, the standard of beauty, and negatively evaluating oneself and one's own group against that standard

Legalistic fallacy: A way of thinking that erroneously assumes that racism is no longer a major problem in society because there are now laws against it

Maintaining relationships: A component of anti-racism in conscious practice—encourages whites to stay in relationships with other whites and make having ongoing conversations with them about race part of their conscious anti-racist practice

Meritocratic ideology (or myth of meritocracy): Popular myth that everyone has an equal chance of making it to the top, which erroneously assumes that those at the top are the most deserving, and those at the bottom thus must not be working hard enough

Microaggressions: "Brief and commonplace daily verbal, behavioral, and environmental indignities, whether intentional or unintentional, that communicate hostile, derogatory, or negative racial slights and insults to the target person or group" (Sue et al. 2007a:273)

Micro-insult: "A behavioral action or verbal remark that conveys rudeness, insensitivity, or demeans a person's racial identity or heritage" (Sue et al. 2007b:73)

Micro-invalidation: "Actions that exclude, negate or nullify the psychological thoughts, feelings or experiential reality of a person of color" (Sue et al. 2007b:73)

Non-racism: Seeking to distance oneself from the label "racist" while remaining uncritical about the ways racism still exists in everyday life, and not taking any particular action to try to stop white advantage

One-drop rule: A rule dictating that even the slightest bit of African American ancestry means an individual is racially classified as black (based on the erroneous pseudoscience of a drop of blood)

Opportunity hoarding: The process by which those who are already privileged seek to hold onto that advantage for their offspring and others like them

Passing: The practice of performing a different "race" than one might typically be classified as, usually/originally practiced in order to gain privileges assigned to whiteness, especially during legal segregation in the United States

Passive racism: Witnessing an actively racist action, such as a racist joke or discriminatory exclusion, and doing nothing to challenge it

Paternalism: In anti-racism, this amounts to a patronizing attitude on the part of whites that they know better than people of color what should be done and how it should be done

People of color: Subordinated racial groups deemed "not white" by the dominant group in power

Prejudice: An assumption (or presumption) made about an individual (whether deemed "positive" or "negative") based on his or her perceived racial group membership. Because prejudice is socially embedded, so that the dominant/advantaged group in society is the group that people are least likely to hold prejudices about, regardless of their own group identity/membership.

Privileged polemics: Double-standard in anti-racist work where whites' statements about race and racism are considered to be more credible and objective than those of people of color (O'Brien 2001)

Race: A pseudoscientific category that focuses on the surface-level genetic variations of skin color, eye shape, and hair texture among people that the human eye is now trained (by many societies) to see and assign meaning to, making it real as a social construct shaped by legal and political restrictions that shape life chances

Racial formation: The process by which sociopolitical interests shape and reshape what constitutes a race (Omi and Winant 1994)

Racial hoaxes: White people have actually committed crimes and then made up stories about unnamed African Americans in order to get the heat of the investigation away from themselves

Racial profiling: Race, ethnicity or skin color is used as a proxy for suspicion—often to justify a traffic stop or other police surveillance activity

Racism: A system of advantage for the dominant group (whites) in society

Resegregation: The process by which curricular placement or "tracking" creates a segregated environment by classroom within the school walls

School-to-prison pipeline: Increase in using criminal justice resources, policies and practices within the schools to handle classroom management and discipline matters once left solely to the schools

Selective enforcement/discretion: Human decisions whether or not to follow a standard policy or to show mercy/leniency

Stereotype threat: When individuals are told that members of their particular group tend to perform better (or worse) on a test, and then indeed their performance on the test tends to conform up (or down) to those expectations (Steele)

Sticky floor: Low-wage, low-benefit, poor working conditions jobs with no room for advancement that women of color are more concentrated in

Subordinated group: The group that controls a disproportionately smaller share of power and resources and lesser life chances in society (as compared to the dominant group)

Symbolic annihilation: The damage caused by the absence or stifling of a multitude of narratives in media

Symbolic ethnicity: When ethnicity is no longer or not part of an individual's everyday life practices

Thick versus thin ethnicity: A thick ethnicity is ethnicity that is part of an individual's everyday life practices, and ethnicity can range on a continuum of thick to thin, where thin ethnicity is only occasionally part of an individual's daily life practices

White privilege: Unearned advantages that whites experience in a racially stratified society that often go unnoticed or taken for granted by them

References

Abdul-Jabbar, Kareem. 2018. "Kareem Abdul-Jabbar: What Sports Have Taught me About Race in America." *Guardian* (August 28). Retrieved on March 3, 2019, at https://www.theguardian.com/sport/2018/aug/28/notes-from-an-ungrateful-athlete-why-race-and-sports-matter-in-america.

Alexander, Michelle. 2010. *The New Jim Crow: Mass Incarceration in the Age of Colorblindness.* New York: New Press.

Allen, Reniqua. 2019. "The American Dream Isn't for Black Millennials." *New York Times* (January 5). Retrieved on January 23, 2019, at https://www.nytimes.com/2019/01/05/opinion/sunday/american-dream-black-millennials-homeownership.html.

Allen, Theodore W. 1994. *The Invention of the White Race.* Vol. 1, *Racial Oppression and Social Control.* New York: Verso.

Allport, Gordon. 1979 [1954]. *The Nature of Prejudice.* New York: Basic Books.

Andersen, Margaret L., and Howard F. Taylor. 2006. *Sociology: Understanding a Diverse Society.* Belmont, CA: Thompson Wadsworth.

Aptheker, Herbert. 1992. *Anti-Racism in U.S. History: The First Two Hundred Years.* Westport, CT: Greenwood Press.

Associated Press. 2019. "Oregon Bill Cracks Down on Racially Motivated 911 Calls." *NBC News* (June 4). Retrieved on August 4, 2019, at https://www.nbcnews.com/news/nbcblk/oregon-bill-cracks-down-racially-motivated-911-calls-n1013721.h

Avery, Beth. 2019. "Ban The Box: U.S. Cities, Counties, and States Adopt Fair Hiring Policies." National Employment Law Project (July 1). Retrieved on July 27, 2019, at https://www.nelp.org/publication/ban-the-box-fair-chance-hiring-state-and-local-guide/.

Badenhausen, Kurt. 2018. "The World's Richest Sports Team Owners 2018." *Forbes* (March 7). Retrieved on January 27, 2019, at https://www.forbes.com/sites/kurtbadenhausen/2018/03/07/the-worlds-richest-sports-team-owners-2018/#2bab325c4622.

Balibar, Étienne, and Immanuel Wallerstein. 1991. *Race, Nation, Class: Ambiguous Identities.* London: Verso.

Balsam, Kimberly F., Yamile Molina, Blair Beadnell, Jane Simoni, and Karina Walters. 2011. "Measuring Multiple Minority Stress: The LGBT People of Color Microaggressions Scale." *Cultural Diversity and Ethnic Minority Psychology* 17(2):163–74.

Barker, Martin. 1981. *The New Racism.* London: Junction Books.

Barrabi, Thomas. 2019. "Colin Kaepernick and Nike: A Timeline of ex-NFL QB's relationship with Brand." *Fox Business* (July 3). Retrieved on May 5, 2019, at https://www.foxbusiness.com/retail/colin-kaepernick-nike-timeline.

Barndt, Joseph. 1991. *Dismantling Racism.* Minneapolis, MN: Augsburg Books.

Beauboeuf-Lafontant, Tamara. 2009. *Behind the Mask of the Strong Black Woman: Voice and the Embodiment of a Costly Performance.* Philadelphia: Temple University Press.

Beetham, Gwendolyn. 2017. "Addressing Passive Racism in the Academy." *Inside Higher Ed* (August 15). Retrieved on July 27, 2019, at https://www.insidehighered.com/blogs/university-venus/addressing-passive-racism-academy.

Beilock, Sian. 2010. "Closing the Racial Achievement Gap: It's Time to Look Beyond the Classroom." *Psychology Today* (August 27). Retrieved on January 25, 2019, at https://www.psychologytoday.com/us/blog/choke/201008/closing-the-racial-achievement-gap-it-s-time-look-beyond-the-classroom.

Bell, Derrick. 1993. *Faces at the Bottom of the Well: The Permanence of Racism*. New York: Basic Books.

Belluck, Pam. 2019. "N.I.H. Head Calls for End to All-Male Panels of Scientists." *New York Times* (June 12). Retrieved on July 24, 2019, at https://www.nytimes.com/2019/06/12/health/collins-male-science-panels.html.

Bembry, Jerry. 2017. "Nine Black Quarterbacks Will Start in Week 13, but Who Has the Juice?" *Undefeated* (December 1). Retrieved on May 8, 2019, at https://theundefeated.com/features/nfl-nine-black-quarterback-will-start-in-week-13/.

Bernstein, Robin. 2017. "Let Black Kids Just Be Kids." *New York Times* (July 26). Retrieved on January 30, 2019, at https://www.nytimes.com/2017/07/26/opinion/black-kids-discrimination.html.

Bertrand, Marianne, and Sendhil Mullainathan. 2004. "Are Emily and Greg More Employable than Lakisha and Jamal? A Field Experiment in Labor Market Discrimination." *American Economic Review* 94(4):991–1013.

Black Lives Matter. 2019. "Build Power." Black Lives Matter. Retrieved on July 20, 2019, at https://blacklivesmatter.com/about/.

Blaec, Jagger. 2017. "Miley Cyrus' Image Makeover Shows Why Black People Fight for Their Culture." *Medium* (May 8). Retrieved on May 14, 2019, at https://medium.com/the-establishment/miley-cyrus-image-makeover-shows-why-black-people-fight-for-their-culture-ada67f9749b5.

Blauner, Robert. 1994. "Talking Past Each Other: Black and White Languages of Race." Pp. 27–34 in *Race and Ethnic Conflict*, edited by Howard Ehrlich and Fred Pincus, eds. Boulder, CO: Westview Press.

Blue Lives Matter. 2019. "Our Mission." Blue Lives Matter. Retrieved on July 20, 2019, at https://bluelivesmatternyc.org/pages/frontpage.

Boboltz, Sara, and Brennan Williams. 2016. "If You Want To See Diversity Onscreen, Watch Netflix." *Huffington Post* (February 26). Retrieved on July 1, 2019, at https://www.huffpost.com/entry/streaming-sites-diversity_n_56c61240e4b0b40245c96783.

Blumer, Herbert. 1958. "Race Prejudice as a Sense of Group Position." *Pacific Sociological Review* 1:3–7.

Bonilla-Silva, Eduardo. 2004. "From Bi-Racial to Tri-Racial: Towards a New System of Racial Stratification in the USA." *Ethnic and Racial Studies* 27:931–50.

Bonilla-Silva, Eduardo. 2017. *Racism without Racists: Color-Blind Racism and the Persistence of Racial Inequality in America*. Lanham, MD: Rowman & Littlefield.

Bor, Jacob, Atheendar S. Venkataramani, David R. Williams, and Alexander C. Tsai. 2018. "Police Killings and Their Spillover Effects on the Mental Health of Black Americans: A Population-Based, Quasi-Experimental Study." *Lancet* 392(10144):302–10.

Bourdieu, Pierre, and Jean-Claude Passeron. 2014. *Reproduction in Education, Society, and Culture*. London: Sage.

Brent, John J. 2016. "Placing the Criminalization of School Discipline in Economic Context." *Punishment and Society* 18(5):521–43.

Brodkin, Karen. 1998. *How Jews Became White Folks and What That Says About Race in America*. Rutgers, NJ: Rutgers University Press.

Brondolo, Elizabeth, Erica E. Love, Melissa Pencille, Antoinette Schoenthaler, and Gbenga Ogedegbe. 2011. "Racism and Hypertension: A Review of the Empirical Evidence and Implications for Clinical Practice." *American Journal of Hypertension* 24(5):518–29.

Brown, Amy. 2019. "Key Findings on Americans' Views of Race in 2019." Pew Research Center (April 9). Retrieved on July 17, 2019, at https://www.pewresearch.org/fact-tank/2019/04/09/key-findings-on-americans-views-of-race-in-2019/.

Brunsma, David, and Kerry Ann Rockquemore. 2002. "What Does 'Black' Mean? Exploring the Epistemological Stranglehold of Racial Categorization." *Critical Sociology* 28:101–21.

Bryan, Nathaniel. 2017. "White Teachers' Role in Sustaining the School-to-Prison Pipeline: Recommendations for Teacher Education." *Urban Review* 49(2):326–45.

Buncombe, Andrew. 2017. "FBI Considers White Supremacist Groups as Much of a Threat as Isis." *Independent*, September 28. Retrieved on January 17, 2018, at http://www.independent.co.uk/

news/world/americas/fbi-white-nationalists-isis-threat-nazis-alt-right-trump-muslim-groups-terrorism-report-a7972136.html.

Bunker, Nick. 2017. "Recessions, Recoveries, and Racial Employment Gaps in the United States." Washington Center for Equitable Growth (July 19). Retrieved on January 21, 2019, at https://equitablegrowth.org/recessions-recoveries-and-racial-employment-gaps-in-the-united-states/.

Burd-Sharps, Sarah, and Rebecca Rasch. 2015. "Impact of the US Housing Crisis on the Racial Wealth Gap Across Generations." Social Science Research Council (June). Retrieved on January 23, 2019, at https://www.ssrc.org/publications/view/impact-of-the-us-housing-crisis-on-the-racial-wealth-gap-across-generations/.

Bush, Lawson, Hansel Burley, and Tonia Causey-Bush. 2001. "Magnet Schools: Desegregation or Resegregation? Students' Voices From Inside the Walls." *American Secondary Education* 29:33-50.

Byrd, W. Carson. 2017. *Poison in the Ivy: Race Relations and the Reproduction of Inequality on Elite College Campuses*. Rutgers, NJ: Rutgers University Press.

Cajner, Tomaz, Tyler Radler, David Ratner, and Ivan Vidangos. 2017. "Racial Gaps in Labor Market Outcomes in the Last Four Decades and over the Business Cycle." Finance and Economics Discussion Series 2017-071. Washington, DC: Board of Governors of the Federal Reserve System, https://doi.org/10.17016/FEDS.2017.071.

Campt, David W. 2018a. *The White Ally Toolkit Workbook*. Middletown, DE: I AM Publications.

Campt, David W. 2018b. "White Ally Toolkit Overview Video." Retrieved on July 20, 2019, at https://www.youtube.com/watch?v=7ghC-4ldfC8.

Cannon, Ada Rose. 2018. "Help! Someone Has Pointed Out My Conference Has Diversity Issues! How Do I Fix This?" *Medium* (April 16). Retrieved on July 24, 2019, at https://medium.com/samsung-internet-dev/help-someone-has-pointed-out-my-conference-has-diversity-issues-c1162a1e8d4c.

Chambliss, William J. 2000. *Power, Politics, and Crime*. Boulder, CO: Westview Press.

Chang, Man-Huei, Heba Athar, Paula W. Yoon, Michael T. Molla, Benedict I. Truman, and Ramal Moonesinghe. 2013. "State-Specific Healthy Life Expectancy at Age 65 Years—United States, 2007–2009." Centers for Disease Control and Prevention. Retrieved on January 3, 2019, at https://www.cdc.gov/mmwr/preview/mmwrhtml/mm6228a1.htm?s_cid=mm6228a1_w.

Charles, Maria. 2011. "A World of Difference: International Trends in Women's Economic Status." *Annual Review of Sociology* 37:355–62.

Childs, Erica Chito. 2005. *Navigating Interracial Borders: Black-White Couples and Their Social Worlds*. Rutgers, NJ: Rutgers University Press.

Chokshi, Niraj. 2017. "Black People More Likely to Be Wrongfully Convicted of Murder, Study Shows." *New York Times* (March 7). Retrieved on January 31, 2019, at https://www.nytimes.com/2017/03/07/us/wrongful-convictions-race-exoneration.html.

Chokshi, Niraj. 2018. "White Woman Nicknamed 'Permit Patty' Regrets Confrontation Over Black Girl Selling Water." *New York Times* (June 25). Retrieved on May 12, 2019, at https://www.nytimes.com/2018/06/25/us/permit-patty-black-girl-water.html.

Coates, Ta-Nehisi. 2015. *Between the World and Me*. New York: Spiegel & Grau.

Coates, Ta-Nehisi. 2017. *We Were Eight Years in Power: An American Tragedy*. New York: One World.

Cohn, D'Vera. 2014. "Millions of Americans Changed Their Racial or Ethnic Identity from One Census to the Next." Pew Research Center Fact Tank (May 5). Retrieved on February 2, 2018, at http://www.pewresearch.org/fact-tank/2014/05/05/millions-of-americans-changed-their-racial-or-ethnic-identity-from-one-census-to-the-next/.

Colen, Cynthia G., Patrick M. Kreuger, and Bethany L. Boettner. 2018. "Do Rising Tides Lift All Boats? Racial Disparities in Health across the Lifecourse among Middle-Class African-Americans and Whites." *SSM—Population Health* 6:125–35.

Collins, Chuck, Dedrick Asante-Muhammed, Josh Hoxie, and Sabrina Terry. 2019. "Dreams Deferred: How Enriching the 1% Widens the Racial Wealth Divide." Washington, DC: Institute for Policy Studies. Retrieved on January 23, 2019, at https://ips-dc.org/wp-content/uploads/2019/01/IPS_RWD-Report_FINAL-1.15.19.pdf.

Collins, Patricia Hill. 2000. *Black Feminist Thought*. New York: Routledge.

Collins, Patricia Hill. 2005. *Black Sexual Politics: African Americans, Gender and the New Racism*. New York: Routledge.

Conley, Dalton. 2009. *Being Black, Living in the Red: Race, Wealth, and Social Policy in America*. Oakland: University of California Press.

Connley, Courtney. 2018. "Reminder: Today Isn't Equal Pay Day for Black, Latina or Native American Women." CNBC (April 10). Retrieved on January 24, 2019, at https://www.cnbc.com/2018/04/10/today-isnt-equal-pay-day-for-black-latina-or-native-american-women.html.

Constantine, Madonna G., and Derald Wing Sue. 2007. "Perceptions of Racial Microaggressions among Black Supervisees in Cross-Racial Dyads." *Journal of Counseling Psychology* 54(2):142–53.

Cooper, Brittney. 2017. "Why It's Important to Recognize That 'Moonlight' Was Robbed of Its Moment. *Cosmopolitan* (February 27). Retrieved on June 2, 2019, at https://www.cosmopolitan.com/entertainment/movies/a8986489/moonlight-was-robbed-of-its-moment/.

Cose, Ellis. 1994. *Rage of a Privileged Class*. New York: Harper Collins.

Cottom, Tressie McMillan. 2019. "I Was Pregnant and in Crisis. All the Doctors and Nurses Saw Was an Incompetent Black Woman." *Time* (January 8). Retrieved on January 9, 2019, at http://time.com/5494404/tressie-mcmillan-cottom-thick-pregnancy-competent.

Cox, Oliver Cromwell. 1948. *Caste, Class, and Race: A Study in Social Dynamics*. New York: Monthly Review Press.

Crawley, Kayla, and Paul Hirschfield. 2018. "Examining the School-to-Prison Pipeline Metaphor." *Oxford Research Encyclopedia of Criminology*. Retrieved on January 30, 2019, at oxfordre.com/criminology.

Creanga, Andreea, Carla Syverson, Kristi Seed, and William M. Callaghan. 2017. "Pregnancy-Related Mortality in the United States, 2011–2013." *Obstetrics and Gynecology* 130(2):366–73.

Crenshaw, Kimberlé Williams, Neil Gotanda, Gary Peller, and Kendall Thomas. 1995. *Critical Race Theory: The Key Writings that Formed the Movement*. New York: New Press.

Crist, Carolyn. 2018. "Police-involved deaths vary by race and place." Reuters (July 31). Retrieved on January 31, 2019, at https://www.reuters.com/article/us-health-race-police-deaths/police-involved-deaths-vary-by-race-and-place-idUSKBN1KL2M4.

Culotta, Elizabeth. 2012. "Roots of Racism." *Science* 336:825–27.

Czopp, Alexander M. 2008. "When Is A Compliment Not a Compliment? Evaluating Expressions of Positive Stereotypes." *Journal of Experimental Social Psychology* 4:413–20.

Darwin, Charles. 1871. *The Descent of Man and Selection in Relation to Sex*. London: John Murray.

Delgado, Richard. 1996. *The Coming Race War?* New York: New York University Press.

Delpit, Lisa. 2006. *Other People's Children: Cultural Conflict in the Classroom*. New York: New Press.

Demnowicz, C. 2017. "Racism Scale." Retrieved on April 1, 2019, at https://racismscale.weebly.com/.

Demuth, Stephen, and Darrell Steffensmeier. 2004. "The Impact of Gender and Race-Ethnicity in the Pretrial Release Process." *Social Problems* 51(2):222–42.

Desmond, Matthew, and Mustafa Emirbayer. 2010. *Racial Domination, Racial Progress: The Sociology of Race in America*. New York: McGraw-Hill.

Diamond, John B. 2006. "Still Separate and Unequal: Examining Race, Opportunity, and School Achievement." *Journal of Negro Education* 75(3):495–505.

DiAngelo, Robin. 2011. "White Fragility." *International Journal of Critical Pedagogy* 3:54–70.

DiTomaso, Nancy, Rochelle Parks-Yancy, and Corinne Post. 2003. "White Views of Civil Rights: Color Blindness and Equal Opportunity." Pp. 189–98 in *White Out: The Continuing Significance of Racism*, edited by Ashley W. Doane and Eduardo Bonilla-Silva. New York: Routledge.

Douglass, Frederick. 2000 [1857]. "West India Emancipation," speech delivered at Canandaigua, New York, August 4, 1857. P. 457 in *Frederick Douglass: Selected Speeches and Writings*, Vol. 2, edited by Philip S. Foner and Yuva Taylor. Chicago: Chicago Review Press.

Dovidio, John F., Kerry Kawakami, and Samuel L. Gaertner. 2002. "Implicit and Explicit Prejudice and Interracial Interaction." *Journal of Personality and Social Psychology* 82:62–68.

Du Bois, W.E.B. 1996 [1903]. *The Souls of Black Folk*. New York: Penguin.

Du Bois, W.E.B. 2016 [1920]. *Darkwater: Voices within the Veil*. New York: Verso.

DuBois, Cynthia. 2016. "The Impact of 'Soft' Affirmative Action Policies on Minority Hiring in Executive Leadership: The Case of the NFL's Rooney Rule." *American Law and Economics Review* 18: 208–33.

Dunbar, Angel. 2017. "Black Pain, Black Joy, and Racist Fear: Supporting Black Children in a Hostile World." *Psychology Benefits Society*, an APA publication (August 30) Retrieved on January 9, 2019, at https://psychologybenefits.org/2017/08/30/encouraging-black-childrens-self-expression/.

Dwyer, Colin. 2018. "What's An Inclusion Rider? Here's the Story Behind Frances McDormand's Closing Words." NPR (March 5). Retrieved on July 24, 2019, at https://www.npr.org/sections/thetwo-way/2018/03/05/590867132/whats-an-inclusion-rider-here-s-the-story-behind-frances-mcdormand-s-closing-wor.

Dyson, Michael Eric. 2005. *Is Bill Cosby Right?: Or Has the Black Middle Class Lost Its Mind?* New York: Civitas Books.

Dyson, Michael Eric. 2017a. "Why White Americans Don't See Themselves When They Hear the Word 'Race.'" *PBS News Hour*. Retrieved on February 6, 2018, at https://www.pbs.org/newshour/brief/216402/michael-eric-dyson.

Dyson, Michael Eric. 2017b. *Tears We Cannot Stop: A Sermon to White America*. New York: St. Martin's Press.

Edwards, Frank, Michael H. Esposito, and Hedwig Lee. 2018. "Risk of Police-Involved Death by Race/Ethnicity and Place, United States, 2012–2018." *American Journal of Public Health* 108(9): 1241–48.

Eichstedt, Jennifer L. 2001. "Problematic White Identities and a Search for Racial Justice." *Sociological Forum* 16:445–70.

Eligon, John. 2018. "Police Killings Have Harmed Mental Health in Black Communities, Study Finds." *New York Times* (June 21). Retrieved on January 9, 2019, at https://www.nytimes.com/2018/06/21/us/police-shootings-black-mental-health.html.

Espiritu, Yen Le. 1993. *Asian American Panethnicity: Bridging Institutions and Identities*. Philadelphia: Temple University Press.

Essed, Philomena. 1991. *Understanding Everyday Racism: An Interdisciplinary Theory*. Thousand Oaks, CA: Sage.

Evans-Campbell, Teresa. 2008. "Historical Trauma in American Indian/Native Alaska Communities: A Multilevel Framework for Exploring Impacts on Individuals, Families, and Communities." *Journal of Interpersonal Violence* 23(3):316–38.

Fadal, Haweya. 2016. "#Black Lives Matter Goes Global," NBC News, August 11. Retrieved at https://www.nbcnews.com/news/nbcblk/blacklivesmatter-goes-global-n618156 on January 17, 2018.

Fanon, Franz. [1952] 1967. *Black Skin, White Masks*. New York: Grove.

Farmer, Ashley. 2017. "Echoes of the 1960s: SNCC and White Liberal Participation in Anti-Racist Movements." *Black Perspectives* (September 12). Retrieved on January 15, 2018, at http://www.aaihs.org/echoes-of-the-1960s-sncc-and-white-liberal-participation-in-anti-racist-movements/.

Feagin, Joe R. 1991. "The Continuing Significance of Race: Antiblack Discrimination in Public Places." *American Sociological Review* 56(1):101–16.

Feagin, Joe R. 2000. *Racist America: Roots, Current Realities, and Future Reparations*. New York: Routledge.

Feagin, Joe R., and Clairece Booher Feagin. 2010. *Racial and Ethnic Relations*. Upper Saddle River, NJ: Pearson.

Feagin, Joe R., and Karyn D. McKinney. 2005. *The Many Costs of Racism*. Lanham, MD: Rowman & Littlefield.

Feagin, Joe R., and Kimberley Ducey. 2017. *Elite White Men Ruling: Who, What, When, Where and How?* New York: Routledge.

Feagin, Joe R., and Melvin P. Sikes. 1994. *Living with Racism: The Black Middle Class Experience*. Boston: Beacon Press.

Feagin, Joe R., Hernan Vera, and Nikitah Imani. 1996. *The Agony of Education: Black Students at a White University*. New York: Routledge.

Fieldstadt, Elisha. 2019. "Black Man in Hospital Gown with IV Arrested Outside Illinois Hospital for Disorderly Conduct." *NBC News* (July 1). Retrieved on July 12, 2019, at https://www.nbcnews.com/news/us-news/black-man-hospital-gown-iv-arrested-outside-illinois-hospital-disorderly-n1025191.

Forbes, H.D. 1997. *Ethnic Conflict: Commerce, Culture, and the Contact Hypothesis*. New Haven, CT: Yale University Press.

Freedman, Samuel G. 2014. "What Work Remains for the Rooney Rule." *New Yorker* (February 11). Retrieved on March 12, 2019, at https://www.newyorker.com/sports/sporting-scene/what-work-remains-for-the-rooney-rule.

Friedman, Sam, and Daniel Laurison. 2019. *The Class Ceiling: Why It Pays to Be Privileged*. Bristol, UK: Policy Press.

Frost, David M., Keren Lehavot, and Ian H. Meyer. 2013. "Minority Stress and Physical Health among Sexual Minority Individuals." *Journal of Behavioral Medicine* 38(1):1–8.

Gaertner, Samuel L., and John F. Dovidio. 1986. "The Aversive Form of Racism." Pp. 61–89 in *Prejudice, Discrimination, and Racism*, edited by Samuel Gaertner and John Dovidio. San Diego, CA: Academic Press.

Gaertner, Samuel L., and John F. Dovidio. 2005. "Understanding and Addressing Contemporary Racism: From Aversive Racism to the Common Ingroup Identity Model." *Journal of Social Issues* 61 615–39.

Gaertner, Samuel L., John F. Dovidio, Jason Nier, Gordon Hodson, and Melissa A. Houlette. 2005. "Aversive Racism: Bias Without Intention." Pp. 377–93 in *Handbook of Employment Discrimination Research*, edited by Laura Beth Nielsen and Robert Nelson. New York: Springer.

Gans, Herbert. 1979. "Symbolic Ethnicity: The Future of Ethnic Groups and Cultures in America." *Ethnic and Racial Studies* 2:1–20.

Gayle, Damien. 2018. "Structural Racism at Heart of British Society, UN Human Rights Panel Says." *Guardian* (April 27). Retrieved on January 31, 2019, at https://www.theguardian.com/world/2018/apr/27/racism-british-society-minority-ethnic-people-dying-excessive-force.

Geena Davis Institute on Gender in Media. 2019. "The Geena Benchmark Report 2007–2017." Geena Davis Institute on Gender in Media. Retrieved on July 26, 2019, at https://seejane.org/wp-content/uploads/geena-benchmark-report-2007-2017-2-12-19.pdf.

Geiger, Abigail. 2018. "America's Public School Teachers are Far Less Racially and Ethnically Diverse than Their Students." Pew Research Center (August 27). Retrieved on January 28, 2019, at http://www.pewresearch.org/fact-tank/2018/08/27/americas-public-school-teachers-are-far-less-racially-and-ethnically-diverse-than-their-students/.

Genius Media Group Inc. 2009. "Fight the Power." Genius. Retrieved on June 3, 2019, at https://genius.com/40473.

Gerbner, George, and Larry Gross. 1976. "Living with Television: The Violence Profile." *Journal of Communication* 26(2):172–94.

Gilbert, Daniel T., and Patrick S. Malone. 1995. "The Correspondence Bias." *Psychological Bulletin* 117:21–38.

Giroux, Henry A. 1993. "Living Dangerously: Identity Politics and the New Cultural Racism: Towards a Critical Pedagogy of Representation." *Cultural Studies* 7(1):1–27.

Gleeson, Scott. 2018. "Donald Trump: What Was Nike Thinking?" *USA Today* (September 7). Retrieved on April 15, 2019, at https://www.usatoday.com/story/sports/nfl/2018/09/07/donald-trump-nike-colin-kaepernick/1221078002/

Glickman, Lawrence B. 2018. "The Racist Politics of the English Language: How We Went from 'Racist' to 'Racially Tinged.'" *Boston Review* (November 26). Retrieved on December 4, 2018, at https://bostonreview.net/race/lawrence-glickman-racially-tinged.

Gonyea, Don. 2017. "Majority of White Americans Say They Believe Whites Face Discrimination." NPR (October 24). Retrieved on July 17, 2019, at https://www.npr.org/2017/10/24/559604836/majority-of-white-americans-think-theyre-discriminated-against.

Gordon, Milton. 1964. *Assimilation in American Life: The Role of Race, Religion, and National Origins*. New York: Oxford University Press.

Goyette, Braden. 2014. "LA Clippers Owner Donald Sterling's Racist Rant Caught on Tape: Report (UPDATES)." *Huffington Post* (April 29). Retrieved on September 15, 2018, at https://www.huffingtonpost.com/2014/04/26/donald-sterling-racist_n_5218572.html.

Grant, Madison. 1916. *Passing of the Great Race: Or, the Racial Basis of European History*. New York: Charles Scribner and Sons.

Graves, Joseph L. 2015. "Great Is Their Sin: Biological Determinism in the Age of Genomics." *Annals of the American Academy of Political and Social Science* 661:24–50.

Graves, Joseph L., and Michael R. Rose. 2006. "Against Racial Medicine." *Patterns of Prejudice* 40:481–93.

Greear, Jade. 2017. "Objectively Speaking: The Privilege of Whitesplaining." *Huffington Post* (June 20). Retrieved on December 5, 2018, at https://www.huffingtonpost.com/entry/objectively-speaking-the-privilege-of-whitesplaining_us_5949bd76e4b0710bea889a5c.

Greenwald, Anthony G., Debbie E. McGhee, and Jordan L.K. Schwartz. 1998. "Measuring Individual Differences in Implicit Cognition." *Journal of Personality and Social Psychology* 74:1464–80.

Griggs, Brandon. 2018. "Living While Black: Here Are All the Routine Activities for Which Police Were Called on African-Americans This Year." CNN (December 28). Retrieved on March 2, 2019, at https://www.cnn.com/2018/12/20/us/living-while-black-police-calls-trnd/index.html.

Gross, Samuel R., Maurice Possley, and Klara Stephens. 2017. "Race and Wrongful Convictions in the United States." National Registry of Exonerations. Retrieved on January 31, 2019, at http://www.law.umich.edu/special/exoneration/Documents/Race_and_Wrongful_Convictions.pdf.

Hackman, Rose. 2015. "'We Need Co-conspirators, Not Allies': How White Americans Can Fight Racism." *Guardian* (June 26). Retrieved on July 18, 2019, at https://www.theguardian.com/world/2015/jun/26/how-white-americans-can-fight-racism.

Hagerman, Margaret A. 2018. "White Progressive Parents and the Conundrum of Privilege." *Los Angeles Times* (September 30). Retrieved on January 30, 2019, at https://www.latimes.com/opinion/op-ed/la-oe-hagerman-white-parents-20180930-story.html.

Harriot, Michael. 2016. "Taken Without Incident: Why White Criminals End Up Alive." The Root (November 3). Retrieved on January 31, 2019, at https://www.theroot.com/taken-without-incident-why-white-criminals-end-up-aliv-1790857544.

Harriot, Michael. 2017. "It's Official: White Allies Are the Worst Wypipo in the World." The Root (August 3). Retrieved on July 26, 2019, at https://www.theroot.com/it-s-official-white-allies-are-the-worst-wypipo-in-the-1797481427.

Harriot, Michael. 2018. "Jasper Williams and the Stupidity of Respectability." The Root (September 6). Retrieved on December 20, 2018, at https://www.theroot.com/jasper-williams-and-the-stupidity-of-respectability-1828824416.

Hellyer, Isabelle. 2015. "Five Things the Founder of #reclaimthebindi Needs You to Know." *i-D* magazine (April 27). Retrieved on June 4, 2019, at https://i-d.vice.com/en_us/article/nebdjd/five-things-the-founder-of-reclaimthebindi-needs-you-to-know.

Helms, Janet E., ed. 1990. *Black and White Racial Identity: Theory, Research and Practice*. New York: Greenwood.

Herbes-Sommers, Christine. 2003. "Episode One: The Difference between Us." *Race: The Power of an Illusion*. PBS/California Newsreel.

Herreria, Carla. 2019. "NY Middle School Faces Scrutiny After Parents Claim 4 Black Girls Were Strip-Searched." *Huffington Post* (January 26). Retrieved on January 30, 2019, at https://www.huffingtonpost.com/entry/students-strip-searched-new-york_us_5c4d1f70e4b0e1872d4476df.

Hill, Jemele. 2019. "The War on Black Athletes." *Atlantic* (January 13). Retrieved on February 27, 2019, at https://www.theatlantic.com/politics/archive/2019/01/why-trump-targeted-colin-kaepernick/579628.

Holcombe, Madeline. 2019. "It May Soon Be a Crime in Grand Rapids to Call the Police on People of Color for 'Participating in Their Lives.'" CNN (April 25). Retrieved on August 4, 2019, at https://www.cnn.com/2019/04/25/us/grand-rapids-racial-police-calls-trnd/index.html.

hooks, bell. 1981. *Ain't I a Woman: Black Women and Feminism*. Boston: South End Press.

Houts Picca, Leslie, and Joe R. Feagin. 2007. *Two-Faced Racism: Whites in the Backstage and Frontstage*. New York: Routledge.

Howard, Tyrone C. 2013. "How Does It Feel to Be a Problem? Black Male Students, Schools, and Learning in Enhancing the Knowledge Base to Disrupt Deficit Frameworks." *Review of Research in Education* 37:54–86.

Howell, Elizabeth A., Natalia Egorova, Amy Balbierz, Jennifer Zeitlin, and Paul L. Hebert. 2016. "Black-White Differences in Severe Maternal Morbidity and Site of Care." *American Journal of Obstetrics and Gynecology* 214(1):122.e1–122.e7.

Hunt, Darnell, Ana-Christina Ramón, and Michael Tran. 2019. "Hollywood Diversity Report 2019." UCLA Division of Social Sciences. Retrieved on May 30, 2019, at https://socialsciences.ucla.edu/wp-content/uploads/2019/02/UCLA-Hollywood-Diversity-Report-2019-2-21-2019.pdf.

Hunter, Margaret. 2007. "The Persistent Problem of Colorism: Skin Tone, Status, and Inequality." *Sociology Compass* 1:237–54.

Hunter, Margaret L. 2011. "Buying Racial Capital: Skin-Bleaching and Cosmetic Surgery in a Globalized World." *Journal of Pan-African Studies* 4:142–64.

Hwang, Victor. 2000. "The Interrelationship Between Anti-Asian Violence and Asian America." *Chicano-Latino Law Review* 21:17–37.

Ignatiev, Noel. 1995. *How the Irish Became White*. New York: Routledge.

Ignatiev, Noel, and John Garvey. 1996. *Race Traitor*. New York: Routledge.

Implicit Association Test. 2011. Retrieved at https://implicit.harvard.edu/implicit/ on September 14, 2018.

Jackman Mary R., and Marie Crane. 1986. "'Some of My Best Friends Are ... Black': Interracial Friendship and Whites' Racial Attitudes." *Public Opinion Quarterly* 50:459–86.

Jacoby-Senghor, Drew S., Stacey Sinclair, and J. Nicole Shelton. 2016. "A Lesson in Bias: The Relationship between Implicit Racial Bias and Performance in Pedagogical Contexts." *Journal of Experimental Social Psychology* 63:50–55.

Johnson, Maisha Z. 2016. "6 Ways Well-Intentioned People Whitesplain Racism (and Why They Need to Stop)." *Everyday Feminism* (February 7). Retrieved on December 5, 2018, at https://everydayfeminism.com/2016/02/how-people-whitesplain-racism/.

Johnson Jr., Odis, Keon Gilbert, and Habiba Ibrahim. 2018. "Race, Gender, and the Contexts of Unarmed Fatal Interactions with Police." Fatal Interactions with Police Study. Retrieved on January 31, 2019, at https://cpb-us-w2.wpmucdn.com/sites.wustl.edu/dist/b/1205/files/2018/02/Race-Gender-and-Unarmed-1y9md6e.pdf.

Jones, James M., and Robert T. Carter. 1996. "Racism and White Racial Identity: Merging Realities." In *Impacts of Racism on White Americans*, Benjamin P. Bowser and Raymond G. Hunt. Thousand Oaks, CA: Sage.

Kailin, Julie. 2002. *Antiracist Education: From Theory to Practice*. Lanham, MD: Rowman & Littlefield.

Kanter, Rosabeth Moss. 1993. *Women and Men of the Corporation*. 2nd ed. New York: Basic Books.

Karlsen, Saffron, and James Y. Nazroo. 2002. "Relation between Racial Discrimination, Social Class, and Health among Ethnic Minority Groups." *American Journal of Public Health* 92:624–31.

Khazan, Omar. 2018. "Being Black in America Can Be Hazardous to Your Health." *Atlantic* (July/August). Retrieved on January 3, 2019, at https://www.theatlantic.com/magazine/archive/2018/07/being-black-in-america-can-be-hazardous-to-your-health/561740/.

King Jr., Martin Luther. 1963. "Letter from the Birmingham Jail." King Institute. Retrieved on July 19, 2019, at https://kinginstitute.stanford.edu/king-papers/documents/letter-birmingham-jail.

Kochhar, Rakesh, and Anthony Cilluffo. 2017. "How Wealth Inequality Has Changed in the U.S. Since the Great Recession, by Race, Ethnicity and Income." Pew Research Center Fact Tank (November 1). Retrieved at http://www.pewresearch.org/fact-tank/2017/11/01/how-wealth-inequality-has-changed-in-the-u-s-since-the-great-recession-by-race-ethnicity-and-income/ on February 2, 2018.

Kochhar, Rakesh, and Anthony Cilluffo. 2018. "Key Findings on the Rise in Income Inequality within America's Racial and Ethnic Groups." Pew Research Center (July 12). Retrieved on January 22, 2019, at http://www.pewresearch.org/fact-tank/2018/07/12/key-findings-on-the-rise-in-income-inequality-within-americas-racial-and-ethnic-groups/.

Kohli, Rita. 2014. "Unpacking Internalized Racism: Teachers of Color Striving for Racially Just Classrooms." *Race, Ethnicity and Education* 17:367–87.

Kohli, Sonali, and Quartz. 2014. "Modern-Day Segregation in Public Schools." *Atlantic* (November 18). Retrieved on January 25, 2019, at https://www.theatlantic.com/education/archive/2014/11/modern-day-segregation-in-public-schools/382846/.

Korgen, Kathleen. 2002. *Crossing the Racial Divide: Close Friendships Between Black and White Americans*. Greenwood, CT: Praeger.

Kühl, Stefan. 2002. *Nazi Connection: Eugenics, American Racism, and German National Socialism*. Oxford, UK: Oxford University Press.

Lake, Gyasi. 2019. "I Have No Interest in 'White Allies.'" Black Youth Project (March 6). Retrieved on July 18, 2019, at http://blackyouthproject.com/i-have-no-interest-in-white-allies/.

Lapchick, Richard. 2015. "The 2015 Racial and Gender Report Card: National Basketball Association." TIDES: The Institute for Diversity and Ethics in Sport. Retrieved on May 1, 2019, at https://www.tidesport.org/.

Lapchick, Richard. 2019. "The 2018 Racial and Gender Report Card: National Football League." TIDES: The Institute for Diversity and Ethics in Sport. Retrieved on July 24, 2019, at https://www.tidesport.org/.

Larrimore, Mark. 2008. "Antinomies of Race: Diversity and Destiny in Kant." *Patterns of Prejudice* 42:341–63.

Lee, Ashley. 2019. "A Year After Frances McDormand's Oscars Speech, Are Inclusion Riders Making Progress?" *Los Angeles Times* (February 27). Retrieved on March 10, 2019, at https://www.latimes.com/entertainment/la-et-mn-inclusion-riders-oscars-year-later-20190227-story.html.

Legewie, Joscha. 2016. "Racial Profiling and Use of Force in Police Stops: How Local Events Trigger Periods of Increased Discrimination." *American Journal of Sociology* 122(2):379–424.

Leight, Elias. 2014. "Macklemore on Hip Hop & Cultural Appropriation: 'I Need to Know My Place, and That Comes from Me Listening.'" Billboard (December 30). Retrieved on June 15, 2019, at https://www.billboard.com/articles/news/6422361/macklemore-race-hip-hop-cultural-appropriation-hot-97.

Leonard, David. 2017. *Playing While White: Privilege and Power on and off the Field*. Seattle: University of Washington Press.

Levin, Sam. 2018. "Warner Bros to Launch 'Inclusion Rider' Diversity Policy with Michael B Jordan Film." *Guardian* (September 5). Retrieved on July 24, 2019, at https://www.theguardian.com/film/2018/sep/05/warner-bros-adopts-company-wide-inclusion-policy-to-boost-diversity.

Lewis, Amanda E. 2001. "There Is No 'Race' in the Schoolyard: Color-Blind Ideology in an (Almost) All-White School." *American Educational Research Journal* 38(4):781–811.

Lewis, Amanda E. 2003. *Race in the Schoolyard: Negotiating the Color Line in Classrooms and Communities*. Rutgers, NJ: Rutgers University Press.

Lewis, Amanda E., and John B. Diamond. 2015. *Despite the Best Intentions: How Racial Inequality Thrives in Good Schools*. Oxford, UK: Oxford University Press.

Light, Ryan, Vincent J. Roscigno, and Alexandra Kalev. 2011. "Racial Discrimination, Interpretation, and Legitimation at Work." *Annals of the American Academy of Political and Social Sciences* 641:39–59.

Lipsitz, George. 1994. *Dangerous Crossroads: Popular Music, Postmodernism and the Poetics of Place.* New York: Verso.

Lisenby, Ashley. 2018. "Unarmed Black Women Are at Highest Risk when Interacting with Police, Study Finds." St. Louis Public Radio (February 12). Retrieved on January 31, 2019, at http://news.stlpublicradio.org/post/unarmed-black-women-are-highest-risk-when-interacting-police-study-finds#stream/0.

Livingston, Gretchen, and Anna Brown. 2017. "Intermarriage in the U.S. 50 Years After Loving v. Virginia." Pew Research Center Social & Demographic Trends (May 18). Retrieved at http://www.pewsocialtrends.org/2017/05/18/intermarriage-in-the-u-s-50-years-after-loving-v-virginia/ on February 2, 2018.

Loewen, James. 1988. *The Mississippi Chinese: Between Black and White.* Long Grove, IL: Waveland.

Loewus, Liana. 2017. "The Nation's Teaching Force Is Still Mostly White and Female." *Education Week* (August 15). Retrieved on January 28, 2019, at https://www.edweek.org/ew/articles/2017/08/15/the-nations-teaching-force-is-still-mostly.html.

Logan, John R., Elisabeta Minca, and Sinem Adar. "The Geography of Inequality: Why Separate Means Unequal in American Public Schools." *Sociology of Education* 85(3):287–301.

Lott, Eric. 1993. *Love and Theft: Blackface Minstrelsy and the American Working Class.* New York: Oxford University Press.

Lyken-Segosebe, Dawn, and Serena E. Hinz. 2015. "The Politics of Parental Involvement: How Opportunity Hoarding and Prying Shape Educational Opportunity." *Peabody Journal of Education* 90:93–112.

Mallott, Krista M., Scott Schaefle, Tina R. Paone, Jennifer Cates, and Breyan Haizlip. 2019. "Challenges and Coping Mechanisms of Whites Committed to Antiracism." *Journal of Counseling and Development* 97:86–97.

Mathias, Christine. 2017. "The First Abolitionists." *Dissent* (fall). Retrieved on July 18, 2019, at https://www.dissentmagazine.org/article/manisha-sinha-slave-cause-history-abolition-review.

Mathis, Joel. 2019. "Trumpism Is Built on Racism." *The Week* (July 15). Retrieved on July 25, 2019, at https://theweek.com/articles/852693/trumpism-built-racism.

McDougal, Serie, and Sureshi Jayawardene. 2013. "Poll Results: Effects of The Trayvon Martin-George Zimmerman Case on American Thought." Afrometrics (September 7). Retrieved on January 31, 2019, at http://www.afrometrics.org/effects-of-the-trayvon-martin-george-zimmerman-case-on-american-thought.html.

McIntosh, Peggy. 1989. "White Privilege: Unpacking the Invisible Knapsack." *Peace and Freedom* (July/August):10–12.

McIntosh, Peggy. 1990. "White Privilege: Unpacking the Invisible Knapsack." *Independent School* (winter). Retrieved on January 9, 2019, at https://www.racialequitytools.org/resourcefiles/mcintosh.pdf.

McMullin, Julie Ann, and John Cairney. 2004. "Self-Esteem and the Intersection of Age, Class, and Gender." *Journal of Aging Studies* 18:75–90.

McTaggart, Ninochka, and Eileen O'Brien. 2014. "Glass Ceiling/Bamboo Ceiling." Pp. 408–10 in *Asian American Society: An Encyclopedia*, edited by Mary Yu Danico. Thousand Oaks, CA: Sage.

Merton, Robert K. 1949. "Discrimination and the American Creed." Pp. 99–126 in *Discrimination and National Welfare*, edited by Robert M. MacIver. New York: Institute for Religious Studies.

Mesic, Aldina,, Lydia Franklin, Alev Cansever, Fiona Potter, Anika Sharma, Anita Knopov, and Michael Siegel. 2018. "The Relationship Between Structural Racism and Black-White Disparities in Fatal Police Shootings at the State Level." *Journal of the National Medical Association* 110:106-116.

Mickelson, Roslyn Arlin. 2001. "Subverting Swann: First- and Second-Generation Segregation in the Charlotte-Mecklenburg Schools." *American Educational Research Journal* 38:215-252.

Mock, Brentin. 2018. "How Structural Racism Is Linked to Higher Rates of Police Violence." City Lab (February 15). Retrieved on January 31, 2019, at https://www.citylab.com/equity/2018/02/the-role-of-structural-racism-in-police-violence/553340/.

Moore, Matthew. 2019. "Children of Doctors and Lawyers Get a Leg-Up to Top Jobs." *Sunday Times* (January 26). Retrieved on January 27, 2019, at https://www.thetimes.co.uk/article/children-of-doctors-and-lawyers-get-leg-up-as-elite-hoard-top-jobs-rr3v6zncm.

Moore, Suzanne. 2017. "The Oscars Mix-up Matters because This Night Was Always about Racial Bias." *Guardian* (February 27). Retrieved on June 1, 2019, at https://www.theguardian.com/commentisfree/2017/feb/27/oscars-mix-up-matters-racial-bias.

Moreno, Carolina, and Riley Arthur. 2016. "25 Times White Actors Played People of Color and No One Really Gave a St." *Huffington Post* (February 27). Retrieved June 2, 2019, at https://www.huffpost.com/entry/26-times-white-actors-played-people-of-color-and-no-one-really-gave-a-sht_n_56cf57e2e4b0bf0dab313ffc.

Muhammad, Khalil Gibran. 2019. "Op-Ed: When Will Hollywood Confront Its Blackface Legacy?" *Los Angeles Times* (February 24). Retrieved on May 14, 2019, at https://www.latimes.com/opinion/op-ed/la-oe-muhammad-blackface-northam-oscars-20190224-story.html.

Mullainathan, Sendhil. 2015a. "Police Killings of Blacks: Here Is What the Data Say." *New York Times* (October 16). Retrieved on January 31, 2019, at https://www.nytimes.com/2015/10/18/upshot/police-killings-of-blacks-what-the-data-says.html.

Mullainathan, Sendhil. 2015b. "Racial Bias, Even When We Have Good Intentions." *New York Times* (January 3). Retrieved on January 25, 2019, at https://www.nytimes.com/2015/01/04/upshot/the-measuring-sticks-of-racial-bias-.html.

Mullan, Brendan P. 2017. "The Sociology of Inequality and the Rise of Neo-Inequality." *Sociological Focus* 50(2):105–24.

Mulligan, Thomas S., and Chris Kraul. 1996. "Texaco Settles Race Bias Suit for $176 Million." *Los Angeles Times* (November 16). Retrieved on September 15, 2018, at http://articles.latimes.com/1996-11-16/news/mn-65290_1_texaco-settles-race-bias-suit.

Neal, La Vonne I., Audrey Davis McCray, Gwendolyn Webb-Johnson, and Scott T. Bridgest. 2003. "The Effects of African American Movement Styles on Teachers' Perceptions and Reactions." *Journal of Special Education* 37(1):49–57.

Neuman, Scott. 2018. "Men Arrested in Philadelphia Starbucks Reach Settlements." National Public Radio (May 3). Retrieved on July 27, 2019, at https://www.npr.org/sections/thetwo-way/2018/05/03/607973546/men-arrested-in-philadelphia-starbucks-reach-settlements.

Neville, Conor, and Phyllis Anastasio. 2019. "Fewer, Younger, but Increasingly Powerful: How Portrayals of Women, Age, and Power Have Changed from 2002 to 2016 in the 50 Top-Grossing U.S. Films." *Sex Roles* 80:503–14.

Newheiser, Anna-Kaisa, and Kristina R. Olson. 2012. "White and Black American Children's Implicit Intergroup Bias." *Journal of Experimental Social Psychology* 48:264–70.

Nittle, Nadra Kareem. 2019. "A Guide to Understanding and Avoiding Cultural Appropriation." *Thought Co.* (July 3). Retrieved on July 12, 2018, at https://www.thoughtco.com/cultural-appropriation-and-why-iits-wrong-2834561.

Nunnally, Shayla C. 2009. "Racial Homogenization and Stereotypes: Black American College Students' Stereotypes about Racial Groups." *Journal of Black Studies* 40:252–65.

O'Brien, Eileen. 2001. *Whites Confront Racism: Antiracists and Their Paths to Action*. Lanham, MD: Rowman & Littlefield.

O'Brien, Eileen. 2003. "The Political Is Personal: The Influence of White Supremacy on White Antiracists' Personal Relationships." Pp. 253–70 in *White Out: The Continuing Significance of Racism*. New York: Routledge.

O'Brien, Eileen. 2008. *The Racial Middle: Latinos and Asian Americans Living Beyond the Racial Divide*. New York: NYU Press.

O'Brien, Eileen, and Kathleen Korgen. 2007. "It's the Message, Not the Messenger: The Declining Significance of Black-White Contact." *Sociological Inquiry* 77:356–82.

O'Brien, Eileen, and Janis Prince. 2015. "Racial Framing of Trayvon Martin and George Zimmerman in *Tampa Bay Tribune* Letters to Editor, 2012–2013." Annual meeting of the Florida College English Association, St. Petersburg, FL. October 8.

Oliver, Melvin, and Thomas Shapiro. 2006. *Black Wealth/White Wealth: A New Perspective on Racial Inequality*. New York: Routledge.

Omi, Michael A. 2001. "The Changing Meaning of Race." Pp. 243–63 in *America Becoming: Racial Trends and Their Consequences*, Volume 1, edited by Neil J. Smelser, William Julius Wilson, and Faith Mitchell. Washington, DC: National Academy of Sciences Press.

Omi, Michael, and Howard Winant. 1994. *Racial Formation in the United States: From the 1960s to the 1980s*. 2nd ed. New York: Routledge.

Ong, Anthony D., Anthony L. Burrow, Thomas E. Fuller-Rowell, Nicole M. Ja, and Derald W. Sue. 2013. "Racial Microaggressions and Daily Well-Being among Asian Americans." *Journal of Counseling Psychology* 60(2):188–99.

Pager, Devah. 2003. "The Mark of a Criminal Record." *American Journal of Sociology* 108(5):937–75.

Pager, Devah, and Lincoln Quillian. 2005. "Walking the Talk? What Employers Say versus What They Do." *American Sociological Review* 70(3):355–80.

Pager, Devah, Bruce Western, and Bart Bonikowski. 2009. "Discrimination in a Low-Wage Labor Market: A Field Experiment." *American Sociological Review* 74(5):777–99.

Park, Madison. 2018. "Police Shootings: Trials, Convictions Are Rare for Officers." CNN (October 3). Retrieved on January 31, 2019, at https://www.cnn.com/2017/05/18/us/police-involved-shooting-cases/index.html.

Patten, Eileen. 2016. "Racial, Gender Wage Gaps Persist in U.S. Despite Some Progress." Pew Research Center (July 1). Retrieved on January 24, 2019, at http://www.pewresearch.org/fact-tank/2016/07/01/racial-gender-wage-gaps-persist-in-u-s-despite-some-progress/.

Pierce, Chester. 1970. "Offensive Mechanisms." Pp. 265-282 in The Black Seventies, edited by Floyd B. Barbour. Boston, MA: Porter Sargent.

Pincus, Fred L. 2002. "The Social Construction of Reverse Discrimination: The Impact of Affirmative Action on Whites." *Journal of Intergroup Relations* 28:33–44.

Pincus, Fred L. 2011. *Understanding Diversity: An Introduction to Class, Race, Gender, Sexual Orientation and Disability*. Boulder, CO: Lynne Reinner.

Pintchman, Tracy. 2007. *Women's Lives, Women's Rituals in the Hindu Tradition*. New York: Oxford University Press.

Powell, Rebecca. 2000. "Overcoming Cultural Racism: The Promise of Multicultural Education." *Multicultural Perspectives* 2(3):8–14.

Powell, Candice, Cynthia Demetriou, and Annice Fisher. 2013. "Micro-affirmations in Academic Advising: Small Acts, Big Impact." *Mentor: An Academic Advising Journal*. 15:1.

Pyke, Karen. 2010. "What Is Internalized Racial Oppression and Why Don't We Study It? Acknowledging Racism's Hidden Injuries." *Sociological Perspectives* 53:551–72.

Qian, Zhenchau. 2005. "Breaking the Last Taboo: Interracial Marriage in America." *Contexts* 4:33–37.

Quigley, Bill. 2010. "Fourteen Examples of Racism in Criminal Justice System." *Huffington Post* (July 26). Retrieved on January 30, 2019, at https://www.huffingtonpost.com/bill-quigley/fourteen-examples-of-raci_b_658947.html.

Randolph, Antonia. 2012. *The Wrong Kind of Different: Challenging the Meaning of Diversity in American Classrooms*. New York: Teachers College Press.

Rankin, Claudia. 2019. "I Wanted to Know What White Men Thought about Their Privilege. So I Asked." *New York Times* (July 17). Retrieved on July 21, 2019, at https://www.nytimes.com/2019/07/17/magazine/white-men-privilege.html.

Ray, Victor. 2019. "A Theory of Racialized Organizations." *American Sociological Review* (Online First).

Reign, April. 2018. "#OscarsSoWhite Is Still Relevant This Year." *Vanity Fair* (March 2). Retrieved June 13, 2019, at https://www.vanityfair.com/hollywood/2018/03/oscarssowhite-is-still-relevant-this-year.

Roberts, Frank Leon. 2018. "How Black Lives Matter Changed the Way Americans Fight for Freedom." ACLU (July 13). Retrieved on July 26, 2019, at https://www.aclu.org/blog/racial-justice/race-and-criminal-justice/how-black-lives-matter-changed-way-americans-fight.

Rockquemore, Kerry Ann. 2002. "Negotiating the Color Line: The Gendered Process of Racial Identity Construction among Black/White Biracial Women." *Gender and Society* 16:485–503.

Roda, Allison, and Amy Stuart Wells. 2013. "School Choice Policies and Racial Segregation: Where White Parents' Good Intentions, Anxiety, and Privilege Collide." *American Journal of Education* 119(2):261–93.

Rodriguez, Clara. 2000. *Changing Race: Latinos, the Census and the History of Ethnicity*. New York: NYU Press.

Roediger, David R. 1991. *The Wages of Whiteness: Race and the Making of the American Working Class*. New York: Verso.

Roediger, David. 1999. *Black on White: Black Writers on What It Means to Be White*. New York: Schocken.

Rogers, Richard. 2006. "From Cultural Exchange to Transculturation: A Review and Reconceptualisation of Cultural Appropriation." *Communication Theory* 16(4):474–503.

Rollock, Nicola. 2014. "The 'Racism Talk': How Black Middle-Class Parents Are Warning Their Children." The Conversation (October 27). Retrieved on January 9, 2019, at https://theconversation.com/the-racism-talk-how-black-middle-class-parents-are-warning-their-children-33221.

Rollock, Nicola, David Gillborn, Carol Vincent, and Stephen J. Ball. 2015. *The Colour of Class: The Educational Strategies of the Black Middle Classes*. London: Routledge.

Roscigno, Vincent J. 2007. *The Face of Discrimination: How Race and Sex Impact Work and Home Lives*. Lanham, MD: Rowman & Littlefield.

Rosenberg, Alana, Allison K. Groves, and Kim M. Blankenship. 2017. "Comparing Black and White Drug Offenders: Implications for Racial Disparities in Criminal Justice and Reentry Policy and Programming." *Journal of Drug Issues* 47(1):132–42.

Ross, Paula T., Monica L. Lypson, and Arno K. Kumagai. 2012. "Using Illness Narratives to Explore African American Perspectives of Racial Discrimination in Health Care." *Journal of Black Studies* 43(5):520–44.

Rowe, Mary. 2008. "Micro-affirmations & Micro-inequities." *Journal of the International Ombudsman Association* 1:45-48.

Royster, Deirdre. 2003. *Race and the Invisible Hand: How White Networks Exclude Black Men from Blue-Collar Jobs*. Oakland: University of California Press.

Rugh, Jacob S., and Douglas S. Massey. 2010. "Racial Segregation and the American Foreclosure Crisis." *American Sociological Review* 75(5):629–51.

Russell, Jonathan. 2016. "Here's What's Wrong with #BlueLivesMatter." *Huffington Post* (July 9). Retrieved on July 15, 2019, at https://www.huffpost.com/entry/heres-whats-wrong-with-bl_b_10906348.

Russell-Brown, Katheryn. 2008. The Color of Crime: Racial Hoaxes, White Fear, Black Protectionism, Police Harassment, and Other Macroaggressions. 2nd ed. New York: NYU Press.

Ryan, James. 2003. "Educational Administrators' Perceptions of Racism in Diverse School Contexts." *Race, Ethnicity and Education* 6(2):145–64.

Saporito, Salvatore, and Deenesh Sohoni. 2006. "Coloring Outside the Lines: Racial Segregation in Public Schools and Their Attendance Boundaries." *Sociology of Education* 79:81–105.

Scafidi, Susan. 2005. *Who Owns Culture? Appropriation and Authenticity in American Law (Rutgers Series: The Public Life of the Arts)*. New Brunswick, NJ: Rutgers University Press.

Schaefer, Brian P., and Peter B. Kraska. 2012. "Felon Disenfranchisement: The Judiciary's Role in Renegotiating Racial Divisions." *Race and Justice* 2(4):304–21.

Schlesinger, Traci. 2005. "Racial and Ethnic Disparity in Pretrial Criminal Processing." *Justice Quarterly* 22(2):170–92.

Schneider, Arnd. 2003. "On 'Appropriation': A Critical Reappraisal of the Concept and Its Application in Global Art Practices." *Social Anthropology* 11(2):215–29.

Schuman, Howard, Charlotte Steeh, Lawrence Bobo, and Maria Krysan. 1997. *Racial Attitudes in America: Trends and Interpretations*. Cambridge, MA: Harvard University Press.

Schwartzman, Luisa Farah. 2007. "Does Money Whiten? Intergenerational Changes in Racial Classification in Brazil." *American Sociological Review* 72:940–63.

Scott, Deena Isum. 2017. "The New Juan Crow?: Unpacking the Links Between Discrimination and Crime for Latinxs." *Race and Justice* (online first).

Seidman, Gay. 1999. "Is South Africa Different? Sociological Comparisons and Theoretical Contributions from the Land of Apartheid." *Annual Review of Sociology* 25:419–40.

Selod, Saher. 2018. *Forever Suspect: Racialized Surveillance of Muslim Americans in the War on Terror*. Rutgers, NJ: Rutgers University Press.

Shafer, Jack. 2019. "How Trump Changed After Charlottesville." *Politico* (July 18). Retrieved on July 23, 2019, at https://www.politico.com/magazine/story/2019/07/18/donald-trump-racist-rally-227408.

Simons, Meredith. 2016. "100 Times A White Actor Played Someone Who Wasn't White." *Washington Post* (January 28). Retrieved on May 14, 2019, at https://www.washingtonpost.com/posteverything/wp/2016/01/28/100-times-a-white-actor-played-someone-who-wasnt-white/.

Sigelman, Lee, and Susan Welch. 1993. "The Contact Hypothesis Revisited: Black-White Interaction and Positive Racial Attitudes." *Social Forces* 71(3):781–95.

Smith, Llewelyn. 2003. "Episode Three: The House We Live In." *Race: The Power of an Illusion*. PBS/California Newsreel.

Smith, Robert J., and Justin D. Levinson. 2011. "The Impact of Implicit Racial Bias on the Exercise of Prosecutorial Discretion." *Seattle Law Review* 35:795–826.

Smith, Stacy L. 2014. "Hey, Hollywood: It's Time to Adopt the NFL's Rooney Rule—for Women." *Hollywood Reporter* (December 15). Retrieved on May 28, 2019, at https://www.hollywoodreporter.com/news/hey-hollywood-time-adopt-nfls-754659.

Smith, Stacy L., Marc Choueti, Katherine Piper, Ariana Case, and Angel Choi. 2018. "Inequality in 1,100 Popular Films: Examining Portrayals of Gender, Race/Ethnicity, LGBT & Disability from 2007 to 2017." USC Annenberg Inclusion Initiative.

Smith, William A., Man Hung, and Jeremy D. Franklin. 2011. "Racial Battle Fatigue and the MisEducation of Black Men: Racial Microaggressions, Societal Problems, and Environmental Stress." *Journal of Negro Education* 80(1):63–82.

Sonnad, Nikhil. 2018. "The NFL's Racial Divide in One Chart" *Quartz* (May 24). Retrieved on May 13, 2019, at https://qz.com/1287915/the-nfls-racial-makeup-explains-much-of-its-national-anthem-problems/.

Spencer, Karen Lutfey, and Matthew Grace. 2016. "Social Foundations of Health Care Inequality and Treatment Bias." *Annual Review of Sociology* 42:101–20.

Spencer, Katherine B., Amanda K. Charbonneau, and Jack Glaser. 2016. "Implicit Bias and Policing." *Social and Personality Psychology Compass* 10/1:50–63.

Spencer, Steven J., Claude M. Steele, and Diane M. Quinn. 1999. "Stereotype Threat and Women's Math Performance." *Journal of Experimental Social Psychology* 35:4–28.

Steele, Claude. 1997. "A Threat in the Air: How Stereotypes Shape Intellectual Identity and Performance." *American Psychologist* 52:613–29.

Steele, Claude, and Joshua Aronson. 1995. "Stereotype Threat and the Intellectual Test Performance of African Americans." *Journal of Personality and Social Psychology* 69:797–811.

Stokes, Melvyn. 2007. *D.W. Griffith's The Birth of a Nation: A History of "the Most Controversial Motion Picture of All Time."* Oxford, UK: Oxford University Press.

Stringer, Chris. 2003. "Out of Ethiopia." *Nature* 423:692–694.

Sue, Derald Wing. 2010. *Microaggressions in Everyday Life: Race, Gender and Sexual Orientation*. Hoboken, NJ: Wiley.

Sue, Derald Wing, Christina M. Capodilupo, and Aisha M.B. Holder. 2008. "Racial Microaggressions in the Life Experience of Black Americans." *Professional Psychology: Research and Practice* 39(3):329–36.

Sue, Derald Wing, Christina M. Capodilupo, Gina C. Torino, Jennifer M. Bucceri, Aisha Holder, Kevin L. Nadal, and Marta Esquilin. 2007a. "Racial Microaggressions in Everyday Life: Implications for Clinical Practice." *American Psychologist* 62(4):271–86.

Sue, Derald Wing, Jennifer Bucceri, Annie I. Lin, Kevin L. Nadal, and Gina C. Torino. 2007b. "Racial Microaggressions and the Asian American Experience." *Cultural Diversity and Ethnic Minority Psychology* 13(1):72–81.

Takaki, Ronald. 2008. *A Different Mirror: A History of Multicultural America*. New York: Back Bay.

Taparata, Evan. 2016. "The U.S. Has Come a Long Way Since Its First, Highly Restrictive Immigration Law." Public Radio International (July 4). Retrieved at https://www.pri.org/stories/2016-07-04/us-has-come-long-way-its-first-highly-restrictive-naturalization-law on January 29, 2018.

Tatum, Beverly Daniel. 1994. "Teaching White Students about Racism: The Search for White Allies and Restoration of Hope." *Teachers College Record* 95:462–76.

Tatum, Beverly Daniel. 2017. *Why Are All the Black Kids Sitting Together in the Cafeteria? And Other Conversations About Race*. 20th anniversary ed. New York: Basic Books.

Taylor, Jessica July 26, 2019. "Supreme Court Lets Trump Border Wall Move Forward, but Legal Fight Still Looms." National Public Radio (July 26). Retrieved on July 28, 2019, at https://www.npr.org/2019/07/26/745785115/supreme-court-lets-trump-border-wall-move-forward-but-legal-fight-still-looms .

Thompson, Brian. 2018. "The Racial Wealth Gap: Addressing America's Most Pressing Epidemic." *Forbes* (February 18). Retrieved on January 22, 2019, at https://www.forbes.com/sites/brianthompson1/2018/02/18/the-racial-wealth-gap-addressing-americas-most-pressing-epidemic/#6571ae537a48.

Thompson, Martha E., and Michael Armato. 2012. *Investigating Gender: Developing a Feminist Sociological Imagination*. Boston: Polity Press.

Thompson, Maxine S., and Verna M. Keith. 2001. "The Blacker the Berry: Gender, Skin Tone, Self-Esteem, and Self-Efficacy." *Gender and Society* 15:336–57.

Thornhill, Ted. 2018. "We Want Black Students, Just Not You: How White Admissions Counselors Screen Black Prospective Students." *Sociology of Race and Ethnicity* 1–15.

Tilly, Charles. 1998. Durable Inequality. Berkeley: University of California Press.

Tomaskovic-Devey, Donald, Marcinda Mason, and Matthew Zingraff. 2004. "Looking for the Driving While Black Phenomena: Conceptualizing Racial Bias Processes and Their Associated Distributions." *Police Quarterly* 7(1):3–29.

Torres, Lucas, and Joelle T. Taknint. 2015. "Ethnic Microaggressions, Traumatic Stress Symptoms, and Latino Depression: A Moderated Mediational Model." *Journal of Counseling Psychology* 62(3): 393–401.

Tuan, Mia. 1999. *Forever Foreigners or Honorary Whites?: The Asian Ethnic Experience Today*. Rutgers, NJ: Rutgers University Press.

Ture, Kwame, and Charles Hamilton. [1967] 1992. *Black Power: The Politics of Liberation*. New York: Vintage.

UNESCO. 1950. *The Race Question*. Paris, France: UNESCO.

U.S. Bureau of the Census. 2017. "Educational Attainment in the United States: 2016." Retrieved on January 25, 2019, at https://www.census.gov//data/tables/2016/demo/education-attainment/cps-detailed-tables.html .

Valencia, Richard. 2002. "'Mexican Americans Don't Value Education!' On the Basis of the Myth, Mythmaking, and Debunking." *Journal of Latinos and Education* 1(2):81–103.

Van Ryn, Michelle, and Steven S. Fu. 2003. "Paved with Good Intentions: Do Public Health and Human Service Providers Contribute to Racial/Ethnic Disparities in Health?" *American Journal of Public Health* 93:248–55.

Vasquez, Jessica. 2011. *Mexican Americans Across Generations: Immigrant Families, Racial Realities*. New York: NYU Press.

Vasquez-Tokos, Jessica. 2017. *Marriage Vows and Racial Choices*. New York: Russell Sage Foundation.

Vera, Amir. 2018. "How National Anthem Protests Took Colin Kaepernick from Star QB to Unemployment to a Bold Nike Ad." *CNN* (September 4). Retrieved on May 1, 2019, at https://www.cnn.com/2018/09/04/us/colin-kaepernick-controversy-q-and-a/index.html.

Walters, Pamela Barnhouse. 2001. "Educational Access and the State: Historical Continuities and Discontinuities in Racial Inequality in American Education." *Sociology of Education* 74:35–49.

Warner, Judith, and Danielle Corley. 2017. "The Women's Leadership Gap: Women's Leadership by the Numbers." Center for American Progress (May 21) Retrieved on March 24, 2018, at https://www.americanprogress.org/issues/women/reports/2017/05/21/432758/womens-leadership-gap/.

Warren Patricia, Donald Tomaskovic-Devey, William Smith, Matthew Zingraff, and Marcinda Mason. 2006. "Driving While Black: Bias Processes and Racial Disparity in Police Stops." *Criminology* 44(3):709–38.

Warren, Jonathan W., and France Winddance Twine. 1997. "White Americans, the New Minority?: Non-Blacks and the Ever-Expanding Boundaries of Whiteness." *Journal of Black Studies* 28:200–218.

Waters, Mary C. 1990. *Ethnic Options: Choosing Identities in America*. Berkeley: University of California Press.

Watts, Charlotte, and Cathy Zimmerman. 2002. "Violence against Women: Global Scope and Magnitude." *Lancet* 359:1232–37.

White, Gillian B. 2015. "The Recession's Racial Slant." *Atlantic* (June 24). Retrieved on January 23, 2019, at https://www.theatlantic.com/business/archive/2015/06/black-recession-housing-race/396725/.

White, Gillian B. 2017. "There Are Currently 4 Black CEOs in the Fortune 500." *Atlantic* (October 26). Retrieved on March 24, 2018, at https://www.theatlantic.com/business/archive/2017/10/black-ceos-fortune-500/543960/.

Wilf, Rachel. 2012. "Disparities in School Discipline Move Students of Color Toward Prison." *Center for American Progress* (March 13). Retrieved on January 30, 2019, at https://www.americanprogress.org/issues/race/news/2012/03/13/11350/disparities-in-school-discipline-move-students-of-color-toward-prison/.

Williams, Stereo. 2017. "The Truth About Elvis and the History of Racism in Rock." *Daily Beast* (July 12). Retrieved on July 2, 2019, at https://www.thedailybeast.com/the-truth-about-elvis-and-the-history-of-racism-in-rock.

Williams, David R., and Ruth Williams-Morris. 2000. "Racism and Mental Health: The African American Experience." *Ethnicity and Health* 5:243–68.

Wise, Tim. 2004. *White Like Me: Reflections on Race from a Privileged Son*. New York: Soft Skull Press.

Witzig, Ritchie. 1996. "The Medicalization of Race: Scientific Legitimization of a Flawed Social Construct." *Annals of Internal Medicine* 125:675–79.

Wren, Karen. 2001. "Cultural Racism: Something Rotten in the State of Denmark?" *Social and Cultural Geography* 2(2):141–62.

Wright, Matthew. 2018. "'These Nicknames Make Dangerous People Seem Cute': Twitter Blasts Using Nicknames Such as Permit Patty and BBQ Becky Because It 'Shields Racist White Women from the Consequences They Should Face for Putting Black Lives in Danger.'" *Daily Mail* (October 20). Retrieved on May 10, 2019, at https://www.dailymail.co.uk/news/article-6298459/Twitter-blasts-nicknames-Permit-Patty-BBQ-Becky-shields-racist-white-women.html.

Wun, Connie. 2016. "Unaccounted Foundations: Black Girls, Anti-Black Racism, and Punishment in Schools." *Critical Sociology* 42(4–5):737–50.

Wyche, Steve. 2016. "Colin Kaepernick Explains Why He Sat During National Anthem." National Football League (August 27). Retrieved on April 16, 2019, at http://www.nfl.com/news/story/0ap3000000691077/article/colin-kaepernick-explains-why-he-sat-during-national-anthem.

X, Malcolm. 1992 [1964]. *The Autobiography of Malcolm X*. New York: Penguin.

Yan, Holly. 2018. "Yale Student Accused of 'Napping While Black' Wants Fellow Student Disciplined." *CNN* (May 14). Retrieved on May 1, 2019, at https://www.cnn.com/2018/05/14/us/yale-black-grad-student-interview/index.html.

Yancey, George. 2003. *Who Is White?: Latinos, Asians, and the New Black/Nonblack Divide.* Boulder, CO: Lynne Rienner.

Yang, Linda. 2018. "How to Be an Ally, According to Black Lives Matter Co-Founder Alicia Garza." *Vice* (February 20). Retrieved on July 26, 2019, at https://www.vice.com/en_us/article/zmwqv8/co-founder-alicia-garza-shares-future-plans-for-black-lives-matter.

Yglesias, Matthew. 2019. "Trump's Racist Tirades Against 'the Squad.'" *Vox* (July 18). Retrieved on July 26, 2019, at https://www.vox.com/2019/7/15/20694616/donald-trump-racist-tweets-omar-aoc-tlaib-pressley.

Yoo, Hyung Choi, Gilbert C. Geeb, and David Takeuchic. 2009. "Discrimination and Health among Asian American Immigrants: Disentangling Racial from Language Discrimination." *Social Science and Medicine* 68(4):726–32.

Zarya, Valentina. 2015. "Women-Owned Businesses Are Trailing in Size and Revenue." *Forbes* (September 2). Retrieved on January 27, 2019, at http://fortune.com/2015/09/02/women-business-size-revenue/.

Zhao, Christina. 2018. "'BBQ Becky, White Woman Who Called Cops in Black BBQ, 911 Audio Released: 'I'm Really Scared! Come Quick!'" *Newsweek* (September 4). Retrieved on July 15, 2019, at https://www.newsweek.com/bbq-becky-white-woman-who-called-cops-black-bbq-911-audio-released-im-really-1103057.

Zimmerman, Amy. 2017. "The Cultural Crimes of Iggy Azalea." *Daily Beast* (April 14). Retrieved on June 3, 2019, at https://www.thedailybeast.com/the-cultural-crimes-of-iggy-azalea.

Zimmerman, Kristin. 2014. "The Unfair Sentencing Act: Racial Disparities and Fiscal Consequences of America's Drug Laws." *Themis: Research Journal of Justice Studies and Forensic Science* 2:160–75.

Zwerling, Craig, and Hilary Silver. 1992. "Race and Job Dismissals in a Federal Bureaucracy." *American Sociological Review* 57(5):651–60.

Index

A

Abdul-Jabbar, Kareem, 91
abstract liberalism, 42–43
active racism, 35
Advancement Project, 124–125
Affleck, Ben, 87
African Americans, 6–7, 11–12, 50–51, 115
  and antiblack prejudices, 26
  and aversive racism, 44
  and criminal justice institution, 38
  BLM. *See* Black Lives Matter (BLM)
  darker-skinned, 18
  lighter-skinned, 18
  one-drop rule, 17
  recession of 2008, 125
  stereotypes, 27
Africans, and slavery, 3–4
Alexander, Michelle, 73
Allen, Paul, 61
Allen, Reniqua, 60
"All Lives Matter," 94, 102
All of Us or None, 126
Allport, Gordon, 24, 57
A Mighty Heart, 82
Annenberg Inclusion Initiative at the University of Southern California, 120
Anti-Drug Abuse Act of 1986, 31
anti-racism, 36, 105–129. *See also* anti-racist practices; anti-racists; anti-racist whites
anti-racist organizations, 121–127
anti-racist practices, 114–121
  inclusion riders, 120
  micro-affirmations, 128–129
  Rooney Rule, 119–120
anti-racists, 36, 105–109
anti-racists of color, 109–114
anti-racist whites, 109–114
apartheid, 6, 20, 34
Arizona State University, 96
Asian Americans, 6, 8, 19, 26–27, 51
Assata's Daughters, 123

assimilation, 9–10
Austin, Erin, 97
authentic relationships, 112
aversive racism, 43–45
Azalea, Iggy, 100

B

Bacon, Nathaniel, 3
Bacon's Rebellion, 3
Ballmer, Steve, 61
Bangerz, 101
Ban the Box campaign, 126
Beatty, Warren, 86
Belichick, Bill, 88
Bell, Derrick, 50
Beyoncé, 103
bias
  correspondence, 25
  implicit, 25–26
  racial, 27, 68, 71–72, 78–79, 96–97
biracial identification, and gender, 22
black blood, 14, 17
Black Feminist Thought: Knowledge, Consciousness, and the Politics of Empowerment (Collins), 47
Black History Month, 1
Black Lives Matter (BLM), 1, 93–96, 102, 111, 122–124
Black Lives Matter Global Network, 94
Black Power (Ture and Hamilton), 11
Black Sexual Politics (Collins), 83
Black Student Union, 37
Black Youth Project, 100, 123
Bland, Sandra, 54
"Blue Lives Matter," 94
Blumenbach, Johann, 4–5
Blumer, Herbert, 24
Bonilla-Silva, Eduardo, 19, 40–43, 52, 58, 106
Bourdieu, Pierre, 84
Braasch, Sarah, 98
Brady, Tom, 88
Breakfast at Tiffany's, 82

CPSIA information can be obtained
at www.ICGtesting.com
Printed in the USA
LVHW061918090421
683897LV00006B/8

9 781516 533374